CHARLESTOWN

The history of a Cornish port

Of Charlestown dock, it has been claimed that in the old days it was possible to walk from one side to the other across the decks of ships. This photograph, c1914, with two steamships loading china clay and nine sailing ships, mostly top-sail schooners, waiting their turn, proves the point.

CHARLESTOWN

The history of a Cornish port

BY

RICHARD & BRIDGET LARN

Published by
Richard & Bridget Larn

Shipwreck & Marine
Ropewalk House
Charlestown
St. Austell
Cornwall. PL25 3NN
England

Distributed by
Tormark Press Ltd,
Islington Press Ltd.
Islington Wharf
Penryn
Cornwall. TR10 8AT
Tel No. 0326-374339

ISBN 0-9523971-0-2

Typeset and printed by
Villiers Publications Ltd
19 Sylvan Avenue
London. N3 2LE

CONTENTS

Books by the same author(s)

Cornish Shipwrecks – the South Coast
Richard Larn & Clive Carter(David & Charles-1969)
Cornish Shipwrecks – the Isles of Scilly
Richard Larn (David & Charles-1971)
Shipwrecks of the Isles of Scilly
Richard Larn (Thomas & Lochar-1993)
Devon Shipwrecks
Richard Larn (David & Charles-1974)
Goodwin Sands Shipwrecks
Richard Larn (David & Charles-1977)
Shipwrecks of the Goodwin Sands
Richard Larn (Beresford Books-1994)
Shipwrecks of Gt.Britain & Ireland
Richard Larn(David & Charles-1981)

Tormark Press series:
Shipwrecks – St.Ives to Bude
Richard & Bridget Larn
Shipwrecks Around Land's End
Richard & Bridget Larn
Shipwrecks Around Mounts Bay
Richard & Bridget Larn
Shipwrecks Around the Lizard
Richard & Bridget Larn
Shipwrecks – Falmouth to Looe
Richard & Bridget Larn
Charlestown – a Visitors Guide
Richard & Bridget Larn

The 'Diver' Guide to South Cornwall
Richard Larn (Underwater World Publications)
Commercial Diving Manual
Richard Larn & Rex Whistler
Sir Clowdisley Shovell's Disaster in the Isles of Scilly
Richard Larn & Peter McBride
Land's End Shipwrecks
Richard Larn & Edwin Mills

in preparation
A 'Diver' Guide to the Isles of Scilly & North Cornwall
A Walking Guide to the Isles of Scilly
A Chronicled Index of United Kingdom Shipwrecks – 10 Volumes
(in association with Lloyd's Register)
Dorset Shipwrecks

Charlestown

Charlestown, a beach between green hills,
A harbour Rashleigh built, that thrills:
Old homes, stone walls and atmosphere
Round dock and lock-gate, Smeaton's pier.
A low boat slews on ropes, loads clay;
Tall masts and a galleon frame the bay.
Regency porches laze in the sun:
A stillness and a life that is fun.
The Harbour-master leans on a wall
By the roundhouse; leat-waters fall.
By the weighbridge stand with Dick Larn
And talk about shipwrecks, and yarn.
Here artists paint and girls serve tea
And light leaps from a sparkling sea;
Here women stroll in summer frocks
And watch the spray dash on the rocks.
The night sky drips with stars, and floods,
The universe like a shower of buds.
Here men can gaze and know, at peace,
A mystery that will never cease.

Nicholas Hagger. 6 April 1994

FOREWORD

If, as has been claimed, national history can only be written from a base of any number of detailed local histories, then the national histories of Cornwall have been particularly well underpinned. The Cornish tradition of the local study – town based or parish based – is longstanding. Some of us would see it also as a grand, independent and eminently worthwhile pursuit: compilation of knowledge for its ownsake, to inform and to delight others, and to give a degree of permanence to what we deem worthy of remembrance.

Charlestown is not a parish (at least, only a parish of convenience since 1846; it lies within the ancient parish of St. Austell and nor is that its original name. Porthmear, or Polmear Cove, a handy south-coast inlet within the greater St. Austell bay, was re-named after, and by, Charles Rashleigh of Menabilly who fashioned a dock harbour here at the end of the 18th century. Because Charlestown was designed to serve the growing china industry, its evolution was linked to easy access from the clay pits just inland, to the servicing and speedy turn-around of cargo ships and fairly soon to a complete infrastructure that could have served some much larger port. Nor was it ever just industrial; homes, some quite substantial, some small but inherently picturesque, huddled around the dock inlet and lined the access road.

In the present century Charlestown was all set to become a fossil; but, in our Age of Leisure, a fossil with a price and one that could be bought and sold as a package. The paradox has been that, on the one hand, constant use of the harbour for television series has allowed millions of people to become familiar with at least one aspect of Charlestown – far more so, probably, than with any other part of Cornwall – yet on the other hand we have never been given a proper study of the place. Some twenty years ago I was with a party of visiting industrial archaeologists, many of them leaders in their field, whose tour included a Charlestown show-around. Their eyes fairly popped. One of them said 'Why isn't there a decent history of all this?' Why indeed?

Well, now we are offered one. It has (we are told) been eighteen years in preparation, and to very good effect. For a local history it helps to be experienced in the appropriate lines of research and it certainly helps to be able to tell a story properly. In this case, maritime expertise, residence on the spot, and a belief in the rightness of the effort, amounting to devotion, would constitute a bonus. Richard & Bridget Larn bring to their task all these things. In planning their book they have had in mind the same 'ordinary reader' who, if he or she knows Cornwall and

Scilly, will long have profited from the Larn archive of shipwrecks and, just as important, the Larn tradition of publishing results in compact and instructive format. We are given a model history of this 'very private place', for which the reader should instantly turn to Appendix 1, a sailor's-eye chronology of Charlestown happenings from 1747 to 1994. After that, read it as a constructive story (which it should be, and is). Cornish historians will encounter a great many familiar names from the 19th century and probably find strange sidelights; at least we get the facts about the Crowders, into whose hands this port and all its tenancies passed under what the Larn's call, with restraint, 'unusual circumstances'.

We have needed this study for a long time. It could be supposed that the right authors simply never came along, and a partial or misleading history would hardly have served. Richard & Bridget Larn fill that need with skill and devotion, in the fine vein of Cornish Local history, and archaeologists of the recent past as well as ordinary deskbound historians have good cause to be grateful to them. I myself am additionally grateful, not only for having been asked to supply this little introductory passage, but because I can now go back to look at Charlestown with comprehension and adequate guidance. I wish this book all the circulation and success that it deserves. Perhaps, for future television series', a discreet puff could be slipped in among the credits.

Professor Charles Thomas, CBE DLitt FBA FSA.

ACKNOWLEDGMENTS

This book, the first comprehensive history of Charlestown and its founder, was intended for publication in 1990, coincident with the port's 200th. anniversary. However, events that year affecting the long term future of the port and village suggested that publication should be delayed, a decision made with great reluctance at the time, but which has since proven to have been correct. Between 1985 and 1994, the port of Charlestown experienced the most significant and traumatic change of its 204 year history, and no book concerning its past could ever be considered comprehensive or complete until its future was reasonably certain.

The purchase of the port by Square Sail Ltd. in October 1993 as a permanent base for its fleet of square-rigged sailing ships, has appropriately 'turned back the clock' so to speak, bringing once again to this unspoilt historic Georgian port, in addition to the continuing china clay coasters, the type of vessels and maritime activity for which it was once famous. Hopefully, their permanent presence has also ended speculation regarding the future of the port, since without question, the port is the very heart of Charlestown, of which many people are justifiably proud.

Consequently, no excuse remained not to complete and publish this book, which has been some eighteen years in preparation. To those who have waited so patiently for it to appear, our sincere apologies, and trust you will appreciate our dilema. We jointly commenced research into the history of Charlestown in 1976, first talking to most of the village elders at length, all of whom were so very co-operative and more than willing to pass on their early recollections of Charlestown. Sadly, time marches on and many of them, whose names will be known to many residents and locals, are no longer with us, and unfortunately never saw their words in print, but their enthusiasm and love for Charlestown became our inspiration. Included amongst those lovely people were 'Goldie' Facey and 'Doll' Brabyn, both of whom had old time seafarers in their families, who worked sailing ships in and out of Charlestown; also 'Dayer' Walkey, dock porter and labourer, who enjoyed the nickname 'Saltwater'; Donald Littleton, estate foreman & carpenter; 'Dobber' Kellaway, porter and labourer; 'Doug' Side, stone mason; 'Bill' Charters, estate painter; Colin Boswarrick, coal man and one time mule-driver; 'Jim' Isbell, stone mason; 'Bill' Doe, harbour master and pilot; Dennis Beynon, pilot; Harold King; Lady Florence Crowder; Bob Mills; John Williams; 'Sid' Averill; Hedley Mitchell; Philip Rashleigh and many others. To all of them we owe a debt of gratitude, and we are only sorry that they did not live long enough to enjoy this publication.

So many residents and locals have made valuable contributions to our story, that it is now difficult to remember them all. To Enoch Walkey; Howard Mills; 'Barnie' Hodge; Fred Glover; Ron Tregonning; Sally and David Williams, and Graham Brabyn. To 'Ted' & Evelyn Busby; John Newey; Pietr Crowder QC; Veronica Rashleigh; William Henry Stark; Charlotte Barry; Dr. John Rowe; John Lydiatt; D.R. Carter; L.J. Tyrrell; Gerald Mutton; Barbara Mummery, Jim Miller and C. Hancock to all of whom we are deeply grateful. If inadvertently we have left someone out, our sincere apologies and grateful thanks and assure you that it was not intentional. In our research we have probably exhausted every relevant indexed file in the Cornwall County Records Office for information on Charles Rashleigh and Charlestown, and thank the County Archivist, Mrs. Christine North and her deputy Colin Edwards, who never waned in their helpfulness, interest and courtesy. At the Royal Institute of Cornwall, Truro, our thanks and appreciation are extended to Harold Douch and Roger Penhallurick, its successive Curators, particularly for the use of photographs from their collection; also to Angela Broome, the librarian, and all the staff. To the Superintendents and staff of the British Library, the Colindale Newspaper Office; British Museum Library; City of London Guildhall Library; Public Records Office, at both Chancery Lane and Kew; the Historic Manuscript Commission; Exeter University Library; Plymouth City and St. Austell Public Library staff, and Hydrographic Office, Taunton, we extend out thanks. Also to John Davies, of Truro, Clive Carter of Penzance, and the late Eric Collins; John Trounson of Redruth; the editors of all currrent and extinct west country newspapers; to Roger Parker of Partech (Electronics) Ltd, Charlestown, for use of aerial photographs; to J.C. Burrow, Frank Connor, English China Clays and T.P. Roskrow for the use of photographs; to Nicholas Hagger for his poem 'Charlestown'; Joy Averill of Charlestown, who carried out some proof reading for us, Professor Charles Thomas, for his Foreword, Mary Richards, for her keyboard work, but most particularly Mary Quantrell of St. Austell, who so ably read our manuscript material several times over, making corrections and suggesting many changes, almost all of which were adopted, thank you all. With so many dates, names and places mentioned, there are bound to be minor errors in this book, and we welcome comments, criticism and contributions, particularly photographs and personal memories that would enhance a second edition.

Our greatest source of 20th. century information concerning the village has been our very dear friend and associate Arthur Hosegood and his late wife Alwyn. 'Nutsy' Hosegood or 'Art' as he is known locally, now one of the oldest Charlestown born residents, has contributed so much information and personal recollections that we unreservedly give him full recognition and sincere thanks. Unfortunately, failing eyesight means that Arthur will never be able to read this book for himself, but will no doubt listen to it many times over as we intend to have it put it on tape for him as a 'talking book', an entertainment medium that may allow other disadvantaged individuals to enjoy it, possibly through the County Library Service. At one stage Arthur despaired that we would never complete and publish this in his lifetime; so, to Arthur Hosegood, 'yer 'tis captain, and many thanks' !

Richard & Bridget Larn
Ropewalk House, Charlestown. 1994

INTRODUCTION

Charlestown, until 1985 was just another quiet, tucked away west country seaport, well known locally but almost unheard of outside of Cornwall. Since its inception by Charles Rashleigh, its founder, in 1790, the most important events in the history of the village were probably Rashleigh's infamous court cases in the early 1800's, the change of ownership in 1825, a visit by His Royal Highness, the Prince Edward, Duke of Kent, in July 1931, a notorious murder after World War II, the opening of the Charlestown Shipwreck & Heritage Centre in 1976 and a period of location film making for cinema and television. Such titles as 'The Eagle has Landed', 'Darwin's Voyage of Discovery', the 'Onedin Line', the 'Day of the Triffids' and more recently, 'The Three Musketeers', all gave Charlestown brief periods of national publicity. In turn, this brought increasing numbers of visitors during the summer, otherwise the village remained a very private place, still owned completely by the Crowder family, but managed through an agent.

Originally the sole property of Charles Rashleigh until his death in 1823, the port and leasehold tenancies changed hands in 1825 in unusual circumstances, passing into the hands of the Crowder family. They managed the estate through an agent as absentee landlords until 1985, when the entire village and port was offered for sale as a lot, including a vast acreage of surrounding greenbelt farmland. The unannounced and sudden change of ownership, dealt with at length in Chapter 9, was traumatic in the extreme for many residents, who had thought occupancy of their homes was guaranteed for life at very low rents, and that nothing would ever change. With 98% of the domestic properties and 100% business premises leasehold, many with no formal agreement, the transition from an easy going absentee landlord, almost pepper-corn rents, many non-maintaining leases, a near Victorian attitude towards management of the village and cosy secure occupancy, came as a nasty shock. Charlestown was literally dragged kicking and struggling out of its complacency into the real hard world of commerce and speculators, of investors, financiers, developers and asset strippers. Between 1985 and 1993 ownership of the village or parts of it, including the dock, changed hands seven times in eight years, and always for six figure sums. Suddenly Charlestown woke up to find itself featured almost daily in the national media. The residents, many of whom were elderly and had lived their entire lives in the village, some as 2nd. or 3rd. generation occupants of the same house, were subjected to several years of unwarranted, unnecessary, uncaring stress and uncertainty as to their future. Now, eight years after the original sale, things have settled down, no longer do properties stand empty and derelict and there is now an air of optimism. Owners have invested in new roofs and improvements, the future of the port appears secure, most of the leasehold dwellings are in the ownership of a national housing Trust. In fact, the entire village looks in better shape than at any time this century, having suffered endless years of neglect and non-investment.

It may come as something of a surprise to readers to learn that no archive of Charles Rashleigh's papers, nor of early Charlestown appears to have survived. The research necessary for this book therefore had no base on which to build, and gathering information has as a result, been piecemeal, protracted and difficult in the extreme, which may explain why so little has been written about the village in the past. What ever happened to all the thousands of letters, accounts, bills, receipts, agreements and documents accumulated over 50 years of Rashleigh business interests, which included two legal practices, a bank, his personal estate, a village and seaport, may never be known; they appear to have simply vanished. Following the death of her father in 1823, Martha Rashleigh, the spinster daughter who had looked after Charles in later life, was forced to leave the family home at Duporth, moving first to Cuddra House and then to Cuddra cottage. The sheer volume of documents relating to her father's estate must have been formidable, but what happened to them? Perhaps Martha took only a selection, or none at all, or simply burnt them? Perhaps the Crowder family as successors-in-title to the village requested their retention, in order to sort out the estate? Despite several formal approaches, the Crowders, their solicitors and agents will admit to possession of but a handful. Perhaps Joseph Daniel, the rogue footman owner of Duporth destroyed them, although they were more likely to have been stored in the old Count House rather than at Duporth; we just do not know.

Our accumulated knowledge of the village and Rashleigh's therefore came together in pieces, like a jigsaw puzzle, but without the benefit of an overall picture. The principal source was the County Records Office in Truro, which proved to have relevant material widely scattered in archives relating to the Rashleigh, Tremayne, Hawkins, Robins, Polkinghorne, Rodd, Fox, Coode and Sawle families, as well as other prominent Cornish landowners of the 18th and 19th centuries. Correspondence in abundance can be found from Charles Rashleigh in all these sources but, regrettably offers the researcher a one-sided view of any situation, leaving you unaware of the circumstance that initiated a letter, or its reply.

Our greatest single find was at Menabilly, Charles Rashleigh's family home and birth place, where Veronica Rashleigh and her now late husband Philip made available to us amongst other valuable material, a copy document, the original of which was at one time in the hands of a Miss Fursden of Exeter, long deceased. Extensive correspondence and searching in Devon failed to discover what happened to Miss

Fursden's estate, believed to have contained much Rashleigh memorabilia, indirectly inherited from Martha Rashleigh on her death in 1847. This document sets out in chronological order as a first hand account, written either by Grace Rashleigh, Charles's wife, or Harriet, his eldest daughter, the events that led to Charles's downfall.

Other material has been gleaned from collections in the Royal Institute of Cornwall, Truro; Devon Records Office; some material held by Charlestown Estate Ltd., private documents which were in the possession of the late Lady Crowder, and accounts published in the now defunct *St.Austell Gazette & Mid Cornwall Advertiser*; *St.Austell News* and *St.Austell Star* newspapers, held in the Colindale Newspaper Office of the British Library, in London. Also the *West Briton and Cornwall Advertiser*; *Royal Cornwall Gazette*; *Sherbourne & Yeovil Mercury*; *Cornish Guardian* and *Western Morning News*.

Charlestown has played a major role in local history, particularly regarding mining and china-clay. The story of Charles Rashleigh and his family, his 'town', its creation, development, social and economic history is fascinating, told here for the first time. Whilst hopefully, the future of the port is now secure, Charlestown is still at a cross-roads. In our opinion, this is possibly the most critical and important point in its history, its fortunes balanced precariously between economic survival and threatened destruction by development, which could so easily destroy the character of this unique village *for ever*. Building applications, most fortunately rejected, have been made on an unprecedented scale in recent years following its sale, at one time representing 35% of all applications received in Restormel Borough Council's Planning Office. There are many small Cornish ports which once looked like Charlestown, where borough and district councils allowed the creeping cancer of over development to change their character irreverisibly. Amusement arcades, fast-food outlets, fish-and-chip shops, ticky-tacky houses, dreadful blocks of flats, flat-roofs, holiday camps and endless stereotype gift shops, have virtually destroyed the character of so many once beautiful Cornish ports. In season, they are to be avoided where possible, out of season, they become ghost-towns and everyone bemoans the lack of permanent residents, children and character, wishing they could put back the clock, but always it is too late.

Charlestown is the one last opportunity in Cornwall for an intact, working, historic Georgian seaport to remain unspoilt, just as it was 125 years ago. It has been saved from modern development only by the chance of 200 years of private ownership, without which Charlestown would already be no different from Looe, Polperro, Mevagissey, or any other small port in the county. Where else in Cornwall can you stand on a granite quay and not see a single new building or flat roof? Where else do green fields still used for animal grazing, reach down to the sea, with a working farm literally yards from the head of the dock, still

3

fully integrated into village life? Surely we owe it to future generations to be able to visit and say, 'so this is how things were'? For Charlestown, it is not too late, but its future lies in the hands of its residents, the Restormel Borough Council planners, and a minority who would destroy it merely for short term financial gain. Whatever the outcome, their decisions will be judged by their children.

CHAPTER 1

Charles Rashleigh, Attorney-at-Law. 1747 – 1784

The founder of Charlestown was born during the early hours of 17 November 1747, at Menabilly Manor, near Fowey, overlooking St.Austell Bay, then known as Tywardreath Bay. Charles Rashleigh was the 10th child and seventh son of Jonathan and Mary Rashleigh, she being the daughter of Sir William Clayton of Marden, Surrey. Tywardreath parish records, which abound in references to the Rashleighs', since it has been their parish church for almost three centuries, show that Charles was baptised there on 7 December [1], when just twenty-one days old.

Of his early days we know virtually nothing. His father Jonathan, was a MP. FRS. and FSA, representing the pocket borough of Fowey at Westminster and wealthy in the extreme, so that the Rashleigh children enjoyed every opportunity. Educated at home, Charles appears to have had a restricted but carefree childhood, escaping the many illnesses and disease of the period, which claimed the life of his brother William in the same year that Charles was born, and another brother, Henry, in 1753. The only recorded incident of his youth was when he was twelve, when he fell from a horse and broke an arm. As to an early likeness, there is but one, a beautiful oval enamel, one of a set depicting all the children, still in family hands, thought to have been painted around 1755, which shows Charles as a cherubic faced, dark haired boy.

As to Charles's family background, the name Rashleigh goes back to 1549, and under the old style spelling of Rayshelegh, as early as 1196 [2]. The presence of crescents on the family coat-of-arms suggest that an ancestor took part in the Crusades, and the family certainly has very deep roots in the west country, since early Raysheleghs lived at a manor of the same name at Wembury, six miles south-east of Plymouth. Possibly the first move of a branch of the family into Cornwall, brought them to Fowey in 1529, when 'Philip of Foy', at the dissolution of the monastries, outdid the rival Treffry family living at Place, by purchasing the priory and lands of St.Andrew's, Tywardreath, from the King for £209. By 1573, Philip's eldest son John had built a fine house in the town centre, now the *'Ship Inn'*[3], which became the family home, at the same time purchasing large tracts of land at Menabilly. Such large land and property holdings entitled John to a Parliamentary vote, and generations of Rashleighs' were Members of Parliament for 260 years without a break. Both John and heir, also a John, died in 1624[4] only nine days apart, probably from some common disease, so that completion of the planned manor house at Menabilly was left to the younger son,

Jonathan, who saw work completed that same tragic year. It may amuse readers that Jonathan then sent his son to Oxford, with instructions that he should, 'have a poor scholar to wait on him, learn to dance and avoid lewd friends!'

Menabilly, made famous through the writing of Daphne du Maurier, later Lady Browning, who occupied the manor from 1944 to 1969, has been witness to many changes. In 1644 it was besieged by the Cromwellians and pillaged after it fell, Jonathan Rashleigh being heavily fined and imprisoned for months for leading the opposition. Fifty years later, another Jonathan started a cartage service from Menabilly, which operated between the ports of Penzance, Falmouth, and Fowey to London, and under heavy armed guard allowed the safe transportation of valuables and money; an early security service in fact. 1824 saw William Rashleigh adding a kitchen and stables to the family home, and it was during these alterations that a seemingly useless buttress was disturbed. Behind the brickwork was discovered a secret staircase leading down to a cell; on a stool were the remnants of a human skeleton, on the floor lay an eating plate and the preserved uniform, gold buttons and epaulettes of a senior Royalist military officer. The identity of the unfortunate individual has never been established, but the story certainly inspired Daphne du Maurier's famous novel[5], 'The King's General'.

At the age of seventeen, Charles Rashleigh set his sights on the legal profession. The children living at Menabilly were now mostly grown up, the family reduced in number to eight. Philip, the eldest was 35 years old; Martha, still a spinster, was 34, John aged 22, Robert 21, Peter and Thomas, 18 and 15 years respectively. Their father Jonathan died that same year, 1764, on 26 November, aged 71,[6] being buried in Fowey church. As to the remaining Rashleigh children, Jane had married taking the surname Duke, her husband coming from Lake House, Wiltshire; Mary was living away from home, later to marry William Stackhouse; and brother Jonathan, having completed his studies at All Souls College, Oxford, had taken holy orders and was rector at Silverton, in Devon, eventually to marry a Catherine Stackhouse of Trehane, who bore him eleven children. Rachael was the outcast, seldom mentioned or visited, having eloped with a Dr. Gould of Fowey. In his will, their father left Menabilly estate to Philip, being the eldest son, which in law deprived Mary Rashleigh of her home. To ensure their mother's position, the children had a legal agreement drawn up, which reads in part, '- her peaceful enjoyment of the Manor, its furniture and contents for her lifetime.' This large document survives, interesting in itself since it bears the signatures and personal seals of Charles and nine Rashleigh brothers and sisters who had reached their majority. Charles Rashleigh started his career as an articled clerk in the office of Francis Polkinghorn, of Trewiddle, Cornwall. Much later, long after Charles had been admitted to the Inns of Court and called to the

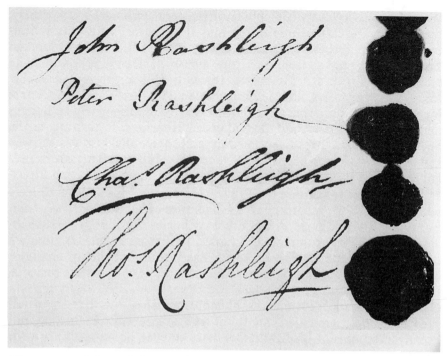

Signatures of four of the Rashleigh brothers, including Charles, on a legal document of 1764, giving their mother Mary Rashleigh, the right of abode at Menabilly for life.

'King's Court of the King's Bench' to become an attorney-at-law, these two men were to form a partnership, taking a joint lease on a writing office with garden in St. Austell. Situated in Churchtown, the old centre of St. Austell, its location remains uncertain but was described in the lease document as *Julyan's Tenement*. As a lowly clerk in those early days, no doubt receiving little or no pay, an early invitation from his brother Philip to assume Stewardship of Menabilly on his behalf offered a welcome income. Intent on maintaining the Rashleigh tradition in Parliament, having inherited a seat at Fowey, Philip sought someone he could trust to manage the family estate and affairs, which included many tenant farmers and the whole of Polkerris port and village. Who better than his younger brother, now training as a solicitor ?

Having qualified in his profession, before returning to Cornwall in 1769, Charles did in fact start a legal practice in the City of London, Rashleigh & Co., situated at 36 Lincoln's Inn Field. Many years later, this became Edward Buller & Co., until it's financial crash, brought about by the embezzlement of trust funds by one of the partners. The practice then became Rashleigh & Smart, then Rashleigh & Son, moving to 63 Lincoln's Inn Field, where it survived until 1916.

Charles Rashleigh obviously set his sights on becoming wealthy at an early age. Certainly his choice of the legal profession was timely, there being a great upsurge in the mid 18th century in property dealing, leases, shares, land registration etc. His first purchase of land in Cornwall appears to have been the manor of Tregorrick, which he bought from Edward Henshaw, through Henshaw's trustees, Sir Edward Dering, Sir William Wynn and William Strickland. This estate was originally the home of the Lowers of St.Winnow, whose heiress married first a Roper and then Edward Henshaw. Returning to the St.Austell area, Charles lived for a time at Menabilly, but was actively searching for a home of his own, where he could entertain his friends and enjoy his bachelor years. He settled on a house in Church Street, St.Austell, later to become the White Hart Hotel. This appears to have been built in 1769, according to an indenture of 'a dwelling, *lately built*, from the Rt.Hon.Lord Arundell, to Charles Rashleigh', dated 26 September of that year, making Charles its first occupant. Originally a two storied property, the building has undergone many changes, including the addition of a third floor, a complete wing on the east side and various extensions at the back.

It was here, in 1774, that Rashleigh established the first St.Austell bank, having persuaded many of the Menabilly, Prideaux and Luxulyan tenants of his brother's estates to open accounts. This town house was also used for a time as a solicitors' office by Rashleigh after his departure to Duporth. At the time of Rashleigh's occupation, this house, identified only as No.3 Church Street, overlooked an area of St. Austell on the east side used as a bull-ring on which was later built the 'White Lion' inn, which in turn was demolished to make way for the National Westminster Bank, known locally as the 'red brick building'. In 1769, the main road into the town from the east led down East Hill, between Rashleigh's house and the church into Fore Street (there being no South Street at the time). The only access to High Cross Street was up past the Market House and through Cross Lane. The area now occupied by the junction of Church Street and High Cross Street was a high banked extension of the churchyard, into which was built the 'Black Hole', a sort of semi-underground chamber used to house drunks, felons and prisoners awaiting transport to Bodmin gaol. This dungeon prison was in use until the old St. Austell Police Station was built in 1866.

Rashleigh decorated and furnished his new home in a most lavish style, with a mahogany table in the dining room capable of seating 40 people to dinner, later taken to Duporth. The drawing-room was hung with beautiful hand-painted French wall-hangings, which remained in place for an incredible 140 years, being removed only when the founder of the St.Austell Brewery, Walter Hicks, purchased the building from a Mr. F.G.A. Pinckney in 1911. At what point in history Rashleigh's town house was turned into an hotel is uncertain, but an entry in the journal of one Christopher Wallis, dated 11 October 1804 reads, 'Went to St.

Charles Rashleigh (1747-1823), founder of the port of Charlestown, in his mid 20s when this portrait was painted c1770.

Austle White Hart, *new house*, and there slept'. Part of the building was used as a legal practice well into the 1800's, when the residential part was sold to a Mr.Dunn, after which it served for a time as an office of the Inland Revenue. It is said that this establishment was named after another 'White Hart', which once stood in Fore Street, dating back to 1735. It is of interest in the Rashleigh story to note that the firm of solicitors Coodes, Hubbard, French & Follett, which until recently occupied premises over the National Westminster Bank, had its roots in Rashleigh's White Hart building, the practice having started as a partnership with Rashleigh all those years ago, literally only the width of a street away. Incidentaly, prior to 1952, the name of this practice included the name Gifford as one of the partners, who along with his wife was tragically murdered at Duporth, on the outskirts of Charlestown, their bodies being wheel-barrowed over the cliffs by their son. Following the death of Francis Polkinghorn, Rashleigh's original partner in St.Austell, the practice became Rashlcigh & Coode, then Rashleigh Coode & Robins, until Charles's death. Robins & Shilson emerged from that practice, which in time became Shilson Coode & Co., and finally Coode & Co. Sections of the famous drawing room wall-hanging in the White Hart were professionally removed by staff of the Victoria and Albert Museum, Kensington, and placed in their collection. Whilst not on public display, details can be found in their catalogue of wall coverings and hangings (V.& A. negative No.75689, Ref.E10/XIXc). Its description reads: 'Anonymous, wall-paper, French. Eight fragments from the panoramic wall-paper "La Baie de Naples", published by Dufour, Paris c1800. Views of Tivoli, Amalfi, Vesuvius and the Bay of Naples, surmounted by frieze of Pompeian arabesques with putti and running pattern imitating a modillion cornice. Colour prints in Grisaille from wood-blocks. From the walls of the drawing room (White Hart Hotel), given by the St.Austell Brewery Co.Ltd.' By prior arrangement with the Superintendent of the Department, the original material can be viewed by the public and is well worth the effort to see this historic link with Charlestown's founder.

During 1774 Charles Rashleigh, now aged 27, met and fell in love with Grace Tremayne of Heligan Manor, a very large and historic estate between Mevagissey and Gorran, near St.Austell. An oil painting of her, probably executed when she, 'sat for my Picture to Mr. Clifford, the limner', in February 1774, shows her as a slight, fair haired young lady. Three years Charles' senior, born on Christmas Day 1744, she had already lost both parents, her father in 1756, her mother Grace, in 1765. The latter was of very old Cornish stock, being a Hawkins of St.Austell before marriage, her grandmother a Clotworthy. Grace kept diaries, always the pocket edition of *The Ladies Own Memorandum Book or Daily Pocket Journal by a Lady*, printed by G. Robinson, No.25 Paternoster Row, London. Four of these diaries survive, covering the years 1774, 1776, 1779 and 1789, having been found hidden in the stables at

At his town house in St. Austell, now the White Hart Hotel, Charles Rashleigh had the drawing room decorated with hand painted wallpaper, which survived for 140 years.

Trebartha House, Cornwall, her daughter Harriet's home after marriage, many years later. Two of these concern her life before marriage and two after, at both her St. Austell town house and Duporth. Enteries for 1776, suggest that romance was very much in the air on the 20th March, 'Mr. Charles Rashleigh came while we were at breakfast and went home in the evening'. The following Sunday, the 24th, Grace's brother Henry Hawkins Tremayne, took tea with Charles at Heligan manor, obviously the day he asked for the young ladies hand in marriage, since pencilled into the margin is the two line poem, 'The day is come you wished so long, love picked you out among the throng.' The period of engagement was very short, just four months, during which time Charles visited Heligan once a week, but every single day during the week prior to the wedding. As was customary with wealthy families, who viewed wedlock as a very serious financial business, a marriage agreement was drawn up, an extract from which reads:

' – Indenture made this 29th day of June in the year of our Lord 1776, between Grace Tremayne of Heligan, spinster, and Charles Rashleigh of St.Austell, gentleman, whereas the said Grace Tremayne is now lawfully entitled unto the sum of £2,500 by

11

virtue of the settlement made on the marriage of her father John Tremayne esq. deceased, with Grace Tremayne, and a further sum of £1,000, a legacy given her by the will of her late mother Grace Tremayne, widow deceased, and also £1,500 given her by the wife of her late brother Lewis Tremayne, deceased, amounting to the whole of £5,000, also several parts and shares of and in sundry tin bounds in the County of Cornwall . . also all that dwelling house (Heligan Manor) and messuage with the stables, courtlage, barns, gardens, orchards, fields, closes and parcels of land and other premises with their appurtenances, also all that meadow behind the outer walled garden called the Tin Pit meadow . . etc.'

The day after the marriage contract was signed, Charles wrote to his brother John, then living at Prideaux, Luxulyan, informing him of events:

'Dear Brother, I paid a visit to Heligan yesterday with a view to settling my future happiness and to give up the idle life of a batchelor with pleasure, hence I acquaint you my offer was well received by Miss Tremayne and the family seemed well pleased with the intended connection. You will give my love to Kitty (Catherine Rashleigh, nee Battie, of London) and appraise her of my step taken and, I hope, you will approve the match, which I assure you is the result of a long connection and sincere regard, and I trust will tie the knot.

I wish it not to be common conversation in the companies, but as I know Mr. Stackhouse's regard for me, you will make him acquainted with the affair and not forget to add my best respects . . '.

That Charles wished his marriage to be a very private affair is obvious from the letter he wrote to his mother on Monday 1 July, *after* the ceremony:

'I was married with the greatest prospect and happiness. Only my brother and sister and Mrs. Rashleigh were at the wedding.'

The ceremony took place at St.Ewe, the nearest parish church to Heligan, used by the Tremaynes for centuries, Mr. Peard officiating. Surviving documentation supports the wedding date of 1 July, although the original marriage certificate is dated 29 June; but this may have been merely the date of application. As was customary in the 18th century, the young couple remained at Heligan for a two week honeymoon, receiving many visitors. On 13 July, Charles took his bride to St. Austell, her diary recording, 'Left Heligan with Mr. C.R. after Breakfast, dined at Kilmouth and got *home* to St. Austell in the evening'. The word 'home' is heavily underlined.

Rashleigh documents surviving in either private hands or the CRO.Truro, bear witness to the hundreds of property deals in which Charles was involved, many on a private basis. Examples of these include a lease of 7 March 1777, 'Hugh, Lord Falmouth, to Charles

Rashleigh, 7/8ths of Higher Menacuddle, late in the occupation of Elizabeth Bligh, then Ann Giles, widow deceased; also 7/8ths of Lower Menacuddle, late in the occupation of Henry Lake, then John Rosevear, then John Carter.' For what purpose Rashleigh wanted Menacuddle in the Gover valley, on the northern outskirts of St. Austell is uncertain; the area was once a rich mining development or the interest may have been connected with water rights. On 29 March the same year, 'Robert Rashleigh, merchant and Thomas Rashleigh, gent. both of London, to Charles Rashleigh, a house and garden called Julyan's tenement in Churchtown, St.Austell, also five fields on the north side of Tregonissey Road'. A year later, 'John Sawle, seven year lease to Francis Polkinghorne and Charles Rashleigh on behalf of their partners in the tin trade, to be carried on in the St.Austell Blowing House, with pinion, mell(mill), tying horse and implements'. Another in 1781, '17th. July, John Sawle, 50 year lease to Henry Lakes and Charles Rashleigh, on behalf of the partners at the old Blowing House. A plot of land where a smelting house is now building in Blowing House Hill, St.Austell, with liberty to use all the necessary water, so as no wilful waste be made of said water, nor injury done to any mill that can be avoided.' Charles took a considerable interest in local mining, buying shares in the Polgooth mine and at Crinnis, where huge deposits of shallow copper were eventually found. Of the Polgooth mine, its captain in 1791, named Phillips, said that 'it now has 23 shafts and the bottom of the mine, 120 fathoms deep, had not been seen for 75 years.'

At about this time Rashleigh fell out with a young man named Nicholas Symons of Hatt, near Botus Fleming, in east Cornwall. His father William had been county Sheriff in 1735 and Charles employed him in his London practice as an articled clerk in 1777. On qualification, Rashleigh 'having taken a great fancy to him, offered Nicholas a partnership in the St.Austell practice in 1782.' In fact they even made a joint purchase of property that same year at Lanascot, ' – Charles Rashleigh esq. and Nicholas Symons, gent, bought of William Cole and Rebecca his wife, I messuage; 1 curtilage; 3 orchards; 30 acres of land; 1 of wood; 10 of firs; 4 of moor, and a moiety of 3 messuages, 3 cottages, 3 stables, 3 gardens, 3 orchards, 10 of firs, 4 of moor & common pasture, for the sum of £120.'

In the meantime Symons had become enamoured with a common milliner and refused to leave London for Cornwall. Disapproving of the connection but anxious that his son should not lose this opportunity, the father spoke to Rashleigh, who is said to have 'flown into a rage and withdrawn his offer.' In November 1783 Symons wrote Rashleigh a letter saying, ' – my prospects are blighted and, for the sake of my family I have sacrificed my interests.' Nicholas Symons then seemingly disappeared and it was not until 38 years later, in 1821, two years prior to Rashleigh's death, that their names were again linked, this time with a happy outcome. It transpired that on leaving London, Symons went to Liverpool, where he changed his name to Nathanial Sherwood, obtaining employment as a coach driver between the port and Manchester. He married a Susan Roberts who bore him six children, but was always poor, and since Susan later maintained she was unaware of his true identity, we can assume that she was not the London milliner. Symons died in 1802 and it was only by chance in 1821, that Susan Sherwood saw the Rashleigh practice nameplate in Lincolns Inn Field, London. Remembering that her late husband had mentioned the name several times, she made enquiries, eventually meeting Charles in person, when she produced a great many papers that her late husband had said were valuable. The matter was taken to the Bodmin Crown Court in August 1822 by Rashleigh himself, which must have been a considerable sacrifice on his part, being very ill at the time. It was proven Symons had indeed been the eldest son and heir of William Symons and, as a result, Nathanial's (Nicholas Symons) cldcst son, who married an Agnes Penn, inherited the family estate and it is believed the family still occupy the property near Hatt. The story of Nathaniel Symons (Nicholas Symons) was published in 1912 by a William Mitchell, a distant relative, living in Philadelphia, USA.

The additional responsibility of Under Sheriff of Cornwall was accepted by Charles in 1778, the first of three such terms of office he was to serve, the second being in 1782-3 under Sheriff Davis Giddy of Treadrea, a celebrated historian, who took the name of Davies Gilbert to write a history of Cornwall. His third term was in 1797-8, but Charles was never appointed County Sheriff himself.

The year 1779 was an eventful one for Charles Rashleigh, now aged 32. On Sunday 7 February Grace Rashleigh gave birth at Heligan to Harriet, the first of their three daughters. She had in fact gone there some three weeks earlier, for what was then known as the 'lying-in'. Grace's record of the event in her diary reads: 'I was safely delivered of my dear little Harriet at 7 o'clock in the Morning. Mr. Stephens came to see me at Heligan about 10 o'clock in the forenoon. My brother baptised my dear child one hour after birth.' Later that spring Charles was appointed Deputy Town Clerk of Grampound; he also purchased 94 acres of land at Duporth, on the coast, south of St. Austell, planning and making arrangements for the building there of his new manor house. Business then had to be put aside whilst Charles travelled to London for the funeral of his favourite brother Robert. A successful merchant in the city, his death at 36 was a considerable shock to the family. The brothers had obviously been very close; Robert's will, proved on 2 March, bequeathed to Charles, '- the sum of £500 and all my books in the English language.'

Less than 12 months later Charles found himself elected Town Clerk at Grampound, then sole partner in his legal practice, when his friend and mentor Francis Polkinghorne died. A proclamation of 29 August

1780 read: 'I, John Hoyle, Mayor of the said Borough of Grampound, have made, nominated, constituted and do hereby appoint Charles Rashleigh of St. Austell in the said county, gentleman, to be Town Clerk of the said Borough in the place and stead of Francis Polkinghorne, gentleman, my late Town Clerk, deceased, for as long as I shall continue Mayor.'

In fact, John Hoyle ceased to be mayor before mid October 1780; however, his successor, Jonathon White, duly reappointed Rashleigh on the 17th of the month without the formality of another proclamation.

The development of Porthmear, known today as Charlestown, although still a decade away, had its roots in the purchase by Charles of clifftop pasture land at Duporth and Duporth farm. To what extent the land here was developed or inhabited is unclear, but amongst the Sawle family documents for Penrice estate, since it was they that sold the land to Rashleigh, are many references that suggest some sort of early occupation. A paper dated 6 September 1731 refers to the 'surrender of a tenement at Duporth'; another of 18 September 1734 headed 'Deed, Duporth lease', reads, 'Thomas Stephens, parish of St. Austel and Richard Sawle of London. In the manor of Tewington, land, tenements, fields, lying and being in the *village* of Duporth, part of the said customary lands of the said manor.' Maps of the period indicate no reference to a Duporth village, nor to any clifftop dwellings other than the original Duporth farm, hence these references pose a number of unanswered questions.

In Chapter 5, reference is made to the fact that in 1828 all the documentation relating to Duporth manor and estate was stolen from a solicitor's office in St. Austell. Hence, details of the original boundaries, the building costs, original lay-out, maps, plans, and details of when exactly the clock tower and entrance lodge were built remains uncertain. The 94 acres of land were purchased in 1779 and assuming that it took at least two years to clear the ground, to build Duporth manor and lay out the drives and garden, it would be reasonable to assume that the large dinner party, mentioned in a letter as having taken place on 7 September 1781, was some sort of house-warming. It was attended by ten Rashleigh brothers and sisters and their spouses, including Dr. Gould and Mrs. Stackhouse, who sat around the 40 seat dining table in the dining-room, at the front of the house on the first floor, overlooking Tywardreath Bay.

No evidence survives to indicate at what point in time Charles disposed of his town house in St. Austell, but it is known he retained some rooms for a legal practice for a number of years. We also know he leased the remainder to an Elizabeth Price for £100 in 1807, and sometime after, the accommodation to a T. Westlake, for the same amount. The year 1781, that saw the move to Duporth house was memorable for other reasons. Early in March, Mary Rashleigh, Charles's mother, died at Menabilly. Three months later he was offered the position of

Steward to the Duchy of Cornwall, a position he held until his death; the family also celebrated the arrival of a second daughter, born at Duporth on 28 July. Christened Martha on 12 October, Charles left reference to the event in a letter by writing, ' – my brother (*the Rev. Jonathan Rashleigh*) breakfasted here and christened my little girl at noon, Mrs. Boscarwane, Miss Rashleigh and my brother stood sponsors'. Throughout her life, Martha was always known to the family as 'Pattie', a nickname given her by Charles, derived presumably from Martha – Mattie – Pattie; as far as we can tell, her father seldom used her proper name in correspondence. That same year Charles took a 50 year lease on a plot at Blowing House Hill, St. Austell, 'where a new smelting house has been erected on behalf of Edward Fox and Charles Rashleigh, partners in the tin trade'. Fox was a member of a well known Quaker family, then living at Wadebridge, whose wife Anna was a niece of William Cookworthy. His involvement with the new trade in china clay probably influenced Charles when he considered the building of a port to service St. Austell. Later, Rashleigh and Fox became joint proprietors of the Polgooth copper mines.

Now aged 53, Philip Rashleigh married his cousin Jane Pole on 16 April 1782, Charles being asked to draw up the customary marriage agreement. His legal assistance was also engaged to represent Philip in a long standing quarrel with the mayor and corporation of the pocket borough of Fowey, led by the Treffry family. They had been at loggerheads with the Rashleigh's for years over 'stick-voters', the Rashleigh's having purchased the rights from the crown during the reign of Henry VIII. During the Reformation the king had seized Tywardreath priory and confiscated its rights, including that of the voters, offering it to the Rashleighs, whereas the Treffry family felt it should have gone to them. In a letter to a friend, Charles commented:

'I would like effectively to crush the Treffry interest; I think the object worthy of expense, but merely to crush the present opposition I do not think worth much attention. I know how far the Prince supports such a contest, and that he will do nothing material to maintain it. I also know that it cannot be successful, yet I very much wish that more of the old conveyance should be used, and feel greatly obliged for the favour done to me by his conduct.'

Another letter, this one to brother Jonathan from Charles, stated:

'I am perfectly satisfied that the business at Fowey must end to my entire satisfaction in every point of the proceedings. I feel as bold as ever about Tregony and Penryn.'

The only surviving portrait of Charles Rashleigh as a young man, which hangs at Menabilly, includes his brother Robert. Dressed in military style clothing and holding a flint-lock musket, some writers have interpreted this as indicating that Charles had served in the regular army, but this is untrue. Close examination of the full portrait reveals dead game birds and a gun dog, suggesting that it is a hunting scene.

Charles was of course involved with the Crinnis Cliff Volunteers, for whom he financed the construction of the gun battery overlooking the harbour, but from a military viewpoint this was temporary, volunteer service, to counter a threatened Napoleonic invasion, much as the LDV. and Home Guard did against a similar German threat in World War II.

The cliffs at Charlestown had in fact served as a look-out point against possible invasion for many years. In 1720-1, men were paid to watch the sea around the clock, a typical watch roster of the period revealing surnames still local to the area:

'Monday   – John Benallack, by day. Joshua Pearse & John Hooper, by night.

Tuesday   – John Edds, by day. John Lake & William Gonde, by night.

Wednesday – John Cummins, by day. Joseph Rosevear & John Cowe, by night.

Thursday   – Thomas Daddow, by day. Nicholas Michell & William Whale, by night.

Friday   – John Harle, by day. Nicholas Michell, snr. & Henry Varco, by night.

Saturday   – Thomas Thomas, by day. Philip Willeton & Nathaniel Gomma, by night.

Sunday   – John Daniel, by day. John Harper & Andrew Gonde, by night.

Additional day watchers: Simon, ye miller at Bolingey. At night:
Peter Nankivell, Matthew & William Walkey, Mordicay Williams, Peter, Philip and Joseph Daniel.'

The men were of course paid by the government for this duty:
'St. Austell, in Powder Hundred. We the Constables of the said Parish of St. Austell, do hereby humbly record that in obedience to a warrant sent about the 29th day of October last did raise watch and wards to be sett 11.00 and 6.00 att three several places in the said parish on the sea coast viz. at Polmeore, Trewarren and Portewan where attended three men by day and six by night from the said 29th October until 1st day of January the following, being sixty-three days and nights in attending, which time were imployed five hundred sixty seven persons at one shilling each man every day night, amounting to £28.7s.0d. Paid powder & ball £0.9s.0d.
Signed: Dennis Russell and Joseph Coad.'

Many Regiments of Cornish Volunteers were raised between 1779

17

and 1783 by the local gentry as the threat of invasion continued, a number of Companies going to make up each Regiment. At St. Austell, Henry Hawkins Tremayne of Heligan, commanded one very large Company, to which arms were issued on 19 July 1779, only six days after the meeting. The receipt for their return at the end of that war reads: 'Office of Ordnance, Plymouth, 30 September 1784.

Received into His Majesties stores within the said office from Henry Hawkins Tremayne esq. of Heligan, in the County of Cornwall, the small arms and accoutrements undermentioned, which were issued to him to arm the Associated Gentlemen of St. Austell and its neighbours for the defence of the coast between Fowey and Mevagissey on 19th. September 1779, pursuant to the Lt.Gen. Sir William Draper's Orders, dated 7th. of the said month:

Item	Useful/Damaged		Item	Useful/Damaged	
Musquets	140	9	Cartouch boxs	126	14
Bayonets	114	3	Belts for same	92	6
Scabbards for do.	70	72	Frogs for the bayonets	111	16
Steel rammers	149				

Signed: Alexander Tho's. Wilkinson.'

It is likely that the original issue had been a set of 150 muskets, issued to two Companies of 84 + 84, ie. drummers not being armed, sergeants and officers having swords only. The Cornish Militia, which were a different organisation, on embodiment in 1778, wore uniform red coats with dark blue facings, and the various Regiments of Volunteers probably wore the same. Receipts dated 1784 suggest that privates wore a buff waistbelt with a bayonet frog on one hip, a cartouche cartridge box on a chest strap, a black tricorn hat and gaitors fitted with instep straps, linking boots or shoes.

The abandoned and until recently derelict gun battery overlooking Charlestown harbour to the west, with its battlemented wall, has fortunately now been listed as a national monument by English Heritage, and during the early months of 1994 was partially restored by Restormel Borough Council. Within the enclosure can be found the remains of a brick magazine, several gun platforms, as well as the bases of two flagstaffs, their granite mounted rigging support rings and the base of the repository drill shed. In 1991, at the instigation of the authors, when application was made through the Residents Association for the battery to be considered for listing, the Cornwall Archaeological Unit visited the site, producing a site drawing and carrying out an excavation of two possible gun platforms. This battery was built at Charles Rashleigh's expense in 1793 to defend the harbour. In 1795, the Crinnis Cliff Volunteers were formed, which surprisingly survived for over 100 years, its fife and drum unit emerging in the late 19th.c. as the Mount Charles brass band. The unit local to the area was a single company formed under Captain John Peter, Lieut's. Henry Luke and Joseph Dingle. When Peter and Luke resigned, Joseph Dingle became their captain, with William Banks as Lieutenant and Ensign J. Geach. This Volunteer force merged with the artillery in 1800, the gun battery thereafter being known officially as the Crinnis Cliff Battery. The overall picture is confused regarding all these volunteer military organisations, which proliferated throughout the county as panic spread regarding possible French invasion.

In June 1798, a single company of Infantry Volunteers was raised, which expanded to three companies, its senior Captain being a Thomas Carlyon and original lieutenant named as John Hearle Tremayne, whose father had commanded the local volunteers during the war of 1779-83 and the French Revolution of 1794. On 28 July, only a month later, a single troop of provisional cavalry was gazetted at St. Austell, Captain A. Hawkins, Lieut. Jeffreyson and Cornet R. Lawrence being its officers, which was disbanded when the threat of war diminished. In 1805, when invasion again looked imminent, Charles personally financed a Crinnis Cliff Company of volunteers, who were all workmen in his employ, paying for their uniforms, horses and equipment.

Immediately prior to the late 1770's, when Charles Rashleigh made land acquisitions at West Porthmear, later to emerge as Charlestown, it is appropriate to take a brief look at the coastal villages already established in the bay. Known certainly since Elizabethan times as Tywardreath Bay, since Tywardreath was the largest of the settlements, it was not re-named St. Austell Bay until the early 1700's, when that town began to assume some prominance. On the 16th century Cott manuscript map, held in the British Museum map room, only Polkerris is named as a coastal place in the bay. Polkerris translates as 'fortified pool or cove' and at the time was an active pilchard fishing community of some 40 inhabitants, in the ownership of the Rashleighs, as it is to this day. It must have been of some importance, since the Cott manuscript depicting coastal defences shows a Tudor watchtower on a rock, just north of the beach. However, written under the tower in secretary script but undated, are the words, 'Not built.' Interestingly, there are still seven muzzle loading iron cannon set into the ground around the harbour as mooring bollards, which have been dated by Colin Carpenter, an armament expert, as being early 17th century. Where these came from is something of a mystery, and may possibily have been taken up from a shipwreck.

Pilchards were the mainstay of Polkerris and a surviving contract dated 1772 for the Polkerris seine fishermen states:

'Contracted with Sainers to go on Polkerris sain to be sent out at midsummer next and restrictions as under, viz. The publick expense to be as in the last preceeding year, 7s.6d.(37p) each. The fishermen to clean the cellars as often as necessary, excepting when so much fish is taken that they have not the time for it; they are also to shoot the ground sain whenever Mr. Rashleigh their employer pleases to have it done, and Mr. Rashleigh to have whatever fish may be chose by him in any of the netts without paying for it, unless when a large catch of mackerel or such like is taken when the men are to have half.

Each Sainer to forfeit one penny for each hour they shall be absent from Polkerris, Sundays excepted, unless employed on the Fishing Account or by the direction of Mr. Rashleigh, which penny shall be deducted out of his wages. Any Sainer who choses to work at such hours as he is not required to attend the fishing may have one penny (0.5p) for each hour he shall so work for Mr. Rashleigh. Any fisherman not being on board one or other of the fishing boats at the time the Stop Saine is put overboard, or absenting himself at any time from the craft without leave of the Master, shall lose his share of the catch which shall be equally divided amongst those who gave their attendance at such catch and any fisherman quitting their attendance or crafts before the expiration of the time agreed for, shall lose his share of the fish.'

The account book for fish sold from the village that year suggests either a poor season, or an industry already in decline:

'To Mr. Carrie – 45 hogsheads at 130/-	£67.10s.0d
deduct short gauge	3. 7s.6d
	£64. 2s.6d
The owners 3/4 share is	48. 1s.10d
The Sainers 1/4 share is	16. 0s. 7d
From the Sainers share deduct	
1/12th tithe	1. 6s. 8d
Towards the expenses of sharing day	5s. 0d
Balance	£14. 8s.11d
Shared by 17 fishermen, each =	17s.00d (85p)'

If this seems little reward for what was probably many weeks work, one benefit was their supposed immunity from the much feared press gang, who roamed the coast looking for likely seamen to press into Royal Navy service. Each man in the pilchard industry was given a document stating, 'By the Commissioners for Executing the Office of Lord High Admiral of Gt. Britain, these are to give notice that no fisherman and others employed in the pilchard industry on the coast of Cornwall are to be imprest into his Majesties service, but permitted to follow their said employment without let, hinderence or molestation.' Despite this supposed protection, one naval lieutenant took the press gang into Polkerris in April 1782, carrying off four or five fishermen on board a navy cutter, tearing up their papers declaring they were forgeries.

The estuary leading from the bay, through Tywardreath and the river into Luxulyan valley was still navigable by shallow draught vessels at this stage, animals, crops, granite and ore being regular exports via the shallow waterway. Par was still only a hamlet situated at the mouth of the river, which was already heavily silted, and with no harbour of its own as yet. On the north-east side of the estuary was the hamlet of East Porthmear, which also belonged to the Rashleighs of Menabilly. It was they who built the little row of almshouses alongside the road to Fowey, almost next door to the '*Ship Inn*', the document relating to their construction reading, 'East Porthmear, in the Parish of Tywardreath, four dwelling houses for the Poor, 1807, cost £133.6s.8d, @ £3 per cent, per annum.' It was Charles Rashleigh's sister Jane, who made it her business to distribute poor pay of 2 shillings a month to the families living there. They also received double pay in March, May, September and December, plus winter fuel.

From Spit Point west to the little inlet known as West Porthmear, the cove that was to develop into Charlestown before the century was out, was a continuous run of high cliffs, the sea lapping almost at its base at high water for most of its length. The mile long beach now at Crinnis was created naturally by siltation and long-shore drift, almost entirely during the 18-19th century, by waste sand washed down from the china clay workings above St. Austell, via streams entering the sea at Par. Apart from one large house at Merthen, and a cliff cellar with accommodation over at West Porthmear, there were virtually no dwellings at all on this stretch of coast until one reached Porthpean, people prefering to live in the shelter of high ground, away from the wind where possible.

Porthpean was in fact two villages, Lower Porthpean which enjoyed a somewhat haphazard economy based on fishing, smuggling, wrecking and a little bit of 'this and that', with the residents living mostly in Higher Porthpean, where agriculture and mining held sway. A little further round the bay, past Silver Mine Point, was Ropehaven or Ropehorn, an isolated and very private, inaccessable seine fishery and smuggling centre, which belonged to the Hext family for generations.

Having mentioned wrecking, shipwreck did play a small part in the local economy, frequently involving the Rashleigh family who owned virtually the whole of Gribben Head. On 16 December 1774, the Dutch vessel *Jaff Johanna Christina* was wrecked near the entrance to Fowey harbour. Dyewood, dyestuffs, 137 elephants teeth (weighing between 30-50lbs. each), iron hoops, a stanchion, brandish, pieces of lead, a pump brake, an old blunderbuss, three cannon, three cutlasses and a pistol iron (barrel), were amongst the goods recovered by a Henry Stephens and Thomas and William Melhuish, of Mevagissey, presumably fishermen, 'which remains in their possession until they have been paid reasonable salvage.' Philip Rashleigh paid five shillings to a Jonas Bennett in 1775, 'for burying a man that was cast ashore in the manor of Trenant, on 21 January.' Sixteen shillings was paid on 30 December 1794 for three pieces of timber from a wreck, which drifted ashore at Polridmouth; amongst the ten named men who shared the reward was one Stephen Best. Philip also paid one guinea for an anker of brandy, 'flung onshore and taken up by John and James Geach, at Par,' whilst a cask of gin, containing 25 bottles found under Trill's Ground by John Bennett and others near West Porthmear on 10 April 1800, resulted in the salvors receiving £1.11s.6d. During the 19th century a considerable number of shipwrecks occurred around and within the outer basin at Charlestown, which will receive mention in due course.

Chapter 1   Reference Sources

No.	Sources
1	CCC.CRO. Tywardreath Parish baptismal records
2	Menabilly mss, Rashleigh family tree
3	The Book of Fowey, Keast. J, 1987 p39
4	ibid p33
5	ibid p33
6	ibid p77
7	Menabilly mss
8	CCC. CRO. DDR.5598
9	Menabilly mss
10	Trebartha, Latham. B. p69
11	ibid p68
12	ibid p75
13	ibid p74
14	CCC. CRO. DDT/811/2
15	Trebartha, Latham. B. p75
16	ibid p75
17	CCC. CRO. DD.CF1/853 (Coode's Index Book)
18	Menabilly mss
19	CCC. CRO. DD.CF/4532
20	Trebartha, Latham. B. p76
21	CCC. CRO. DDR/5557
22	ibid DD.CF/46871-3
23	ibid DD.CF/184
24	ibid DD.CF/127
25	ibid DDT/1908
26	ibid DDT/1911
27	ibid AD/448/45
28	Magna Britann, Lyson (Cott mss)
29	CCC. CRO. DDR/5025
30	ibid DDR/5088
31	ibid DDR/5085
32	ibid DDR/5088
33	ibid "
34	ibid DDR/5085
35	ibid "

CHAPTER 2

Porthmear becomes a Town. 1785 – 1804

Prior to 1790, the year that work commenced on the stone pier at West Porthmear, St. Austell, now a growing town, was supplied mostly by road with its necessities. As more work became available in the local mines and china clay industry, so the population of St. Austell grew, from 1,380 in 1745, to 3,290 by 1779. Mevagissey, Tywardreath and Fowey, all open to shipping, were some distance away over hilly country, and whilst a proportion of materials in and out of the town passed by sea through these ports, the addition of road transport costs caused the merchants to seek an alternative. This was West Porthmear, the little cove midway between Porthpean and Crinnis, less than two miles from St. Austell's town centre. The early history of West Porthmear is therefore that of an open sandy cove, with two or three families living either above a cliff-top pilchard cellar (still standing, once named *Content* Cellar, now *Salamanda*, after a World War II minesweeper), or in a couple of run down cottages that have since disappeared. Its nine or so adult residents earned a living from fishing, hovelling, or ship and cargo handling, tending the small wooden sailing coasters of up to 250 tons that unloaded their cargoes of timber, coal, grain, manure, limestone and groceries after running ashore at high water. As the tide fell, so horse drawn carts could get alongside, which transported the discharged goods up the long hill to the Turnpike road running across St. Austell Downs, then on to the town or surrounding countryside. Ever more frequently, there was outgoing cargo to load consisting of barley, malt, copper or tin ore, straw, hay, granite, lead or sand and, towards the end of the 18th century, the first shipments of china clay for the Staffordshire potteries. The ships however, were always at the mercy of the elements. With no national weather forecasting service or radio communication and the beach sheltered only from certain winds, ship's captains relied entirely on experience and time honoured weather lore, to determine if and when they dare risk their vessel being hard and fast ashore, often for 24 hours, handling cargo. During that time the wind could easily increase and shift into the locally much feared south-easterly quarter, blowing hard onshore, bringing huge breakers that could destroy a vessel in a matter of minutes. It was a risky business and we are told that many a coaster came to grief on the foreshore here, but it seemed there was no alternative. Four ships were wrecked here, one of which was the *Three Friends*, captain McMelcheran, lost on 22 January, 1788. It has been claimed by some writers that Charles

Rashleigh lost one of his own ships here on the foreshore, which inspired him to build the port, but in fact Rashleigh was neither whole nor part owner of any ship until the late 1790's, after the port of Charlestown was built.

The earliest reference found to a land transaction covering the ground on which Charlestown now stands, dates back to 1784. Whilst there is the very old Polmear Farm in Charlestown, still being worked, and a much younger West Polmear farm, now converted into two dwellings (No's. 91 & 92 Charlestown Road) as well as the 20th. century Tewington farm, also now a dwelling (No.99 Charlestown Road), many locals consider Polmear or West Polmear as being the original place name, but it was in fact West Porthmear. However, no less than ten variations of the name and spelling exist in various references, some examples of which are:

1682 *Palmere.* Captain G. Collins, English Channel chart

1755 *Polmere.* Kitchin's map of the district

1784 *West Porthmear*, original land agreement

1820 *Higher Polmear/Lower Polmear*, Duporth documents

1845 *Polmear*, Channel Sailing Directions manual

     Porthmear, Smith's map of Cornwall

     Portmeor, C.R.O. Truro, documents, various

     Porthmeor,   "   "   "   "

The name Porthmear or Polmear translates from the old Cornish language as Porth-meur, meaning 'Great cove, or pool,' whereas nearby Porthpean means 'Little Cove, or pool', with Duporth, sandwiched between the two, being 'Black cove, or pool.' The document relating to the transfer of land at Porthmear is dated 19 July 1784, and reads:

'Special Court of the Manor of Tewington, held at Porthmear on 19 July, before Charles Rashleigh, Deputy steward of the said Manor, also at this court came Emblin Tucker, widow of Macklin Tucker, late of the parish of St. Austell, gardiner deceased, who at his death was one of the customary tennants, surrendered into the hands of His Royal Highness George Augustus Frederick, Prince of Wales, all that one cellar with the appurtenances built on the pasture of Gwallen and also two acres of land lying near to Porthmear. That parcel of pasture of Gwallen and said two acres on which a coal yard has lately been made, to the intent and purpose that Macklin Tucker, of the Parish of Pilton, in the County of Devon, nephew and heir in law to the said Macklin Tucker deceased, shall pay a yearly rent of 3s.4d for the cellar and 2d for the two acres.

25

To this same Court came Macklin Tucker, yeoman, nephew and heir at law of Macklin Tucker, gardiner deceased and one of the customary tennants of the aforesaid manor of Tewington, and surrendered into the hands of the same as the others surrendered, to the purpose that Neville Norway of the Borough of Lostwithiel took of his Royal Highness, the cellar and two acres at 3s.4d and 2d per annum.'

The initiative to develop Porthmear's sandy cove to a more formal trading place with storage facilities, probably originated with Macklin Tucker, who appears to have built a coal yard there. This was in turn taken over by Neville Norway, a merchant banker, born in 1739, who was made mayor of Lostwithiel in 1811. Of Tucker we know nothing, other than that on 11 January 1765, acknowledgment was sent to Mrs. Grace Tremayne of Heligan, mother of Charles's future wife, confirming that Tucker had taken lease of pasture land at High Cross, St. Austell, known as the Mowhay meadow. In return Mrs. Tremayne was to have a 'sufficient supply of turnips for her needs.'

Whether Rashleigh's acquisition of land at Porthmear was part of a predetermined development is impossible to say, but in 1789, along with a grant for 1,000 years of part of Tregrehan common, he took over all the leased land at Porthmear previously held by Norway, including use of the foreshore from the Duchy. All this land was eventually purchased outright by him in 1798, when the port was almost completed; at the same time Charles bought the Manor of Tewington from the Duchy under the Land Redemption Act:

'Manor of Tewington, 27th. November 1798. Certificate of Contract, of a sale in fee to Charles Rashleigh esq. of the Manor of Tewington, in the County of Cornwall, excepting nevertheless, reserving unto his said Royal Highness, his heirs and successors, Dukes of Cornwall, all wrecks of the sea, and all mines and minerals within and under the said manor lands & premises, with full liberty of ingress, egress and regress.'

Hence total freehold ownership of some 600 acres passed into Charles's hands, stretching from Par to Porthpean, including the valley running down to the sea at Porthmear, apart from the foreshore, ownership of which was retained by the Duchy of Cornwall. To add to the burden of responsibility undertaken by Charles, the sheer volume of which was a contributing factor in his eventual downfall, he accepted the appointment in 1785 of Receiver of Fowey and, by 1788, that of Recorder for both Fowey and Grampound, which required his attendance at every magistrates court held in those towns. The year end accounts for the joint legal practice of Rashleigh and Edward Coode, jnr. for 1788, show that the rent and fuel for their joint office totalled £15, both partners receiving a personal sum of £626.2s.10d. At Michaelmas the following year, the account showed a remarkable change:

26

Sophia Rashleigh, Charles's youngest daughter, born 1781, with her husband, the Rev. Gervays Grylls.

'Stamps in the office £121.10s.0d

Bills due at Michaelmas 1788 unpaid £262.1s.0d

Bills not yet made out £588.11s.0d

        other matters etc.   Total £2262.10s.1d

Share at 3 October 1789, Edward Coode £5745.5s.3d

Charles Rashleigh   . . . . £5745.5s.3d.'

In September 1790 each partner received £1949.1s.10d, and in the October of 1791, £1019.7s.6d. Charles's increased income from the practice in 1789 was probably welcome, since his third and last daughter Sophia was born at Duporth on 17 March. Named after Lady Mount Edgcumbe, she was christened on 11 July, her god parents being Charles's sister and sister-in-law. The following winter in Cornwall was particularly cold and hard, with heavy snow. The poor of St. Austell had to be given free wood for fuel, to save them from freezing to death, Charles adding a sum to the £50 given by the town 'to relieve the acute distress'. In fact the weather was so bad that the Polgooth mine had to shut down completely for a time.

Ten years later, in 1798, Charles was made Common Clerk or Recorder for Bodmin, then Recorder and Town Clerk for St. Austell, at the same time buying the joint Lay Representative of St. Austell

Church and a family pew, since this was where Charles and his family worshipped, since Duporth had no private chapel. In 1791 he was also appointed Recorder for Tregony, near Truro. At the same time, work progressed on improvements to Duporth Manor, as witness his letter to George C. Fox, merchant of Falmouth, concerning mahogany, possibly for interior use around the house:

> 'The mahogany would suit me best, the price I leave entirely to you, what they spoke to me was 4 shillings a foot, but then they account the square foot and not common inch measure, as is the custom with mahogany. If you can supply me with the wood soon do, and word of it to my servant Joseph Dingle, St. Austel, who has my directions to send for it immediately.'

The name Joseph Dingle, which has already emerged in connection with the volunteer militia, was linked with Charles Rashleigh's affairs for the best part of 45 years, a relationship between two men that remains obscure, very controversial, and possibly homosexual. Joseph Dingle was taken out of the St. Austell Workhouse as a boy aged twelve, jointly by Francis Polkinghorne and Charles Rashleigh, who apprenticed him to a carpenter some two years later; why we will never know, possibly a philanthropic gesture, common amongst gentry of the period. The boy's parents, Martha and Joseph Dingle, both natives of St. Austell, appear to have been in the workhouse for some considerable time, Martha having died there on 21 January 1767, the father on 7 February 1786. Whilst Dingle was a very common name in the district, after considerable research into parish and workhouse records, it has been possible to establish that Joseph Dingle died at Trevarrick, on 9 February 1845, aged 88 years, destitute and in receipt of parish pay. He was therefore born in 1757 and is likely to have been apprenticed around 1770-71, at the age of roughly 14 years.

Eleven years later Dingle's name appears on the list of house servants at Duporth Manor, as Rashleigh's personal footman/servant, now aged 24. It is impossible now, almost 200 years later, to determine what sort of relationship existed between the two men, which was so obviously far deeper than just master and servant, as will be seen. One writer has suggested that Charles took a paternal fancy to him, seeking to bring him up as a son, but Charles was still a young man, well capable of and possibly still anticipating a son of his own, so one must question if that was likely ? What ever there was between them, Charles was certainly to rue the day he allowed Dingle to enter his household.

Until now, it has always been accepted that it was Charles Rashleigh who conceived the idea of creating a seaport at Porthmear, but this may not be true, since it would appear from records that it was Dingle who gave him the idea. The family document at Menabilly outlining Charles Rashleigh's troubles, makes it quite clear that it was Joseph Dingle who made the suggestion to Rashleigh, and may well have been the motivation for Rashleigh to obtain the lease of the necessary land

Duporth Manor, Charles Rashleigh's country house and estate of some 90 acres, situated half a mile west of Charlestown, photographed in the 1920s.

from Neville Norway in 1789. Dingle's suggestion that a protective stone pier would greatly facilitate the unloading of cargo and offer shelter to shipping, and that excavation within the pier to create a basin would offer sufficient depth of water for ships to remain afloat at all states of the tide, was perfectly sound and very necessary if further shipwrecks were to be avoided. Whereupon Rashleigh sought the advice of John Smeaton, the first man to style himself as a civil engineer, since it was he who designed the second Eddystone lighthouse, the Forth and Clyde canal, several bridges in Scotland, the harbour at St. Ives and, in 1774, the Ramsgate Harbour scheme – obviously a man who understood his business. Smeaton went ahead, presumably after visiting the area, designing first a suitable outer arm for the proposed haven at West Porthmear, to be built with locally quarried granite, which in fact came from Luxulyan valley. His original sketch plan for the stone arm once hung in the office of Stratton Creber Ltd., in Charlestown, and the plans for the remainder of the harbour and basin may still survive somewhere. Called back to Ramsgate by its Harbour Commissioners in 1787, to solve serious silting difficulties within the basin, it did not escape Smeaton's attention that Porthmear would eventually suffer similar problems, since apart from size, there are many similarities between the two ports. This explains the reason for the eventual cutting of an eleven mile water course or leat in 1794,

known as the Port leat, between Luxulyan and Porthmear, a not incon-
siderable achievement in itself, considering that some of it involved
tunnelling through rock for a considerable distance. In addition, huge
upper and lower ponds were dug in the village, which today still act as
header reservoirs, feeding the dock with fresh water on demand via
sluices, not only to maintain the water level, compensating for any leak
in the lock gates, but also to flush away silt from the outer dock from
time to time, a similar scheme to that still employed at Ramsgate.
Smeaton summarised the requirement succinctly, when he wrote in a
letter:

> 'To remove silt, there must be either a natural river or other
> means, or to artificially produce the same. The recourse is to
> construct a basin to take in water, diverted through sluices,
> to cleanse the harbour on release.'

Unfortunately, Smeaton was not to see the Porthmear project completed. He died at the age of 68 on 28 October 1792, one of his many
achievements being the founding of a small select club of engineers,
called the 'Smeatonians', which later merged with other groups to
become the Institute of Civil Engineers. In 1789-90, just before Charles
and Grace departed for a visit to London, Dingle approached his master requesting a lease for life of East Polmear Farm, along with other
land, where he intended to live, which Rashleigh foolishly granted.
This in itself may seem strange, that a gentleman living in a manor
house should allow a then unmarried footman, his personal servant, to
live some half mile distant, when such a position was very much a 'live-
in' situation. But then it may have been that Rashleigh wanted him
'on-site', to supervise the building of the quay and port. In those terms
it is understandable that Charles not only furnished the empty property at his own expense, but also stocked the farm with animals.

Work commenced on the harbour project in 1790, lasting for the best
part of nine years, during which time Joseph Dingle, no longer a footman, acted as Superintendent of Works throughout! Rashleigh appears
to have placed every trust in him, allowing him to produce the initial
estimate and costings, leaving him to supervise not only the building,
but paying wages, organising materials and labour and, on completion
of the first phase, financial control of the running of the emerging port
complex. From workhouse, through apprentice carpenter, footman,
small-holding farmer to Superintendent of Works was meteoric
advancement indeed, which Rashleigh was soon to regret.

The building of the port was of course undertaken with no official
permission, since none was required at the time. In fact only seven
years after its completion regulations concerning such work were introduced, possibly due to the continued threat of French invasion:

> 'Act. 46 George III, dated 23rd. July 1806. After the passing of this
> Act it shall not be lawful for any person to make, construct or
> erect any pier, quay, wharf, jetty, breast or embankment communi-

30

A portrait of Grace Tremayne of Heligan Manor, believed to have been painted by Clifford in 1774, when she was 32 years of age, two years prior to her marriage in July 1776.

cating with the tide flow without giving at least one months notice to the Secretary of the Admiralty and lay same before the Lord High Admiral or Lords Commissioners.'

Dingle's marriage certificate, dated 3 June 1792, when he took as his bride Jenepher Bennett, 'parish spinster', who was in fact a house-maid at Duporth Manor, presents an interesting diversion. Both parties legalised the document by putting as their 'mark' a rough 'X' in the case of Dingle, and Bennett a mark similar to a '?'. Was this a not uncommon gesture of kindness to an illiterate wife, so that she would not feel embarrassed in front of the vicar of St. Austell church, or was he truly incapable of signing his name at that time? A few documents survive seemingly written by Dingle and certainly signed by him, as do a number of payment receipts, as well as a letter or two relating to the poor condition of Porthmear pier and Mevagissey harbour, all signed with a strong literate signature. Surely, it is inconceivable that he could have costed out Porthmear harbour works, materials and labour, and managed the affairs of the dock and its finances for so long as an illiter-

31

ate? Work commenced in earnest on the outer arm in the spring of 1790, levelling the shale outcrops of rock and setting down the foundation blocks of granite, work being limited to low water springs initially, then normal low water until the height of the stonework was above the tide, progress always dictated by the weather.

In order to give the reader as accurate a picture of events as possible, there follows verbatim the relevant paragraphs of the original document concerning Rashleigh's troubles. This is followed by supporting research material, elaborating, often with fascinating detail, on what would otherwise be only a brief clinical account. It is believed to have been written by Mrs. Harriet Rodd, Charles Rashleigh's oldest daughter, who died in 1866:

'Charles Rashleigh. The following is an account of Charles Rashleigh's troubles with his servant Dingle who virtually ruined him. A plan of the proposed pier was then made under Mr. Smeaton's direction, the estimate of the expense was made by Dingle, who being on the spot, and a person to whom Charles Rashleigh thought he could fully rely, was made superintendent of the works.

It was in the year 1791 that the excavation of the rocks, and the building of the pier began. The money for the undertaking, Dingle was directed from time to time to take from the Rashleigh chest, giving cheques for the same, and at the end of each week to deliver particular accounts as to how the sums were expended. This plan was adopted from the time of its commencement until it was completed. After the pier and the basin were completed, a number of houses were built in the same manner in or about 1794 and the place was named Charlestown after him.

At this time the Rashleigh's had no reason to believe that Joseph Dingle was anything but a sober, honest and industrious man. Indeed, so high an opinion did they hold of the man's integrity and ability than no sooner was Charlestown sufficiently advanced he not only gave him the sole trading rights, but advanced him considerable sums of money to enable him to carry it on to advantage, on no other security other than notes of hand, or cheques. In the year 1798, after the place was completed, an account was made out and was balanced by Dingle, in which he gave Rashleigh credit for the whole money received from time to time, as the work was being carried on and debited him with the total of the weekly accounts. In the account he also gave Charles Rashleigh credit for the rents he received for the buildings, for quay dues from the pier and the basin, leaving a balance in Mr. Rashleigh's hands of £14,000. The account was afterwards continued by Dingle to the year 1805, by which time the balance due to Charles Rashleigh had risen to upwards of £25,000, which Joseph Dingle afterwards admitted was a just and true account. After this year, no other balances were struck by Dingle, although Mr. Rashleigh was beginning to feel very uneasy at the conduct, frequently pressing him to do so. The sum was now upwards of £30,000. Now, unfortunately too late, Mr. Rashleigh saw that he had been placing his property in the hands of a person unworthy of competence and who was coming openly to bid him defiance.

Mr. Rashleigh was therefore obliged to recourse to law, in the hope that by a verdict he might at least be able to free himself from a man who had thus swindled him of his property. This action came to trial in the Bodmin assize before Mr. Boyer, defendant Dingle, and a verdict was given by Mr. Rashleigh for upwards of £20,000. To defeat the verdict a conspiracy was then formed by Mr. Boyer, the solicitor, Mr. Dingle the bankrupt, Mr. Butterfield of Charlestown, and William Mallet Thomas, the bankrupt's nephew and principal creditor. Mr. Rashleigh, seeing that this was a scheme to defeat his claim protested against the formation of the commission. After many harassing proceedings, Mr. Rashleigh sent his clerk and all his books to dock, and two days were spent in their examination, but at last it was determined to place the whole matter before Mr. Wingfield and Mr. Abercrombie, gentleman of the Bar, but at the meeting with the bankrupt and his nephew, the latter of whom swore to a debt of some £15,000, although never worth so many shillings, but was subsequently admitted. He swore on one side of the account only and this being held sufficient to defend the object, this part of the proceedings ended. Mr. Charles Rashleigh, knowing that his accounts, by who so ever investigated them could not withold from him the sum he had before shown, and proved, was justly due, laid his accounts before Dr. Carpenter and abide by his decision, but Carpenter being ill at the time, died before anything was done in it. At length, these vexations and fraudulent litigations ended in everything going back into the hands of Mr. Boyer and an appeal to the Court of Equity was the only remedy left to Charles Rashleigh. It is needless to say that such long legal proceedings still more impoverished Mr. Rashleigh, beside the great pain caused to Mr. & Mrs. Rashleigh in the treacherous and deceitful conduct of one whom they had brought up and treated with such lavish and unwise kindness. The trial and the worry killed Charles Rashleigh.'

Those protracted court proceedings which commenced in 1813 and lasted several years, obviously took a heavy financial and physical toll of Charles, then aged 68, but it is untrue to say it actually killed him. Charles lived for a further eight years following his eventual success in getting Dingle declared a bankrupt, and it was the outcome of a second, even more desperate and expensive court case, involving yet another footman/servant, that broke his heart, sending him to his grave in 1823.

Returning to 1791, the first year of construction work on the pier or jetty, at the end of twelve months it was already high enough to offer protection to fishing boats which could now land their catches in safety. Larger vessels could also get alongside at high water and West Porthmear was now importing serious tonnages of coal, iron, timber, mining requirements and lime for both farming and construction work. That same year saw three new houses built in the village, many labourers in full employment and the population rise from nine to twenty-six. More importantly, regular shipments of china clay were being exported to the north country potteries via Liverpool, the beginnings of a trade for Charlestown with exports to most of Europe and with an unbroken history now over 203 years.

With the pier undamaged following its first winter seas, it was further strengthened and its height increased in 1792, whilst workmen commenced to dig out and deepen the outer basin as well as excavate an inner dock. The shipping trade continued to expand, several more houses, stores, sheds and workshops were built and, to support a new pilchard seine which had been fitted out, more pilchard cellars were constructed, now used as woodwork and wrought iron workshops. In addition, a rope and twine manufactury was started and the population rose to ninety-seven. The following year, 1793, saw work progressing on the eastern enclosing arm of the outer harbour, a second pilchard seine was financed and installed and seven more houses were built, bringing the number living in West Porthmear to 109. Many acres of adjacent common land were also enclosed, but more importantly, the inner basin was opened for the reception of small ships, a shipwrights' yard was established and 'some small vessels were built and launched that year.'

Looking at the port today, in which the loading of ships is undertaken within the dock behind lock gates, one would imagine this was how it has always been, but you would be mistaken. The sole purpose of the then much shorter inner dock, which did not have lock gates for some years, was ship-building and repair work, the handling of cargo being mostly carried out on the outer arms. From the high ground immediately in front of where two weigh-bridges now stand, there was at the time a long sloping ramp running down into the dock, its lower end underwater at high tide, which reached almost level with what is now the Harbourside Inn. On this ramp a great many ships were built over the next eighty years, the associated carpentry, shipwright and blacksmith work being undertaken in a scatter of sheds around the top end of two slipways. At low tide, vessels in the mouth of the dock would sit on the bottom, where they could be scraped, cleaned, repainted or have underwater repairs carried out. When a ship was ready to be launched, it was only necessary to clear other vessels out of the way and it would be gently slid down the ramp into the sea, no doubt restrained from going too far or too fast by heavy iron chains and weights.

During the next twelve months the shipyard was enlarged and improved so that vessels of up to 500 tons could be built, but it should not be overlooked that Thomas Shepheard of Mevagissey, was also building ships on the west beach at Porthmear. In 1794 he completed the big lugger *Speedwell* there, followed by four more before moving into the inner basin shipyard in 1798. Yet another pilchard seine was established, cellars and storehouses blossomed, a further seventy acres of common land was enclosed and broken in for farming and the lime trade was greatly increased, over 11,000 bushels (a bushell being the old dry measure of 8 gallons) being burnt in 1794. Incidently, during the same year, the church in St. Austell which then had a steeple, was struck by lightning and the steeple collapsed, falling across the old Market House, and in so doing destroying its roof and part of the facade, Charles donating a sum of money towards its restoration. This was of course the old, much smaller market house, the present building having been erected on the same site in 1842.

The first lime kiln in the village was built on the edge of the outer basin, a two storey granite building with two hearths at quay level, enabling vessels to discharge rough lime stone for treatment and to load burnt lime in barrels, immediately alongside, with minimum handling. Today, nothing of that lime kiln survives except for one hearth, hidden inside a small lean-to store close to the steps leading from the quay to the harbour master's Round-house. The upper part of the lime kiln, where the stone was fed into the kiln under cover, which also served a second and unusual purpose, was demolished sometime around 1885, making way for the flat area on which the Round-house and flagstaff now stand. The original purpose of a mast near the entrance to the harbour was to fly appropriate signals, a 6ft. diameter black ball or a red ensign by day, with red and green lights at night, indicating whether it was safe for vessels to enter, or not. A second lime kiln was built around 1794-5, inland past the head of the dock, on the western side of the road leading out of the village. This was a most ambitious construction, possibly one of the finest surviving six hearth, back-to-back lime kilns in the county. This consisted of two kiln areas, separated by a splendid granite building, still intact, the lower part of which was the 'gun-shed' for the best part of the 19th century. In here the four iron, long 18 pounder cannon, weighing 25cwt. each were stored in the dry on wooden blocks, along with their garrison truck carriages, shot and powder, wagon type 'dillies' and necessary tackle and accoutrements to install them in the battery. The guns were not left in the battery during the worst winter months, nor during periods of peace, when they were taken out for repository drill and practice firing only. More will be said about the battery and its cannon in chapter 5. We know that the overall quantity of lime handled and burnt in 1795 was 21,000 bushells and this activity continued right up until 1925, the last lime-burner in the village being Henry Netting, who lived in Ash Hill. By the end of 1795, Polmear's population had increased to 175.

As the harbour complex grew, so did the problems, it being necessary to put in temporary flood-gates to protect the dock in 1796. The population increased that year to 190, then 205 in 1797, the year when two ships were built and launched. More stores and houses went up in

1798, the number living in the village rose to 220, and the basin and dock were 'so much enlarged that several vessels can enter and receive repairs'. Evidence that the shipyard was no small undertaking, making all its iron work instead of buying it in ready made, can be found in the 15 April 1799 edition of the Sherborne & Yeovil Mercury, one of the first west country provincial newspapers. In an advertisment, Thomas Hocking, a St. Austell blacksmith, sought 'a foreman ship's anchor smith, for Charles's town.'

If any one year in the history of the village can be described as a turning point, it was 1799, since by the end of that year it could truthfully be said that the port was finished; it was also the year in which it is thought the village changed its name. Who conceived the idea, or when, has been lost, but it appears that by mutual agreement within the village, a collection was started to purchase a very special piece of commemorative porcelain, to be known as the Duporth Cup. This consisted of a saucer some 8ins.(20cms.) in diameter, designed to hold a two handled cup fitted with a domed lid. Dark blue in colour, with a small white flower pattern and gilt rim, the centre of the saucer is inscribed, 'The Rise and Progress of Charles's Town'. The cup and lid both show miniature paintings of views from Duporth, the construction of the dock at Porthmear, the beach before work commenced and the harbour wall under construction. Made in great secrecy at the Wedgwood factory, it was delivered into the village, a deputation taking it up to Duporth House. Here it was presented to Charles, from the villagers, in gratitude for employment and what seemed a prosperous future for everyone. Showing surprise at the wording on the saucer, perhaps exclaiming, 'What's this all about then?', the locals asked his permission to change the name of the village from Porthmear to Charles's Town, in his memory. Looking back, having accepted such a valuable and unique gift, already bearing the proposed new name, it would have been churlish to have refused and from that day on, Charles's Town it was. No authority other than Rashleigh's permission was sought; it just happened, and by usage was quickly accepted, contracted today as Charlestown. Readers may well ask what happened to the Duporth Cup, where can it be seen? Following Charles's death, the Duporth Cup went with his daughter Pattie to Cuddra House, then Cuddra Cottage and on her death to a family named Fursden in Exeter. Following the death of a Miss Charlotte Fursden in 1929, (who held many items of Charles Rashleigh memorabilia including documents) it seemingly disappeared. It is now known to be in the hands of a branch of the Rashleigh family in Devon, but they decline to let it be seen or re-photographed.

That same year, Charles wrote to a friend, on 10 March, 'all our fisheries are at an end, our good folk did not take care when the salt bill was passed', referring to salt as the necessary preservative used in the pilchard industry, on which a prohibitive and unpopular tax had been placed. However, by 28 May he was writing to George Fox, 'I have no cellar vacant at Charlestown, but will engage one such as you will approve', suggesting things had been sorted out. The continued enlargement and deepening of the outer basin brought realisation regarding potentially destructive south-easterly gales, which plague the port to this day, prohibiting vessels from remaining alongside in the outer basin and the opening of the dock gates. Whilst speculation, it is possible that the period 1790-5 saw no really severe weather from that quarter, but something untoward happened in 1798-9 that made it necessary for Rashleigh to have wooden gates fitted to the dock. We know that the very last set of wooden oak gates for the dock were built by Messrs. Hall & Lester of London and Plymouth, and were fitted in 1890 by Mr. Inglis, the engineer responsible for the building of the breakwaters at Newlyn and Mevagissey. The dock was closed to shipping for two weeks that August, whilst the gates were not only replaced but their hangings reversed, since there is every reason to believe that the original gates of 1799 opened outward, ie. seaward, making the inner basin a dry dock, thus allowing ship-repair and building to continue regardless of weather conditions.

In support of this, a summary of Charlestown events which appeared in an early newspaper mentions, 'flood-gates were erected that vessels within might always be afloat in the absence of the tide . . in the inner extremity another excavation . . to form a dry dock.' This would make the flooding and general operation of the dock the reverse of what it is today, since the gates had to open seaward, otherwise tidal water pressure would force them open. As will be seen in Chapter 4, all inner dock shipbuilding and repair ceased completely in 1870, the dock being doubled in size. During these changes it would not have been difficult to reverse the direction in which the gates closed, to turn it from a dry to a wet dock as it is today. Admittedly, early photographs of Charlestown show the gates opening inwards, but these are generally post 1890 and even the earliest Frances Frith pictures, taken c1885, were taken long after these changes had taken place.

Near starvation and the suffering of a great many poor people in St. Austell during the summer of 1800, came to the attention of Charles, who utilised his new port to relieve the situation somewhat by ordering a shipload of barley. His letter to George Fox of Falmouth reads, 'the consignment has arrived, it cost me £1.4s. a bushel, but I am selling it to the poor for £1.0s.' By 1801 the people living in Charles's Town numbered 300 and the area enclosed – either cultivated or in other commercial use, was not far short of 1,000 acres, the greater part belonging to Charles Rashleigh. This land was leased to village tenants for three lives at seven shillings and six pence (37.5p) per acre, per annum. Whilst a very low rent indeed, Charles recognised that for this sum the occupiers would be willing to improve the ground at their own expense, using old pilchard salt, broken (ie. damaged) pilchards, dung, sea sand and seaweed, removing the rocks and bringing the land eventually to a more realistic value of 30-40s. per acre.

Throughout all this development and expansion, which must have been a very exciting and stimulating period, Joseph Dingle appears to have balanced the books satisfactorily, at least up until 1798. The port derived income from rents, quay and harbour dues (ships paying 6d. a ton in 1801), the sale of pilchards, train-oil and so on, which was balanced against sums drawn from Charles for materials and labour. Following such a large undertaking, with initially little or no income, it is not surprising that by 1801 the account showed Rashleigh out of pocket to the tune of £14,000. Whether or not Dingle set out to fleece his employer from the outset we do not know, but there are some strange aspects of the whole business. As the basin and dock work took in more and more land, the records reveal that some of this actually belonged to Dingle, who commenced to charge a rent for its use. As housing was built, so Dingle's name suddenly appears as the owner, and by 21 March 1799 he had moved out of Polmear Farm, sub-letting it to someone else of course, and into Jardan Cuddra, paying a land tax of £1.18s.4d. This was presumably Cuddra House, at Crinnis, a substantial residence.

Charles took Dingle's account of affairs at face value, not doubting his honesty, otherwise it would have been a relatively simple task for William Tallack, Rashleigh's clerk in his St. Austell legal office, to have checked the figures, reached a true balance and from then on to have managed the finances himself. Charles appears to have been content either to let things slide, or perhaps to give Dingle's many business interests more time to repay the large sums of money advanced to him. Rashleigh's many business interests included the buying and selling of tin through the Far East, a common practice in Cornwall at the time, evidenced by a letter from George Unwin, Supercargo to the Honourable East India Company:

'Stamford Street, London. 23 April 1793. Gentlemen, I have the pleasure to send you the sale of your tin shipped last year for China, which I hope will give you the most pleasing satisfaction. The following statement of the price of tin in the China market from 1781 to 1792, a space of 12 years, will show that the expectation of £76 per ton is reasonable and fair, and with respect to the quantity it clearly appears that it would be in the interest of the Company to send out every year 1,200 tons to China, provided there was so much surplus in the county.

Sale of tin to China these past 12 years.

800 tons, £76 per ton, at Prime cost	£1,216,000
800 tons, £88 per ton, sold in China	£1,408,000
Balance to pay all charges	£192,000

Harriet Rashleigh, Charles's eldest daughter, born 1779, and her husband, the Rev. Edward Rodd, painted by A. Stephens in 1842.

They expect to invest from China £1,494,580 yearly, producing a profit of £500,000 after paying freight out and home.'

With two legal practices, several Stewardships, including a new appointment as Steward to Lord Dunstanville's Tehidy estate in 1800 and by letter patent, dated 26 February 1801, Steward to the Duchy of Lancaster, attendance at various magistrates and crown courts, social engagements, the buying and selling of property and commodities, the running of Charlestown itself and Duporth House, Charles was too busy to attend to details. He preferred to put his trust in others, and was probably unwilling to admit his faith in Joseph Dingle was possibly misguided. With the port more or less finished, most men at the age of 53 would have begun to slow down, but Charles now directed his attention to his family and improvements at Duporth and its immediate surroundings, correspondence giving some fascinating insights into his private life. One of his big undertakings was the planting of many hundreds of trees of all types and the creation of wind breaks around Charlestown and Duporth, introducing a wide range of saplings from different countries. No one alive today could have seen Duporth garden at its best, its entrance and driveway a canopy of broad leaf trees of every type, with pines and conifers of gold, greens and blue-greys a wonderful contrast against the deciduous trees. Once there were any number of boweries, streams, waterfalls and fountains, secret hidden places, summer houses, a splendid grotto almost the equal of that at Menabilly created by Philip Rashleigh. Other attractions, all joined by

39

beautifully kept paths, winding through an abundance of shrubs and exotic sub-tropical flower gardens were fruit gardens, melon houses and walled-gardens, as can be seen in the 'Lost garden of Heligan', only recently restored. Unfortunately, they are virtually no more, since like Duporth Manor, which was pulled down in the 1980's, the maintenance became prohibitive. However, Rashleigh's tree planting in and around the ponds and elsewhere in Charlestown, which proved that oak, beech and pine-easters could best withstand the wind, have left a legacy of woodland and mature trees which, although poorly managed, still survives, and greatly enhances the character of Charlestown, particularly the steep hill from Duporth, officially Duporth Road, but still known locally as Brick Hill and sometimes Charlestown Avenue.

Illness, bereavement, Emperor Boneparte and domestic matters seem to have been prominent in the life of the Rashleigh family between 1800-3, as witness various letters of the period;

'Mrs. John Rashleigh died this morning, Tuesday 4th.November 1800.'

'Charles Rashleigh to George Fox, 9th. October 1801. My family are rather better, but yet invalids.'

'Charles Rashleigh to George Fox, 26th. October 1801. I have asked Mr.Norway and some others about the pay to Masters of vessels when the ships have been taken (by the French); they assure me the wages have always been considered as due. I really think William Hoppins a hard case, and know the distress of his family, the sum due to him from Messrs.Lanyon & Fox is £36.16s. May I trouble you once more, I think the amount should be paid. My poor brother John continues in the same helpless state, with little hopes of speedy attention. I left my wife very unwell, and neither Harriet nor Pattie so well as I would wish.'

'Charles to George Fox, 21st.February 1802. I write to appraise you of sending by my clerk, Mr.Tallack tomorrow, a few grafts of the orange and lemon trees, I believe it a little early for grafting. I forgot to say my brother Rashleigh wishes to have a hogshead of the sherry wine. I understand that Mr. Dingle's fish got a good market and sold for above 4 guineas a hogshead . . My dear Pattie is very poorly.'

'Charles Rashleigh to George Fox, 24th. February 1802. My dear Pattie continues very poorly . . Mr. Tremayne also feels the gout very heavy on him.'

'Charles Rashleigh to George Fox, 4th. March 1802. My dear Martha still coughs sadly and seems a little changed which we hope is favourable, yet the strength of it does not appear to abate.' (nb. this is the only letter found written by Charles, in which he uses his daughter's proper name of Martha instead of Pattie.)

'Charles Rashleigh to George Fox, March 1802. I am particularly obliged for your kind attention to, and supply of my wants for linen, it contributes much to my personal comfort. At present Mr. & Mrs. Edward Rodd are living with me, their house not being yet ready to receive them (at St.Just). I lament your having the gout again.'

'Charles Rashleigh to Philip Rashleigh, MP. 27 Norfolk Street, Strand, London, 27th. August 1802. I am most grateful to hear the favourable account of my sister, and which we hope will proceed to her perfect recovery. Typhus is one of the plagues, not of Egypt, but of England .'

' my spinster sister Martha has died.'

'Charles Rashleigh to Philip Rashleigh, 26th. October 1803. I hope Boneparte will not come in June, to partake of the pheasants. I fear whether my health nor time, will allow me to shoot again, but should a chance day come, for my taking that diversion . . '

'Mrs. Rashleigh, the maiden sister, a great invalid, who lives with her brother at Menabilly.'

As this period in Charlestown's history comes to a close, there are only three aspects remaining which deserve a mention. The odd reference is found to an inn and a hotel at Charlestown, some as early as 1793, which should be clarified. It is probable that the isolated pink washed cottage (No.21 Charlestown Road), level with the dock on the west side, was once an inn. However, inn's during the 18th and 19th. centuries were generally much larger establishments, offering food, drink and accommodation, for which this particular building was totally unsuitable. However, any small private house could call itself an 'ale house', provided they had the necessary licence to brew beer which they then sold in their front parlours. Porthmear's first 'inn' or 'ale house' was therefore probably only a private cottage, any one of the thirty-six houses in the village. As to the hotel, this was the existing *Pier House Hotel*, then known as the *Charlestown Hotel*, or simply *The Hotel*. By 1800 it had an attached malting house, brewing beer for their own trade, probably the ale-house, and for sale to ships in and out of the dock. The hotel ceased as such when the Rashleigh Arms was built, being turned into a farm, with one family living in the front part, another in the back, the stables becoming cow sheds and mangers. Later still it became a boarding house, then reverted to a hotel under its present name, the *Harbourside Inn* being created out of its lounge/cafe in 1992.

Finally, a Charlestown Sunday School was formed in 1804, whose original banner still hangs in the Methodist Sunday School Room. This begs the question, where did they meet, since there was no church of any creed in the village at that time? The answer was found on page nine of the *Survey of Charlestown Estate, 1825*, item 102. This shows that there was once a village Meeting House, built directly behind what is now the Rashleigh Arms, itself previously a china clay cellar. This public building was leased to a Matthew Vounder for 5s., on the three lives of J. H. Tremayne, Charles Geach and Jonathan Peters. This Meeting House was in turn, demolished and replaced by the Wesleyn Methodist Church in 1827, built on the foundations of the old building, giving it an even older connection with Charlestown.

Chapter 2   Reference Sources

No	Source
1	CCC.CRO. CF/133/4
2	" DD.CF/134
3	" ibid
4	" DDR(R)(5)13
5	" DDR.5088. Act.46 Geo.III, 1806
6	" St. Austell Parish marriage certificates
7	MB. Mss
8	ibid
9	CCC.CRO. DDR(5)13
10	" ibid
11	" ibid
12	" DDR.5304
13	" DD.CF/4532
14	" DDR(5)13
15	" ibid
16	" ibid
17	" DDR.5304
18	" ibid

CHAPTER 3

Charles Rashleigh versus Joseph Dingle. 1805 – 1814

If Charles Rashleigh was uneasy about Dingle's handling of his affairs at Charlestown prior to 1805, events beg the question as to why he continued to lease him land and property, as well as draw money from the port account, thereby adding to an ever-increasing debt? In an account of 'Rental and land in the Parish of St. Austell, belonging to Charles Rashleigh, dated Lady Day (25th March) 1805,' amongst a wealth of detail concerning place names and individuals, there is clear evidence that Joseph Dingle continued to prosper. (nb. *the order in which various properties are listed in the original document have been altered, to bring those leased to Dingle together for clarity*.)

Description of property	Rent, pa.	Arrears
Cuddra and Cuddra tenament (Joseph Dingle)	£37	£194.6s.8d
House and garden, part of Cuddra (Dingle)	£1.10s	£9.1s.3d
ditto ditto	£1.10s	
Holmbush tenament (Joseph Dingle)	£4.10s	£9.0s
Jardan Crowder (Joseph Dingle)	£10.0s	£52.10s
Porthmear & Crolls & Daniells (Joseph Dingle) and tenaments with Trehawkeys Park.	£110.0s	£525.0s
Warricks & Libby's Cellars at Porthmear,	£12.7s	
Lost-by-the Sea Cellar & field at do. (John Organ) Puckeys tenament at Porthpean Fields	£7.10s	
House and garden	£2.12.6d	
Field	£2.0s	
Field and linhay	£5.5s	
House and garden	£3.0s	
Dwelling house (John Walkey) Cartolls with tenament	£7.4s	
Sundry fields and houses	£80.0s	
House and cellars at Porthpean	£2.10s	

Two houses and a plot of land	£7.0s	
House (William Walkey, since 1795, 20.5yrs lease)	£4.4s	
Elliotts & Hoopers cellars (Walkey & Co.)	£10.10s	
Nap Parks (Nicholas Walkey)	£10.10s	
House, late Matthew Walkey	£10.0s	
House, garden & meadow called the Hop Yard (Ann Walkey)	£2.10s	£6.12s
Dwelling house & remises (Margaret Walkey)	£5.0s	
Biscovallack	£10.0s	
House in St. Austell	£6.8s	
Field called Crapps, in Tregonissey Lane, dwelling house and Brewhouse	£1.4s	
Houses in Menacuddle Lane	6s.	£2.3s.6d
Buck House	£8.8s	
West Park, Francis Polkinghorne	£2.2s	
Part of tenament at Carvath	18s.8d	
Mill at St. Blazey bridge	£2.2s	
The Moiety of St. Austell Gt. Tithes (Mrs. May Sawle)	£1.10s	

Reference was made in the previous chapter to the fact that by 1805 Dingle owed Charles Rashleigh the sum of £25,000. In order to appreciate the equivalent value of that amount today and to equate it with rents and earnings generally of the period, it is necessary to employ a suitable price-indices covering the intervening 189 years. Inumerable references to prices and inflation can be found scattered throughout literature, but a good yard-stick is the 100 base system outlined in *Seven Centuries of Building Wages*, Brown & Hopkins, 1955. In this the authors take as a base 100 (or 1)in the period 1451-75, so that from their graph it can be shown that the cost of that same unit had risen to 600 (or x 6) by 1805 and some 150,000 (or x 1500) by 1990. Whilst only a rough guide, it would appear that Rashleigh's £25,000 in 1805 would be worth about £6m today. This is probably a reasonable costing to place on the building of an entire port, along with its infrastructure and dwellings, plus fifteen years income and interest. By the same yardstick, rents quoted in 1805 as £5.0s. pa. would today be £1,250 and, as will be seen later, Joseph Dingle's receipts for 'pay myself' sums amounting to £760 in one year alone, would have a current value of roughly £62,000. A selection of these receipts for 1806, reveal that Dingle was claiming for

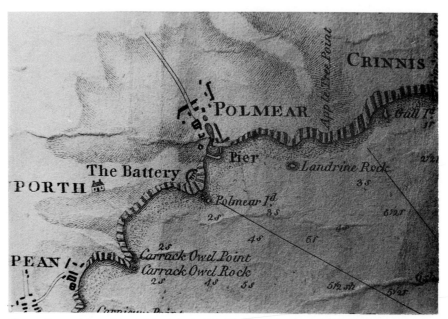

Part of an early chart of St. Austell Bay, c1798, showing development of the port of Polmear or Porthmear, later renamed Charles's Town, with the gun battery and Duporth Manor house to the west.

repairs to Polkerris pier, sums surely in excess of what the pier cost to build initially ?

> 'St. Austell. 16th. May 1806. Messrs. Rashleigh Coode & Co. Pay myself or bearer One Hundred & Fifty Pounds on account of repairing Polkerris Pier for Philip Rashleigh Esq. Joseph Dingle.'

> 'St. Austell. 5th. June 1806. Messrs. Rashleigh Coode & Co. Pay myself or bearer One Hundred & Fifty Pounds on account of repairing Polkerris pier for Philip Rashleigh Esq. Joseph Dingle.'

> 'St. Austell. 7th. August 1806. Messrs. Rashleigh Coode & Co. Pay myself or bearer One hundred & Fifty Pounds on account of repairing Polkerris Pier. Joseph Dingle.'

> 'St. Austell. 17th. September 1806. Messrs. Rashleigh Coode & Co. Pay myself two hundred & Fifty Pounds on account of repairing Polkerris Pier for Philip Rashleigh Esq. Joseph Dingle.'

> 'St. Austell. 20th. November 1806. Messrs. Rashleigh Coode & Co. Pay myself or bearer Sixty Pounds on account of repairing Polkerris Pier for Philip Rashleigh Esq. Joseph Dingle.'

Charles was probably in some financial difficulty already, since on Christmas Day, 1805, he took out a mortgage for £5,000 (£1.25 million

45

by current standards) by an agreement that read:

> 'Charles Rashleigh, of Duporth, to William Praed, of Buckinghamshire; Jonathan Rogers, of Penrose; William Tweedy, of Truro Vean and Thomas Nankivell, of Truro, mortgage of the Manor of Tewington in the sum of £5,000.'

As will be seen later, bitterness developed between William Rashleigh, who was both his nephew and brother Philip's heir, and Charles Rashleigh, over finances. Charles was still the legal Steward for the estate at Menabilly at the time of Philip's death, and took exception to suggestions that all was not well with the accounts, which in time proved true. Also he was accused of using his position to advantage concerning the estate, even attempting to get brother Philip committed to a lunatic asylum. With Dingle drawing huge sums from Charles's office against Philip's account, no wonder Menabilly was experiencing financial difficulties. The amount drawn by Dingle supposedly for repairs to the quay at Polkerris in one year was prodigious, to say the least, particularly when the entire quay dues for Polkerris for the year ended 19th March 1847 amounted to only £9.6s.0d. The sums Dingle was drawing appear even greater when compared with other labour and material costs:

> 'Estimate for the labour of carpenters and joiners work for the building of a new farm house at Menabilly for William Rashleigh esq. (in 1823) to be finished according to the plan and specifications, the sum of £91.13s.5d and likewise to a necessary house with two apartments to be included in the same. And for the labour of painting the house, three coats inside and out £4.1s.6d.
>
> Signed: John Trewin.'

Other evidence of Dingle's continued business dealings in the area, in addition to running the port and Charlestown, can be found in numerous legal documents scattered throughout different collections in Cornwall's CRO and the Royal Institute of Cornwall:

> '3rd June 1806. Bargain and sale with mortgage for £600. Jon. Parnall, of St. Austell, brazier, and William Andrew of St. Mewan, butcher, to Joseph Dingle of St. Austell, merchant,
> a farm at Tregonissey, (leased by Edm. Carthew to Jon. Parnall in 1797, Manor of Treverbyn Courtnay), waste land by Jon. Parnall, part of Boscundle (leased by Thom. Carlyon to Jon. Parnall in 1800); waste land at Gwellyn, Portmellyn and Town, alias St. Austell Foredown leased by Charles Rashleigh to Jon. Parnall in 1802.'

> '2nd June 1812. Reassignment of Mortgage, Joseph Dingle of St. Austell, merchant, to Charles Rashleigh of Duporth, to Jon. Parnall of St. Austell, brazier, property as above.'

'24th October 1806. Lease and Release for one year, Charles Rashleigh to Sir Chas. Morice Pole, of Cavendish Square, Middlesex, Bart., house and out-houses, garden and field in St. Austell, also Porthmeor, Cuddra and Blewetts tenament at Holmbush, now occupied by Joseph Dingle, house and linen-drapery, in Menacuddle and Carwallen.'

Meanwhile, Charles had a wedding to organise, that of his eldest daughter Harriet, who married the Rev. Edward Rodd, of Trebartha Hall, near Launceston, on the 25th April 1805. If we can believe an account of that day, it would appear that Harriet, now 26 years of age and four years younger than Edward, was baptised at St. Ewe that same day before going on to her wedding ceremony at Heligan manor. Her husband became Vicar of St. Just-in-Roseland, Cornwall, and of Lamerton, in Devon. She was described as being 'a gentle sweet nature, but not strong, spending much time in her own room, writing little stories for the poor and entered very little into society'. The couple had seven children, all 'coached in poetry and prose by their mother'.

The threat of French invasion again loomed large in 1805, and was sufficiently serious for the government to send Lt.Col. Enys of the Royal Artillery to inspect the combined Fowey, Par and Charlestown companies. The Crinnis Cliff Artillery Volunteers were inspected on the 21st June, its senior officer being Captain Joseph Dingle, described as the Captain Commandant of the Battery. Its 1st Lieut. was Captain W.J. Bowles; 2nd Lt William Quickhard; 3rd Lt Edward Hannah, with four sergeants, four corporals, eight bombadiers, 80 gunners, of whom three were sick, seven absent and two wanting, making a total of 92 men. Lt Col Enys's report on the men, equipment and the Crinnis Cliff gun battery read as follows:

'This is a very good and useful Company, consisting principally of men in the employment of Charles Rashleigh, of Duporth, between whose house and the village of Charlestown is situated the cliff and the Battery from whence they take their name. None of the officers have ever been in service but they derive great advantage from having the use of four, 18 pdr guns which are kept here in charge of a sergeant and two men of the Royal Artillery, by whom they have been instructed both in the Battery and field artillery, at which they equal to any in the country. When the field pieces are out, they are provided with horses by Mr Rashleigh who has large works of various kinds in Charlestown, which is a place built by him and wholly his property. Their fifes, drummers, arms and appointments and clothing are all very good. The men are active young men and act as infantry as well as artillery.'

Whilst Charles may have had financial problems concerning the port, the business of Rashleigh & Coode looked healthy at Michaelmas (29th September) 1809:

'Balance brought forward £6,822.16s.3d
Bills due at Michaelmas 1802, still due   £17.17s.7d
Costs at do. for which no bills were made   £110.15s.6d
out and still due:
As (1)1803 .. .. £123.14s.8d
As (2)1803 .. .. £53.2s.0d
As (1)1804 .. .. £124.18s.9d
As (2)1804 .. .. £138.14s.0d
As (1)1805 .. .. £271.13s.0d
As (2)1805 .. .. £296.2s.6d
As (1)1806 .. .. £163.3s.1d
As (2)1806 .. .. £565.5s.0d
As (1)1807 .. .. £394.6s.1d
As (2)1807 .. .. £553.1s.0d
As (1)1808 .. .. £381.17s.6d
As (2)1808 .. .. £1001.14s.0d
As (1)1809 .. .. £745.5s.6d
As (2)1809 .. .. £2038.9s.6d

Total £13,362.16s.11d

Due to Mr. Kempthorne £2,000
Due to Mr. Kempthorne, 1809, £1,000'

Amongst the many properties, manors and large houses that passed through Charles Rashleigh's hands during this period was Prideaux, in Luxulyan. Having passed from the Hearle family to the Kendalls, it was bought by Charles in the 1780's, who in turn sold it to his nephew John Coleman Rashleigh, in 1807. What further progress was being made at Charlestown by way of housing or business at this time is not recorded. It was probably a period of consolidation, new businesses becoming better established, with both trade and ship building on the increase. The shipbuilder in Charlestown in 1805 was still Thomas Shephard, who employed four shipwrights and six apprentices, in addition to eight shipwrights and seven apprentices at his other yard in Mevagissey. Residents in the village were also settling down, grateful for employment and a degree of security, but not Joseph Dingle, whose world was about to collapse.

In addition to financial problems, that were eventually to see Dingle bankrupt, there was outside criticism of building work he had supervised:

'Joseph Dingle, Charlestown, to the Rev'd. Mr. Tremayne, 23 August 1809. Hon'rd. Sir, As you have always been kind and very kind to me I hope and trust you will not now be offended at my troubling you with a few lines. Mr. Shipheard has told me this morning that you at a publick meeting (about the bridge at Mevagissey) very much censured the building of Charlestown pier.

The head of Charlestown dock, as it appeared in January 1870, showing the shipyard with associated workshops and stores. The smaller vessel on the left by the flagstaf, was the smack Little Fred, *waiting to be launched. The larger vessel on the slipway was the unfinished, 78 ton schooner* Challenge, *launched the following August.*

Was I the master of language to explain my ideas, I think I could satisfy you that its present state is not from any defect in the building – and if you will have the goodness to ride round it one day at low water, I hope I shall be able to prove to you that the present appearance of its weakness is a proof of its strength. I am, Hon'd sir, your much obliged and ob't and humble servant.'

Dingle appears to have occupied a great deal of Edward Coodes time and thought on behalf of Charles, with visits to London to meet with council: 'From London, 25th Jan. 1811. Edward Coode to Charles Rashleigh esq., Duporth. My dear Sir, I arrived this morning by the mail and had a tolerably pleasant journey, except that I found the night very cold. I have just seen Jacabank for a minute, who says he has sent you details and notice of Debtor and that he has declared in debt as was supposed. Eight days after service of the notice, if he does not appear which I conclude he will not, but I advise you in case he attempts to ascertain the balance by arbitration before you levy a shilling. Dingle has huge debts to a very large amount. Obtained credit for a shilling, but for your consideration & support, it makes it more and more necessary in my opinion (which I sincerely give you to be extremely circumspect), & I am sure you would rather have every shilling of your money .. I advise that you should have no further communication with a man who has so sorely cheated and deceived you. Yours very sincerely, E.C.'

No doubt well aware that Charles intended to take him to court, Dingle made a point of calling at the office of Rashleigh & Coode to see his master, only to find him not there, as Edward Coode reported:

'21st Nov. 1811. Half past 10 at night. Edward Coode to Charles Rashleigh esq., Duporth. My dear Sir, I have been awakened at the office this morning by Joe. Dingle, who says he called in consequence of your saying today, that you wd. consult me as to your account with him, that he had no opportunity of saying a word to you.

He says that he believes in his conscience that on a settlement of accounts he is not a shilling in your debt, that he is willing and desires of settling his accounts with you as soon as he can make them out, but that with his other engagements he can not undertake to do so, in less than a year, and that this was started by you that he never gave you any statement of his payments.

I have written you what he says, and you will let me know your determination.

Would it not be better to forward all the accounts to Edwd. Fox, Rawling's, or any other qualified person; he says he will leave it to any one you will name, or if proper leaving it to yourself and attend you any time for that purpose. Yours very sincerely, E.C.'

Another strange aspect of this whole affair is the fact that as late as 1810, five years after Charles became aware of the vast amount of money owed to him, he had still not stopped Dingle drawing on the account. Even then, it was Edward Coode who had to point this out to him:

'4th Feb. 1810. London. EC. to CR. . . which will be time enough to give the proper notices to Dingle, and to have a conference with you about his account, but I advise you to put an immediate stop to the drawing of cheques, anyway they are illegal and subject both the drawer and the person paying to heavy penalties. I mentioned this to you before, but I conclude it escaped your recollection.'

Unfortunately, no legal documentation appears to survive concerning the actual court proceedings against Dingle, despite extensive searches in the Western Circuit Assize Records, Minute Books, Pleadings and Indictments for Bodmin in the PRO, London, so they must be presumed lost. However from correspondence, provincial newspapers and account books, the scale of his embezzlement can be judged, from which emerges considerable detail and certainly the outcome. From account books of Rashleigh, Coode & Kempthorne, we learn that the practice represented clients in no less than fifteen cases involving the one defendant, Joseph Dingle, most, if not all, of which were successful, judging by the relatively modest legal fees, suggesting they were not protracted hearings. It is also reasonable to assume that all were creditors:

Date	Client	Amount
19 Dec. 1810	Paid Samuel Phillips, for arresting Dingle.	£2.12s.6d
12 Oct. 1810	Blake v Dingle, by costs of two writs	£6.6s.
3 Nov. 1810	Veake v Dingle, by cash	£5.13s.0d
16 Aug. 1811	Bint v Dingle, the like	£7.6s.6d
16 Aug. 1811	Melhuish v Dingle, & bail, the like	£22.6s.6d
17 Mar. 1811	By Received of Dingle, costs	10s.6d
17 Mar. 1811	Phillips v Dingle	£44.4s.11d
28 Sep. 1811	By Received of Dingle	£0.10s.6d
25 Jan. 1812	Melhuish v Dingle, by taxed costs	£37.15s.0d
05 Feb. 1812	Mill v Dingle, costs	16s.9d
08 Feb. 1812	Treffry v Dingle, by costs	£4.14s.6d
02 Apr. 1812	Gill v Dingle, by costs	£18.18s.0d
21 Apr. 1812	Crossman v Dingle, Sheriff on writs of inquiry	£3.3s.0d
20 Aug. 1812	Dingle v Rowe, paid Will. Rawle of Plymouth for viewing notice	7s.6d
05 Dec. 1812	Melhuish v Dingle, Re'cd. extra costs	£15.15s.0d
21 May. 1813	Eastcott v Dingle, by costs	£23.0s.0d
24 Jun. 1813	Tilkins(?) v Dingle, by costs	£5.18s.0d
06 Aug. 1813	Rashleigh v Colenso, paid Will. James his fee	£2.0s.0d
20 Nov. 1813	Received of Mr. Charles Rashleigh for special jury v Dingle, and retaining two	£8.16s.0d

Of these names only Treffry, the wealthy Fowey family; John Colenso, Charles's office clerk, and James Melhuish, a well known Mevagissey shipbuilder, can now be identified.

The first newspaper reference to the trial appeared on 17th August 1811, in the Royal Cornwall Gazette (p3), but gave only outline details of the impending case, which was to last one week:

'Assizes for the County commenced Tuesday (13th), before Sir Robert Graham, Knight, at the Crown Bar and Sir John Bayley, Knight, as Nisi Prius. Twenty-two causes were entered for trial of these. Rashleigh v Dingle. This action was for money lent and advanced by the plaintiff to the defendant, who was the agent at Charlestown, and for money received by the defendant to the use of the plaintiff, in which the plaintiff had a verdict of £23,000.'

'Also another case, Bint v Dingle. Verdict for the plaintiff.' A full account appeared in the press on Friday 23rd. August 1811, when the trial was over:

'Rashleigh v Dingle. This was a very important trial, before a special jury, and excited considerable interest. Mr. Serjeant Lens opened the case. He stated that about 25 years since the plaintiff placed the defendant at the port of Charlestown in the Parish of St. Austell as his agent to manage and superintend the commerce, building and co. of the place; that the defendant had received of the plaintiff from time to time divers large sums of money which were had by the defendant for carrying on the plaintiff's concern at Charlestown: that no general settlement took place till 1805, when it appeared the arrangement was made, and the defendant acknowledged under his own hand that he was indebted to the plaintiff in the enormous sum of £24,000. That from 1805 up almost to the present moment, the defendant had been increasing the debt by receiving the quay dues, rents of the various houses and premises at Charlestown and also receiving of the plaintiff a large sum of money making the total about £35,000 (£8.75m by current standards).

The first witness, John Williams Colenso stated that he is clerk to the plaintiff, he proved the identity of the defendant, acknowledging that in 1805 he was indebted to the plaintiff, on both of their accounts, £24,000, that he has since paid the plaintiff various sums of money by the plaintiff's directions.

Thomas Randell said he was for many years clerk to the defendant, that he for several years collected the dues of Charlestown quay, by the defendant's desire and paid him the money but that he always understood the quay belonged to the plaintiff.

Mathew Vounder, resides at Charlestown and had known for many years the defendant occupied several lime kilns, cellars and other premises for about 20 years. Witness rented several houses of the defendant and regularly paid his rent to him.

Sam Drew of St. Austell, held a fish cellar at Charlestown of the defendant, and always paid him the rent.

Captain Melhuish deposed that, he had regularly paid the defendant the rents of premises occupied by him at Charlestown.

Edward Coode esq. stated that in 1807, he being then Under Sheriff, on executed writs levied on the defendant's property, and that the plaintiff paid him £700 to discharge the execution. The defendant called no witnesses.

Mr. Jekyll addressed the jury in a neat but pointed speech on

52

the part of the defendant. He remarked that this case, take it all and all, was the most extraordinary and wonderful that he had ever met with. It was rather astonishing, that a gentleman in the plaintiff's situation should suffer an agent to manage his concerns for such a long period without calling him to settle. In 1805 something like an arrangement took place, but said the learned counsel, "what kind of settlement that was it is altogether impossible for me to determine." It appeared, that when the arrangement was made, an immense quantity of accounts were given to the plaintiff by the defendant and were now in the plaintiff's possession, and he regretted that these papers were not produced in court, as they might and no doubt would, upon mature investigation, weigh in favour of the defendant. "Was it reasonable to suppose that if the defendant really owed the plaintiff such an amazing balance, he would increase the debt by paying so many large sums to the defendant ?" No further back than 1807, the plaintiff paid the Under Sheriff £700.

Mr. Jekyll said, it was to be lamented that this affair had not been brought into another court, when, in all probability, the defendant would get that redress which here it was not likely he would obtain. Verdict for the plaintiff in the sum of £30,000.'

Dingle immediately declared himself bankrupt. Within three days of the trial ending, public notices were appearing announcing:

'Bankrupt's Effects to be sold at Charlestown: To be sold by auction by order of the Assignees of Joseph Dingle, a bankrupt, on Monday 10th May next, by 4 o'clock in the afternoon, at the Charlestown Hotel, all those stop and tuck pilchard sean, boats and materials, with their stocks of salt, viz the *Porthmeor* sean, one 16th in the *Friend's Endeavour* sean, the *Charlestown* sean, the *Three Sisters* sean and one 32nd in the *Parr* sean and also all the cellar utensils, viz: washing troughs, buckets, press-poles, oil stand, lode-buckets, fish stands, scoops, barrow etc. etc.'

How much of the £30,000 debt recognised by the court, which Charles insisted was nearer £35,000 was repaid, apart from £700 is not recorded, but judging by events, it was probably little or nothing, which is why Charles proceeded against Dingle by suing him for the outstanding amount. Taking into account the additional creditors, whose individual claims we do not know, but which must have come to a considerable sum in total, plus the huge amount owed to Rashleigh, one cannot help but wonder what on earth Dingle did with all that money ? Whilst he seemingly disappeared from Charlestown from then on, we know he continued to live at Cuddra for a time, and was still there when Charles finally won his law suit in 1820, but had left by 1823, when it was occupied by Martha Rashleigh. From there on he vanished completely from public notice until his death, at Trevarrick in 1845, in receipt of parish pay, presumably rendered penniless by the courts. Probably for the first time in his life, Charles, now aged 66, found himself very short of capital, at a time when he should have been enjoying the fruits of his labour. With property to maintain in Charlestown, the upkeep of his family and estate at Duporth, business interests and a high level of social life, to find himself deprived in later life of the equivalent of some £8 million must have come as a considerable shock. His financial situation probably dictated his behaviour for many years to come, his forthcoming actions those of a once wealthy man seeking only to regain his position. Despite having lost a considerable amount of capital, one consolation was that the port of Charlestown was proving to be more than successful, as witness the number of ships entering the port during part of 1811:

'Charlestown 6th Feb.1811. Arrived the Samuel,(M) Moffard; the Mary & Betsey,(M) Couch; the Thames,(M) Tarrant; the Grace,(M) Hodge, all ex Plymouth; Venus,(M) Mellurish, from Newport.

Charlestown 13th Feb.1811. Arrived the Susan,(M) Johns, from Mevagissey.

Charlestown 6th Mar.1811. Arrived the Ann & Elizabeth, (M) Moyse, from London; Ann & Elizabeth,(M) Clymo, from Plymouth, and the Susan,(M) Johns, from Mevagissery.

Charlestown 27th Mar.1811. Arrived the Charlestown,(M) Williams; Mary & Betsey,(M) Couch, from Plymouth; Mariner, (M) Banks, for Swansea; Sisters,(M) Greenfell, from Bristol; Nottingham,(M) Harvey, from Fowey.

Charlestown 3rd Apr.1811. Arrived the Active,(M) Pidgeen, from Plymouth; Hope,(M) Allen, from Mevagissey, and the Unity,(M) Bone, from London.

Charlestown 10th Apr.1811. Arrived the Charlestown,(M) Williams; Flora,(M) Fuse, from Plymouth; Betsey,(M) Hodge, from Fowey; Fame,(M) Chiswell, from Bristol.

Charlestown 1st May 1811. Arrived the Joker,(M) Thomas, from Bristol; Fox,(M) Melhuish, from Swansea; sailed, the Charlestown, for Plymouth and the Joker, for Fowey.

Charlestown 8th May 1811. Arrived the Lamb,(M) Melhuish, from
Falmouth; Stag,(M) Lee, from Plymouth; sailed, the William & Nancy; Four Friends; Mary & Betsey and the Stag.

Charlestown 15th May 1811. Arrived the Mary & Betsey,(M) Couch;

Agnes,(M) Harvey; Speculation,(M) Powett; sailed, the Fox; Lamb; Agnes; Mary & Betsey.'

For one particular day that September, ship movements were particularly numerous:

'Charlestown 11 Sep 1811. Arrived, the Betsey,(M) Rollin; Fortune, (M) Jolly; Ann & Elizabeth,(M) Moyse; Fox,(M) Melhuish; Mariner, (M) Banks; Sisters,(M) Hodge; Industry,(M) Lelean; Betsey,(M) Slade, and the Lydia,(M) Cooper. Sailed, the Active,(M) Rickard; William & Alexander,(M) Pollard; Betsey,(M) Rollin; Ann & Elizabeth,(M) Moyse; Fortune,(M) Jolly; Mary & Betsey,(M) Couch; Lydia,(M) Cooper.'

The Rashleigh family had in fact suffered a considerable blow shortly before the business of Dingle came to a head, when Philip Rashleigh MP, the eldest brother, now a widower, died at Menabilly on 26th June 1811, aged 82. An obituary published in the West Briton newspaper of 28th June 1811 (p3) said of him, 'he was one of the last of that respectable order of men, the old English Gentleman which is so far wearing away, and was distinguished by independence in public life, and by integrity and hospitality in private.' His will, consisting of twelve pages plus seven codicils, reads in summary as follows:

'The last will and testament of . . . give and devise all my manors, mesuages, lands, tythes, tenements and estate . . together with rectories or Parish Churches of Wickham in the County of Hampshire . . to the said Charles Rashleigh and Thomas Rashleigh, and their heirs, for and during the life of the said William Rashleigh, upon trust to support the contingent uses and estates hereafter limited from being defeated and destroyed and for that purpose to make entries and bring actions as occasion shall require but never the less to permit and suffer the said William Rashleigh to receive and take the rents, issues and profits thereof to and for his proper use and benefit and . . after his decease . . use of the 1st, 2nd, 3rd, and every other son . . of the said William Rashleigh, lawfully to be begotten severally successively and in remainder one after another in order and course as they shall be in the priority of birth . . of heirs male . . respective bodies of such 1st, 2nd, 3rd, . . every other sons . . every elder of such sons . . heirs, male. of his body . . '

Philip left his estate to the use of his brother Jonathan Rashleigh, his sole executor, for his lifetime. On his decease he wished Menabilly to pass to his nephew William, Jonathan's eldest son, and should anything happen to William whilst Charles, Thomas or Jonathan were still alive, then they were to reassume its responsibility.

Although he represented the Borough of Fowey for several successive Parliaments, rising to become Father of the House of Commons, Philip suffered a severe decline in intellect in his twilight years, which forced him to leave public life. His entire business and financial affairs were therefore managed by Charles who, either through impotence, a poor understanding of his brother's affliction or a desire to line his own pockets, sought a Commission of Lunacy against him. On consulting counsel however, Charles found he could not achieve this without the agreement of William, who standing to inherit the estate, and being fond of his uncle, would never have approved such an action. Philip's will was dated 5th March 1803, with brother Jonathan appointed his executor and trustee, but Jonathan died in 1806, five years before his brother, and it looks supiciously as if Charles either negligently or deliberately, failed to ensure that Philip made a new will. Consequently, on Philip's death, Charles was announced executor, entitled to the legal estate of Menabilly in the several leases for 500 years, but was he Trustee of the leases for William? That question was the nub of what became a serious family dispute, from the moment William took occupancy of Menabilly manor 'with its household furniture, farm, stock, pictures, minerals, fossils, shells, coins, cabinets, linen and the implements of husbandry in or about the Barton of Menabilly.'

When William asked Charles to furnish a schedule of the many grants in fee he held and deliver the conveyances, he refused to do so, which was only the beginning of the deep financial rift between the two men. It was not until April 1814, that William was advised his uncle's trusteeship might be in question, it being suggested he file a Bill of Equity against Charles Rashleigh, in an attempt to compel him to assign the leases to another trustee.

The contest for control of Menabilly and its finances resulted in an enormous amount of correspondence between the interested parties, which lasted for well over two years. It began with a letter from William (WR) to Thomas Robins (TR), a solicitor friend in Liskeard, dated 23 March 1813, requesting: '. . will you please act on my behalf. Charles Rashleigh as late Steward . . William Rashleigh as heir at Law and Devisee, My *RIGHT* I certainly do claim, but not a jot beyond it, and to ascertain this is the object of my employing your assistance. You will of course give me a day at Menabilly before the meeting takes place.'

Another letter from William, living at Maidstone, dated 2nd August 1813 reads: 'Dear Sir, Charles Rashleigh has interpreted my letter to him very differently to what I intended. Having studied to express my wishes in the kindest manner possible, at the same time confessing the anxiety I have long felt to hold my property true and independent of his control, and only intended him to consult his own comfort and conscience as to the time of resigning the Stewardship if he resolved in giving it up. I begged he would consider what was most congenial to his own feelings & should not at this time, when his mind has been so much harassed by Dingle and his associates, no one can feel more sincerely more than I do for all the vexation his mind has suffered, and it will give me the utmost satisfaction if this change (which I deem so essential to my own comfort) should be effected without his love and esteem as a relative and a friend.

Mr. Charles seems to imply from his letter that all the Deeds and other writings at Menabilly were his property. If such a claim should be persisted in, I shall feel it a duty to *contest it to the utmost*. I feel obliged by your enquiries for Mrs. Rashleigh (William's wife), who remains in so weak a state as to deprive me of all hope of recovery. Thank God! she does not suffer pain.'

In fact William's first wife, Rachael Stackhouse, who he had married in Probus church, died at Maidstone shortly after that letter was written. It also seems his aunt, widow of Jonathan Rashleigh, died about the same time since he wrote in a note to Thomas Robins, '4th Sept. 1813. This day I quit this place to accompany the remains of Mrs. Jane Rashleigh to the family vault.' That September, 1813, TR. communicated with WR: 'I shall feel much pain if Mr. Charles Rashleigh should resign your stewardship under any unpleasant sensations.' But William was determined, sacking Charles, who in turn wrote to Robins saying: '30 Dec. 1813. Mr. Rashleigh dismissed me from the Stewardship before Michaelmas last'. Charles, determined not to give up without a fight, prompted another letter from WR. to TR.: '20th Jan. 1814. All my friends are surprised at Mr. Charles Rashleigh persisting in his claims, and fear his character must inevitably suffer from such an exposure as must be the consequence.' The fight continued: '2nd Jan. 1814, TR. to WR. I have received a letter from Charles Rashleigh respecting the Fowey lands in which he says, "I have no authority to send you any papers re deeds deposited in my hands by the very persons who claim the interest in the Estate." The Steward of the Manor of Fowey has the rentals of that manor and to him I refer you. He is very pressing for settlement of his accounts without further delay.' The Rashleigh & Coode partnership in St. Austell received the large sum of £1,000 from William on the 18th Jan.1814, with note of a further sum, 'the £500 due', which we can reasonably presume was the amount owing. Progress in the dispute appears to have frustrated William, since he then wrote: '24 Jan. 1814. WR. to TR. You will oblige me by a letter to say what progress has been made with respect to Mr. Charles Rashleigh and what answer you would advise my making to him and Mr. Kimber. It will be a great disappointment if the case is not laid before Sir J. Romilly to enable him to give an answer previous to the meeting of Parliament. I hope you will deem it wise to let much of the prior case remain. It is strange indeed that Mr. Charles should not be satisfied that Dr. Goulds deed is not at Menabilly. The Dr. says he remembers it was sent from Menabilly to London, and from thence it was conveyed in a bag with many other Fowey papers to the office at St. Austell where, as the Dr. rightly insists, it may still be found.' On 3rd Feb. Robins told Charles in a letter, that William was 'offering to buy lands held by the Corporation of Fowey, if you will fix a price on them.' In reply, Charles wrote on 5th Feb. that he wanted 'to sell all his property in Fowey, at public auction and would not offer it to William.'

The first suggestion that the Menabilly accounts may have been wanting arose on 5th March: 'WR. to TR. That false reports have gained circulation of the harshness of my conduct towards Charles Rashleigh as to render it necessary for the justification of my own character, then a statement of the whole transaction between us should appear before the public, and I am advised, by a reputable friend, acquainted with both parties, to take such measures as may prevent Mr. Charles from casting me all blame (that may hereafterappear) from his shoulders to those of his clerk, which has been deemed likely from his abstaining from any inspection of the accounts himself.' More accusations were to follow only three days later: '8th Mar. 1814. WR. to TR. *Another* material error I have detected in Mr. Charles Rashleigh's accounts which I am unwilling to mention till the fact has been ascertained by a reference to Mr. Jonathan Rashleigh's account books at Lincoln Inn from whence I have just returned. In the statement No.3, dated October 1813, you will find the last article under the head of annuities as follows:

"To Mrs. Jane Rashleigh, two years quarters annuity due Mid'r 1813, £90.0s.0d."

Now it appears from the enclosed transcript from Mr. Jonathan Rashleigh's books that no money has been received by him from Mr. Charles Rashleigh since March 1813. I am therefore charged with the sum of of £10 a quarter due on Midsummer which has neither been paid by Mr. Charles nor ever received by my sister. It was by the merest accident that this error was discovered by my general suspicion of every money transaction from that quarter that induced me to desire an inspection of my sisters accounts during my stay with her at Bath.

This is additional proof (although God knows none is wanting), to render a minute enquiry into any doubtful point in discussion between us and call for decisive evidence that every item is strictly due that appears on the different documents.'

By April things were becoming serious: '30th Apr. 1814. TR. to WR. I have received the case with Sir Samuel Romilly's opinion and have sent to retain him as your leading counsel. I think Charles Rashleigh will be much surprized to find a Bill of Equity will be filed against him. You must also apply to your two brothers to become party in the Bill proposed to be filed & which I would recommend your doing immediately.'

Presumably not wanting to involve more members of the family in the dispute than necessary, William asked of Robins '. . my brother at Wickham most readily agrees to joining me as co. plaintiff, must I apply likewise to my two other brothers?' Such legal matters were protracted even in those days, and by June William was again expressing frustration: 'It was by anxious desire that the business with Mr. Charles Rashleigh might have gained a little progress, but I fear my patience

The Duporth Cup, a breakfast-cup and saucer with lid, made by Wedgwood, presented to Charles Rashleigh by the residents of Porthmear in 1800, with the request that the port be renamed Charles's Town, after its founder. It bears five miniature paintings showing the early development of Charlestown.

must be exposed to a further trial.' One month later William had the necessary co-operation: 'My brother George has consented to be a co. Plaintiff in the Chancery suit against Mr. Charles and has written him to that effect.' In other correspondence William mentioned: 'Mr. Charles Rashleigh's behaviour ceases to give me surprise. I sincerely pity him.' That October, one month before the hearing, William was in correspondence with the Rev. Peter Rashleigh, his brother, of Southfleet, Gravesend, in Kent: 'It appears that Mr. Charles Rashleigh at first approved of my brothers decision of joining me as a co. Plaintiff, but Mr. Charles has recently told him that he shall consider all those who join me, as leagued against him and his character. No pains have been spared to make the case clear. The 6th. November is now at hand when I conclude the Bill will be filed (at the Exeter Sessions), if Mr. Charles persists in his claims.'

As that day drew nearer, Charles probably realised he could not possibly win: '31st Oct. 1814. WR. to TR. Mr. Carew Pole has just called on his return from Duporth. Mr. Charles Rashleigh told him it had long been his wish that the differences between us should be settled amicably, he has in consequence written Mr. Tho's. Rashleigh fully on the subject from whom we shall shortly hear further. Of course, all further proceedings in Chancery must stop. I have not been well lately, but am considerably better.'

He was not the only member of the Rashleigh's who had been ill; the strain of the Dingle case and now a pending suit must have been a considerable burden on Charles's family: '12th Aug.1813. CR. to WR. Our last accounts of my dear Pattie are much the same. A return of her sad disorder . . my business with Dingle is in Status Quo, nothing done.' Three weeks later, he wrote: '9th Sept. 1813. CR. to WR. I wish I could say my own dear Pattie was much better, her disorder seems rather to have changed of late, yet it continues with mostly the same effect.

Dingle and his creditors, namely Mr. Butterfelt and Mr. Thomas, his nephew, refused to comply with the terms of their Petition, and refer the dispute with me to Mr. Wingfield and Mr. Abercrombie and I am as much at sea as ever.' In fact, the Dingle affair dragged on through solicitors until 1820, before some sort of satisfactory outcome was achieved. As to Charles's differences with William, the threatened Chancery suit was never filed, being withdrawn at the very last moment. It was left to Thomas Rashleigh, of No.18 Devenraux Court, Temple, London, to instruct Thomas Robins in a settlement between the two parties:

'12th Nov. 1814. . . as you are now fully authorised to act for Mr. William Rashleigh & I am fully instructed to meet you in the most amicable friendly manner on the part of my brother Charles, I trust and hope our united efforts will not be unsuccessful in bringing about a happy reconsiliation between two such near relatives and neighbours, and I may add, men of such exemplary and worthy character. We are all frail and fallible on this side of the grave and therefore there must be occasional misunderstandings amongst even the dearest Relations and Friends; such unfortunately is the present case & you and I are called in to do justice to the parties and reconsile all differences between them. I beg therefore my dear Sir, that you will forward by every possible means the settlement of all cash accounts without prejudice to any question arising out of my late brothers will and in doing so you will I trust not dwell on trifles – they are both men of spirit and liberty.' The accounting problems concerning Rashleigh & Coode were resolved quite simply: '1st Dec. 1813 TR. to WR. I have had Mr. Carbis & Mr. Colenso with me two days this week about the accounts, and the partnership account under the name of Messrs Rashleigh & Coode has been closed in which the errors I pointed out have been admitted, and there is a balance of £465.6s.9d due to you.'

In February 1815 fresh problems arose: '7th Feb. 1815. WR. to TR. Mr. Charles Rashleigh has opened a discovery of what may be expected; there is opposition to my interest, which I do not feel at liberty to disclose, but am most anxious to wipe my hands clean of the whole concern – you would indeed be surprised to hear what has been going on – Charles Rashleigh & Mr. Coode still continue partners and Steward of the Manor!!' Another month passed and still Charles had not released the relevant documents he held for Menabilly estate: 'TR. to WR. 7th March. Charles Rashleigh has not yet sent me the original leases for 500 years, but I will avail myself of your friendly hint.' Also, there was a concerted move to break the hold that the partnership Rashleigh & Coode had over the district: 'TR. to WR. 6th. March. As to Mr. Coode, I perfectly agree with you, that he ought not to continue Steward of the Manor and Borough of Fowey.' Another problem seems to have arisen that month, provoking the response: '25th March. WR. to TR. What eventful times we live in! That kind Providence who has hitherto preserved us, will not I firmly trust, withdraw his protecting arm at this awful crisis.' It was May 1815, before there was any positive sign that the end to the dispute was in sight: '23rd May. WR. to TR. It is with great comfort that I inform you of my seeing a letter from Duporth this morning, wherein my Uncle complies with my ernest wish that a perfect reconsiliation should take place between us. It is therefore my intention to call on him soon after my return home.' The matter was at last resolved, four long years after Philip's death: '17th July 1815. WR. to TR. Charles Rashleigh and myself have exchanged visits cordially on both sides.'

So ended a period of almost ten continuous years of legal wrangling, relating initially to Joseph Dingle and then Menabilly estate, which must have taken a considerable toll on Charles Rashleigh's health, who by now was 68 years old. In financial terms, he lost heavily on both accounts, a fortune to Dingle and now not only his fee as Steward of Menabilly, but what ever other income the estate yielded him, as well as all the rents he previously enjoyed from Fowey.

Chapter 3 Reference sources

No	Source
1	CCC. CRO. DD.CF/3333
2	ibid DDR/5040
3	West Briton & Cornish Advertiser
4	ibid
5	ibid
6	CCC. CRO. DDR/5557
7	ibid DDR(8)1/188 p11
8	ibid DDR/5304 (Correspondence misc)
9	ibid DDR/5306
10	ibid "
11	ibid DDR/5307
12	ibid "
13	ibid "
14	ibid DDR/5306
15	ibid DDR/5307
16	ibid "
17	ibid "
18	ibid "
19	ibid "
20	ibid "
21	ibid "
22	ibid "
23	ibid DDR/5306
24	ibid "
25	ibid DDR/5307
26	ibid "
27	ibid DDR/5308
28	ibid "
29	ibid "
30	ibid "
31	ibid "
32	ibid "

CHAPTER 4

Charles Rashleigh's Troubles. 1815 – 1823

The next nine years saw a continuing decline in Charles Rashleigh's health and financial situation, whilst at the same time the port of Charlestown prospered beyond all expectations. Had Charles employed someone other than Joseph Dingle to look after his interests regarding the port, someone honest enough to give him the return on his huge capital investment that he deserved, then without doubt he would have become one of the wealthiest men in Cornwall.

Unfortunately for him and particularly his family, his capital base had almost vanished by 1810, so that whilst his basic income continued to grow, allowing him to continue his life style, there was no longer cash to invest in new ventures. As a consequence he missed the greatest investment opportunity mid-Cornwall has ever seen, that of the great boom in copper mining, which took place towards the end of the tin mining era, right on Charlestown's doorstep.

Both Charles and his friend Edward Fox, of Wadebridge, had become the principal partners in the Great Polgooth tin and copper mine after a new company was set up in 1783. This was a successful working which as early as 1695 was recorded as having 'at least twenty mines (shafts) all in sight, which employs a great many people at work, almost day and night'. It grew to become the most important working east of Truro and had its own smelting house prior to 1700. By 1741, it was rich enough to have its own Newcomen atmospheric pumping engine and, by 1797, no less than fifty individual shafts had been opened up, the deepest of which was 110 fathoms(660ft/201m), employing over 1,000 people. In 1802, its wages alone were costing £1,000 a month. This great venture ended temporarily in 1804 when the partners, which included Boulton & Watt, the engine manufacturers, closed the workings with a profit of £100,000 (£25 million by current standards). Closure was due to expiry of the lease, which became a legal matter between the adventurers and Lord Arundell, owner of the mineral rights. During this dispute part of the mine was deliberately flooded. A scheme to re-open the mine in 1812 came to nothing, because 'the owners, being the proprietors of the smelting-house in St. Austell, sold tin raised from the mine on terms not always satisfactory to those adventurers who had no interest in the smelting business.' Shortly before 1820, the mine was re-opened under John Taylor, a Norwich-born mining engineer, prominent in the Crinnis area mines. Charles Rashleigh also had shares in the Pentewan valley mine known as the *Happy Union*, so named after a 'happy union' between three parishes. The source of the tin worked here was that washed down over many centuries from the hills above St. Austell, which was mined most successfully between 1813-15. Mr. Colenso, who worked for a time in Charles's office, described the lode in a letter as: 'a wide belt, 700 fathoms (4,200ft/1,280m) long, with an average production of 180lbs per sq. fathom of surface area, which yielded 11.25lbs of black tin per ton, or 15lbs per cub.yard of gravel. This represents 2 tons of tin per mile of valley deposit, some of the metal being found in 10lb lumps.' This mine was abandoned in 1829, although a revival was attempted further up the valley in 1837, just south of the *London Apprentice Inn.*

Whilst ore from both the Polgooth and Pentewan mines was shipped out of Charlestown, their combined output was soon to be dwarfed by that of new discoveries made within half a mile of the port, an investment opportunity in which Charles could only afford a minor participation. Copper mining was nothing new to the St. Austell area of course, having been worked locally since the mid-18th century, with workings known as Wheal Treasure, Wheal Fortune, Wheal Regent (in Crinnis Woods), Wheal Commerce, Wheal Chance, Cuddra and the old Mount mines, of which little is known. The first 19th century underground discoveries in the Carlyon Bay area were made in 1808. From that year onward until the 1870's, when mining in the area virtually ceased, due to foreign competition, attention was drawn to a coastal strip of killas, running from Par to Charlestown. The *Crinnis Cliff* mine was the first to open here in 1810, when a rich deposit of copper was found commencing at a depth of only 6 fathoms (36ft/11m), so shallow in fact that the ore was brought to the surface in its early days by a hand operated windlass!

During the first four months of 1813, no less than forty-nine ship loads of copper ore were despatched from this one mine through Charlestown, representing 3,792 tons, proving to be the richest lode this side of the great *Dolcoath* mine. By the end of 1814 it had produced 10,000 tons of ore and by 1816, 40,000 tons, with a profit of £168,000 (£4 million) already paid to its shareholders. By 1820, the number of mines being worked in the Carlyon Bay area, now covered by Beach and Sea Roads, Crinnis Wood and the Carlyon Bay golf course, included the *Great Crinnis* mine, *Little Crinnis, Higher Crinnis, East Crinnis, Pembroke, Lanescot, Fowey Consuls* and many others. In fact, the area proved so rich that it broke the dominance of the great Camborne, Redruth and Gwennap mining area. Despite a great upsurge in mining and other employment, there were Cornish people keen to seek their fortunes abroad, tempted by higher wages or by a taste for adventure. Many foreign mining concessions, particularly in the New World, sought their skilled mining labour in Cornwall, but the loss of these men bore no relation to the emigration caused by sheer necessity which commenced in the late 1830's. With the ending of the wars with France, over a quarter of a million fighting men were released from the army and navy, many of whom were unable to find work. Certainly, if one was unemployed in Cornwall, times were very hard indeed. At Christmas 1814, William Rashleigh gave £50 to be distributed amongst the poor of Fowey, at 1 shilling each. Later, in June 1817, he gave 'a labouring man, a one gallon loaf and 6 pence; women and children above 12 years of Age, a gallon loaf and 4 pence; children between 8 and 12 years, a gallon loaf and 2 pence; children below 8 years, a gallon loaf only.' Some chose to leave their native county on board a vessel appropriately enough named *Charlestown*, on 22nd May 1818:

> 'On Wednesday morning, sailed from the Port of Charlestown, the *Charlestown*, Williams, master, with about 50 persons on board as passengers for America, amongst whom are some families including infants at the breast. In the number of those who have thus bid adieu to the land of their nativity in pursuit of better fortune in a distant shore is a woman 70 years of age, whose husband emigrated seven months since'.

The *Charlestown* was in fact only a 70 ton sloop-rigged barge or lighter, built by Thomas Shepheard, her initial owner, who sold shares in her to Joseph Dingle, described as a merchant, as well as Richard Williams and John Nancollas, both mariners of St. Austell. The *Charlestown* was in service out of Fowey for fifty-five years, longer than any other vessel of the period, rigged as a sloop from 1824 and finally 'going absent' in 1850. She was of a class designed to carry bulk limestone from Plymouth to the many south coast lime kilns, as well as granite cargo, and probably assisting in the construction of Charlestown harbour. Very basic in design and devoid of all except the most rudimentary accommodation for her three man crew, whilst 70 ton sloops and brigs took emigrants to America, that the flat-bottomed lighter *Charlestown* would attempt to cross the Atlantic was most improbable. It is more likely that she made passage to Plymouth, where upwards of 150 emigrants left in June 1818 alone on much larger vessels. The fare to Canada was from five to six guineas, to the United States £7 (without provisions, or £11 with), children going half price. The account of the *Charlestown's* sailing is in fact the only record of emigrants leaving via the port in its entire history. Although Cyril Bunn, in his excellent *Book of St. Austell*, suggests that many emigrants sailed from Charlestown for America, Australia and South Africa, this cannot be substantiated.

When Charles Rashleigh, Joseph Dingle and John Smeaton drew up designs and plans for the port only twenty-six years earlier, their one failing was that their plans were 'for the day', with no vision for the future and no allowance for potential expansion. The angle at which the main quay comes out from the shore and the enclosing arm on the east side, made for a relatively narrow entrance with an unfortunate but necessary 'dog-leg' before access could be gained to the inner dock. The port was also built on the shoreline, so that within a matter of only ten

A view of the dock and entrance, taken from the path leading up to the Gun Battery. Photographed around 1890, very little had changed since Rashleigh's time over 100 years. The building with the lean-to veranda was the Content *pilchard cellar, the large white building far right, a lime kiln, which was later utilised for 'hot and cold seawater baths'.*

years, by which time the tonnage of individual ships using the port must have almost doubled, it was still only a 'shallow water' port, whose outer basin to this day dries out completely at low water springs. The 'dog-leg' is still necessary to offer protection to the dock gate(s), to break the strength of any heavy south-easterly swell, which could otherwise force the gates open. In fact the port of Charlestown was never built large enough in the first place, which became patently obvious by 1813, if not earlier. By then, some 25-30 pack mules were constantly employed carrying ore between the *Great Crinnis* mine and the port alone, in addition to hundreds of wagons handling outgoing china clay and incoming coal, timber, lime etc. causing enormous congestion. So much so, that a Mr.J. Rowe wrote to Charles in October 1812: ' . . requesting more room at Charlestown for sampling the copper ore.' Had the port been designed differently, it could have expanded, perhaps with an outer basin similar to that added to Mevagissey harbour in 1889-90 which enclosed 10.25 acres of water. A glance at a map or chart of the area, shows clearly that a breakwater arm could easily have extended out from Polmear island on the western side. To the east, the rocks off Appletree Point could have served the same purpose, enclosing an area of relatively 'deep' water, which if dredged and deepened, would have offered the inner harbour even more protection. In fact the owners of the port following Charles's death in 1823, Messrs. Crowder, Sartoris & Co., drew up plans in 1864 for just such an extension. Due to the enormous cost of £8,691.12s.10d (which today would equal some £1.8 million) the harbour was never enlarged, but would in any case have been far too late, since by then two competitive ports had been built, at Pentewan and Par. Had Charles Rashleigh never suffered the financial problems he did, he would without doubt have had the capital necessary to carry out a planned development of Charlestown, with additional or enlarged outer basins, deep water berths and more quay space. It is then likely that neither the port of Pentewan or Par would never have been built. When Joseph Dingle embarked on systematic embezzlement from his employer, neither he nor Charles could ever have appreciated the long term implications, nor the way it would directly affect the history of the St. Austell area.

During 1814, Sophia Rashleigh, Charles's youngest daughter, met and fell in love with the Rev. Richard Gerveys Grylls, of Helston, she being 25 years of age, Richard four years her senior and a man of considerable means. They were married in St. Austell Church by the Rev. H.H. Tremayne, on the 29th August 1816, with their reception at Duporth manor. Richard, after graduating LL.B at Cambridge, had been instituted Vicar of Breage, Germoe, Gunwalloe & Cury on the Lizard peninsula. He later acquired a fifth living at Luxulyan, near St. Austell, as Vicar of the parish church of St. Cyriac & St. Julitta. With church responsibilities in two distinct areas, some forty miles apart, he must have employed several junior clergy as curates, since he only relinquished the latter two livings near Helston in 1846. He retained the remainder until his death on the 4th November 1852, by which time he had been rector of Luxulyan for thirty-nine years. Before moving to Luxulyan in November 1813, his curate advised him that 'the house of residence (the vicarage) is not in good repair'. In reply to an episcopal enquiry he stated that he would 'order it to be repaired immediately'. In fact he had a whole new house built, of three floors, set in five acres. Displaying conspicuous affluence for a clergyman, he then added an extension, presumably just prior to his marriage, almost doubling its size; a second in 1843 added new servant's quarters and a dairy, until it became literally a mansion, now named *King's Acre*. The property ceased to serve its original function in 1968 when it was sold by the church, its maintenance burden having become too great. Since then, the old vicarage has served variously as a hotel, restaurant, and holiday flats, the main building now being a private residence. This was Sophia's one and only married home, but they had no children, possibly due to her indisposition. Not long after her marriage, during a visit to the Houses of Parliament, where repairs were being carried out,

Sophia slipped on a loose plank and broke her leg badly. She never totally recovered from the shock of this injury, which left her partially disabled. Following the death of her husband, she went to live in Helston with her in-laws, where she died at the age of 71 years on the 5th March 1860. She was buried in Luxulyan, alongside her husband within the churchyard. Of Sophia's nature we know very little, except that she loved dogs, keeping a great many at any one time. She also loved needlework, one of her pieces, depicting both the Rashleigh & Grylls' coat of arms, being kept at Lewarne in a glass case.

Misfortune had meanwhile befallen William Rashleigh of Menabilly. Only five months after his wife Rachel had laid the foundation stone for the family Chapel of Ease at Tregaminion, near Menabilly, in April 1813, she became ill and died on the 2nd September. Aged thirty-seven, she died at their town house in Maidstone, the *Gentleman's Magazine* commenting: 'Her remains were removed down to Cornwall by her husband, but the scenes on the road were very painful.' The little chapel at Tregaminion, which took two years to complete, in fact became her memorial. 'In Memory of Rachel', reads her epitaph 'whose remains are interred in the family vault at Tywardreath, with those of her children Rachel and Charlotte' (who died aged 12 years and one year respectively). William wrote to Charles in reply to his letter of condolence on the 17th September:

> 'My sincere thanks are due to yourself, Mrs. Charles and Sophia for your affectionate concern on the death of my dearly beloved wife. I am also obliged for your assistance relative to the funeral, which I had the unspeakable comfort of attending myself and allotted a space to accommodate my own form when it shall please the Almighty in his mercy to take me hence.'

Three years later William married again, taking as his bride Caroline Hinxman, of Wiltshire, who lived until 1842. This was the same year in which he ceased to be a Member of Parliament, selling his interest in the Manor of Fowey to a George Lucy.

By 1815, Charles was having to capitalise on some of his investments, since there was still the problem of the mortgage taken out on Christmas Day 1805 on the Manor of Tewington, now outstanding. One of several properties to go was Menacuddle:

> 'Title deed, Charles Rashleigh to Joseph Sawle of Penrice, 31st August 1815. Higher & Lower Menacuddle with houses, fields, barn, linhay, poultry yard, stables and farmyard; fields near the blowing house and at Tregonissey, cottages at Tregonissey, Carnwallen, in the Manor of Treverbyn Courtenay; Biscovellet; gardens in Kiln Lane and adjacent dung pools, nursery, gardens near the Vicarage, house and buildings at Tregarrick, all in St. Austell.'

Perhaps this sale was in anticipation of a demand on Charles to repay the mortgage on Tewington, since on the 15th June 1816, he signed a document for his bankers stating:

'Charles Rashleigh, of Duporth, to bankers Wm. Praed, Bucks; Jn. Rogers, Penrose; Wm. Tweedy, of Truro Vean; Thos. Nankivell, of Truro. Agreement to make payment, or forfeit the estate'.

In a private letter written to their son-in-law, Edward Rodd, in 1817, Rashleigh's wife, Grace, made reference to 'the heavy financial losses my husband has sustained both by Dingle and the court cases, having just been sustained by the bankrupsy of Goodell and the miner's house'. What that implies is uncertain, but we do know that following his death, Charles's estate lost yet more money when Philip Ball & Sons Bank, in Mevagissey, which commenced operation in 1807, crashed in 1824, causing wide-spread financial problems in the area.

The year 1820 was one that Charles could not easily forget, since in a short space of time he lost his wife, and received news that a rival port was to be built close at hand. Also, the circumstances that were to lead to his second large court case came to a head. There was however one piece of good news, which was the end of the sorry Dingle affair, since Charles appears to have been finally successful in suing Dingle and his associates, making Dingle totally penniless. This brought to an end the huge financial burden he had borne throughout many years of trials and court hearings:

'From WR. at Menabilly, to the Rev. Rodd, at Duporth 22nd. May 1820. It will give Mrs. Rashleigh and myself gratification to hear that it has pleased a kind and merciful Providence to administer every support to my uncle and cousins which they must so much need under their present heavy affliction, that Mr.Charles gout has not been increased by the weight of anxiety he must naturally have suffered, we hope also that you have had good accounts of Mr.Tremayne who must have sincerely felt the loss of his sister (Grace Rashleigh). The death of so pious and exemplary a christian as I have always understood my good aunt to have been should cheer her surviving friends with the humble hope that she is at this present time – translated to that endless state of life which the blessed Jesus has prepared for his faithful disciples.

I took it very kind and friendly of you to send me the message you did by my servant, that my aunt had had the great consolation of knowing that the affair with Dingle has been finally and completely settled. Most sincerely, do I hope that my uncle's peaceful enjoyment of the fruits of his labours may tend to make the evening of his life tranquil and happy. Mrs. Rashleigh unites with me in condolence and best wishes to all the family at Duporth, and beg you to believe me very sincerely. Yours, William Rashleigh.'

Grace Rashleigh died in her own bed at 3.30am, in one of the two bedrooms occupied by her and Charles, linked by a dressing room, at the front of Duporth manor overlooking the bay, on 19th May 1820, aged seventy-five. The St. Austell churchyard being full, all burials there had ceased from 1793, therefore a new walled cemetery was created up the hill from the church. It was here that her body was interred, in a large, square, stone family vault, close to the entrance gate, on the 25th May. It was in fact still possible for burials to take place within the churchyard provided relatives were prepared to pay a fee of £4.4s, or £50 to be buried inside the church. Even for that sum (the equivalent of some £12,000 today), the dead were not left in peace for long, since during the 1870 restoration of the interior, those buried within the church were taken up and reburied in the cemetery. It is perhaps worth a comment that of all the Rashleigh family members, we know least about Grace. Her name was only mentioned in correspondence if she was ill, which was seldom, and she appears to have taken no part in her husband's business affairs, remaining always in the shadows.

Meanwhile, the port of Charlestown became more and more busy, with seemingly no end to the increase in trade it was enjoying. Until now of course, it had enjoyed a complete monoploly on shipping for nigh on twenty years, but it is a fact of life and human nature, that if a business is successful, someone will set up in competition; should that business be very successful, then more than one competitor can be expected. Charlestown was one such business which, until now, had not considered competition as even possible. In addition to rapid growth in the export of china stone and clay from the port, there was now the enormous output of the Carlyon Bay area copper mines, a commodity now more important than tin. By 1805 the price of copper had doubled over twenty years; by 1825 the output was twice what it had been forty years earlier. Between 1831 and 1840 Cornish copper accounted for half the world's production, with more than half of the ore mined in the Charlestown area – no small wonder the port was busy! Now would have been the time for Charles Rashleigh to have increased the size of the port, proving to would-be competitors that he intended to maintain his monopoly at all cost, so that they could only watch in envy the seemingly endless stream of animals or horse drawn wagons that negotiated Fore Street in St. Austell to Charlestown, or from Crinnis over Camp Downs. But he had no capital base with which to fund an expansion and Charlestown was already heavily mortaged. One gentleman who did have investment money and was keen to benefit from those boom years was Sir Christopher Hawkins, of Trewithen, who had his eye on Pentewan.

Pentewan, equi-distant south of Black Head as Charlestown is north, had long been a sandy cove where ships could be beached, bringing in supplies for the mines and taking away ore and locally quarried stone. Its location was if anything, no worse than Charlestown's, since it also faced south-east, but as yet had no port and was isolated and remote from most of the copper mines and china clay quarries. But delays at Charlestown due to congestion were becoming intolerable and as a

Two gangs of dock-porters and helpers man the capstans on either side of Charlestown's dock gates. If as is generally believed, this photograph was taken prior to 1890, then the wooden gates are the original pair, fitted in 1799. The estate Agent or Steward is probably the gentleman in the top hat, with the Harbour or Dock Master to his right.

potential port, Pentewan had two advantages; namely its approach road was flat, and clay could reach there without going through the centre of St. Austell. In 1820, Sir Christopher Hawkins bought all the land at the mouth of Pentewan river and embarked on the building of a granite basin, dock gates, an approach channel and quay, warehouses and stores, a terraced row of houses and a church, spending £22,000 on the project. It was not to open in Charles Rashleigh's lifetime, but from the moment Hawkins announced his plans, the writing was on the wall for Charlestown, and things would never be quite the same again.

William Rashleigh, on the death of Charles's wife Grace, had hoped that events would 'tend to make the evening of his life tranquil and happy', but that unfortunately was wishful thinking. The final tragedy for Charles was the affair of Joseph Daniel, which broke his spirit, brought on illness and probably sent him to an early grave. Unlike the Joseph Dingle affair, which received considerable local publicity and was mentioned widely in correspondence by Charles's friends and associates, the Daniel case was, we understand, held in isolation in London, where it excited little interest and certainly was not reported in west

71

country newspapers. In fact, Joseph Daniel is such an elusive figure that whilst researching for this book we were for a while quite convinced that Joseph Dingle and Joseph Daniel were in fact one and the same person! Documentary sources for this court case are, as far as we can tell, from searches made in the Public Records Office, Chancery Lane, non-existant. Only the family records at Menabilly, and the certain knowledge that it was Joseph Daniel who sold Duporth Manor to Dr. Pattison following Charles's death, cast any light on what can only be described as a most strange affair. Recalling the words of Mr.Jekyll, Counsel for the defence in the case of Rashleigh v Dingle, who stated: '. . this case, take it all and all, is the most extraordinary and wonderful that I have ever met with,' one wonders what comment he would have made in this instance?

Joseph Daniel, like his predecessor Dingle, was a personal man servant at Duporth to Charles Rashleigh, having been in his service for many years, presumably long enough to have won his employers confidence and trust. He was also his confidential clerk in the office and a great personal favourite. Some time in 1820 Charles, anxious that Daniel should become a magistrate, found that this was impossible unless he owned some land or property, in other words, that he was a man of means. What followed is almost unbelievable, particularly since the ink was hardly dry on the verdict document of his last court case against Dingle. Whatever induced Charles to go to such an extreme on behalf of a servant, no matter how fond he was of him, is beyond comprehension, particularly since by his very actions he became party to a legal deception – if we can believe what is recorded in the Menabilly manuscript. If only title to land or property was required to help Daniel, why on earth did Rashleigh not sign over some part of the village, or any of his many other land holdings, instead of making over the title deeds of Duporth manor and grounds, his personal home?

There was only one condition, and that was that after a short period of time, Daniel would sign a release, handing back the documents. Charles Rashleigh then had a deed drawn up, 'selling' the property to his man servant, with a suitable release whereby Daniel could restore the property to its rightful owner. Since no money actually changed hands, it was in fact a deliberate conspiracy to defraud the authorities, hardly the act of a sane man in Rashleigh's position. Why Charles behaved in this manner we shall never know, perhaps the only sensible explanation being blackmail. It was such a strange, totally irrational, dangerous and unnecessary thing to do. As an attorney-at-law he must have realised the implications of the matter becoming public, which unfortunately is exactly what happened. Worse still, what if Daniel then refused to sign the release, surely that possibility had not escaped him?

Few authors have attempted to get to the bottom of these affairs concerning Dingle and Daniel, and none of them successfully. Canon

Hammond, in his book, *A Cornish Parish*, written in 1879, was uncertain whether the matter of Dingle's debt ever went to court, thought that it was Dingle who wanted to be a magistrate and left out Daniel completely. In Hammonds own words, 'I have experienced great difficulty in getting at the truth as to this transaction; I can only hope that I have reached it. I am not sure there was a trial.'

With the transfer documents duly signed and witnessed, Daniel was shown the release and off he went, the proud recipient of a beautiful manor house, farm and gardens – for nothing! When a demand was eventually made that he sign the release, returning the title deeds, he denied all knowledge of the agreement, saying that as far as he was concerned Duporth had been given him as a gift. Charles tried everything in his power to regain his property, taking the matter to court after court in London, where on each occasion the judgement was for the defendant. Each judge pronounced, rightly, in the circumstances, that Charles was a victim of his own actions, the new ownership deeds were totally legal and could not now be undone. The cost of more counsel, journeys to London with various employees from Charlestown to swear that Duporth rightly belonged to Rashleigh, time in court, costs and the like, dragged on for almost two years, until finally they bankrupted poor Charles.

Without the benefit of full details of the case, it is difficult to understand various comments made by friends and relatives in their letter writing, but their overall thoughts were the same as the following extracts indicate:

'I hope Mr. Charles Rashleigh will be comforted, his case is lost, and I certainly think never ought to have been brought to Court. It will be said . . people all swore falsely . . I have no doubt of the justice of the verdict . . do not state this to Mr. Charles, if he asks my opinion I will give it.'

'Mr. Charles Rashleigh's other Counsel was Denmar, whose abilities in that line I believe are not thought highly of and who is by no means a favourite of the bench.'

'There is no hope of anything favourable to Mr. Charles Rashleigh from the event of the case in the King's bench.'

'The judges have intimated a strong opinion as to the validity.'

Life of course went on as normal in Charlestown itself, the residents and workers ignorant of what was going on 'up at the big house', since it did not affect them in any way, then or later. In 1822 the question of ownership of the water from Luxulyan came to light in a letter, from William Rashleigh to Thomas Robins:

'Please enquire of Charles Rashleigh whether my late uncle's conveyance to him of Luxulyan mill included all his rights in the River that runs through my land in that Parish, was it included in the transfer to Charles, that we may know how we stand in regard to the diverting of the river from its present channel for the use of Mr Austin's mines, Wheal Treasure. I am led to think that the late Philip Rashleigh's right to the river may have been sold to his brother for the use of Charlestown.'

A snapshot of port activity in early 1822 comes from The West Briton newspaper of the 15th January, reporting ship movements: 'Arrived, the *Active*, the *Charles* and the *Rashleigh*, all from Swansea. The *Duporth* and the *Fowey*, from Fowey; the *Fame*, the *Charlestown* and the *Lark*, all from Plymouth. Sailed: The *Pheasant* and the *Parry*, for *Swansea*; the *Ann*, the *Elizabeth* and the *Lark*, for Mevagissey.' The same source reported on the 15th March, that 'a fine schooner, the *Swan* was launched at Charlestown'. The following winter of 1822-23 was particularly severe; Robins wrote to William Rashleigh: 'my wife is ill, all have troublesome colds', and mentioned that a Mr. Lake had advised him, 'I have had the rheumatism in my hand this last fortnight which is a new complaint to me'. He continued, 'I send for your perusal a letter this instant received from Mr. Walker, by which you will find Mr. Charles Rashleigh has for some time been seriously unwell.' Walker's letter read, 'I had a letter from Charles Rashleigh yesterday not written by himself, stating that he was too ill to write, so that the report of his illness you had heard when I had the pleasure of seeing you at Menabilly, was well founded.'

In February, William was able to report to Robins on the 3rd that, 'Dr Fox was unable to attend Mr Charles Rashleigh, he was attended by Mr Bawen of St Mawes and was much better on Saturday.' On the 14th, 'Mr Charles Rashleigh's illness proves to be gout, which has happily settled in his foot', Followed on the 3rd March, by 'My letter is this instant returned from Duporth, poor Mr Charles Rashleigh continues just the same; Dr. Gould is a little better.'

Charles Rashleigh's life ended on the 9th March 1823, aged 76, and, like his beloved Grace, he died in his own bed at Duporth. Dr. Edward Rodd broke the news to William Rashleigh in writing:

'The recent accounts you have received from this house must have prepared you for the melancholy tidings of the death of your worthy and beloved uncle which took place this afternoon at 3 o'clock. Though his last illness has been extremely distressing, yet for a few hours previous to his dissolution he did not appear to suffer severely and he resigned his valuable life into the hands of his maker without a struggle, patient and resigned to that Divine will and full of hope of a joyful resurrection that is the meditator of a merciful redeemer. His daughters and I have the comfort to stay as well or better than I dared to hope under their severe affliction.'

William Rashleigh passed the news to Robins the following day:

'Poor Mr Charles Rashleigh died yesterday. Though his illness was extremely distressing Dr. Rodd writes me that for the last few

A miniature portrait of Charles Rashleigh in his latter years, probably painted around 1820, three years prior to his death.

hours preceding his dissolution, he did not appear to suffer much. Excuse haste, as I have many letters to write on this melancholy occasion.'

The West Briton & Cornwall Advertiser of the 14th March 1823, carried the following announcement regarding Charles's demise:

'Died, on Sunday 9th March 1823 at his seat, Duporth, near St. Austell, Charles Rashleigh esq. His Majesty's Receiver General for the County of Cornwall. Throughout his long life, Mr. Rashleigh was distinguished as a man of strict integrity and was deservedly esteemed and respected by all ranks and all parties throughout the County.'

Details of the funeral were conveyed to William by Dr. Rodd, who wrote from Duporth on the 14th March:

'By the will of your late uncle, the funeral is directed to be quite private, but the family here readily acquess to your wishes to knowing the time appointed for the last sad ceremony and feel much gratified at your concern and intention of attending. Mr Grylls and myself hope to meet you at St. Austell tomorrow morning at half past 7. We all feel much obliged to you and Mrs Rashleigh for your kind enquiries for us both now and during our late anxious suspense. Patty, I am sorry to say is not quite well, and Harriet and Sophia are tolerable. They unite in kind regards to yourself and Mrs Rashleigh.'

Charles was laid to rest alongside his wife in the large square family tomb, just inside the gate leading into the cemetery, on the 15th March, at 7.30am. Only three years later, with the consent of Charles' chief executor, Dr. Edward Rodd, the tomb was demolished by the church authorities to make way for a small chapel or shed, in order to give the Vicar shelter from the weather when conducting burial services. As a consequence, the Rashleigh tomb was levelled, its sides used to make a floor over their grave which bore only their initials, the stonework slabs probably now hidden beneath the turf. The top of the tomb was placed against the wall, where it still stands today, only a few feet from their grave. Fourteen years later, on 31st October 1847, five days after she died, Pattie,(Martha) Rashleigh was also interred in the family grave, her name being added to that of her mother and father on the commemorative stone.

Chapter 4   Reference Sources

No	Source
1	West Briton & Cornish Advertiser
2	CCC. CRO. DD.CN/2178 p403
3	A Short History of Luxulyan Parish, Rowe. Dr. John
4	Menabilly mss
5	CCC. CRO. DDR(S)1/215
6	ibid DD.CF/1-853 p151
7	Menabilly mss
8	CCC. CRO. DDR(S)1/215
9	Menabilly mss
10	CCC. CRO. DDT/2537
11	ibid DDR/5314
12	ibid DDR/5316
13	ibid DDR/5314
14	ibid DDR/5316
15	ibid DDR/5314
16	ibid "
17	ibid DDR/5316
18	ibid DDR/5314
19	Menabilly mss

CHAPTER 5

New owners and opportunities. 1824 – 1850

Charles Rashleigh's will was read to the executors on 13 March 1823, by Edward Coode. Dated 11 February 1809, it had of course been made at a time when his financial circumstances and expectations were altogether different. Strangely however, despite all his problems, this will had remained unaltered, and without codicil, for over fourteen years. The large, single page parchment document survives and reads in part:

'This is the last Will and Testament of me Charles Rashleigh of Duporth in the parish of Saint Austell, in the County of Cornwall. I desire that my funeral may be private and no mourning be given of any sort but that the usual . . and that my remains may be placed in a plain wooden coffin. If I should die at or within ten miles of Saint Austell Parish I desire to be buried in the new burying ground belonging to that parish and to be carried to the grave by twelve of my own Labourers, but if I shall die at a greater distance from Saint Austell I desire to be buried in the churchyard in which I may die, and in that case the bearers may be selected from the industrious poor of that parish and I give to the Bearers, whether my own Labourers or strangers half a Guinea a piece. . I give, desire and bequeath all and singular my freeholds and copyhold Manors, Messuage, Farms, Lands, Tenements, Tithes and Heredaments whatsoever and wheresoever . . also all my Estate and tin bounds whatsoever and wheresoever. . and also all and singular my monies and securities for monies . . all my goods, chattels, and personal estate . . into and to the use of the Reverend Henry Hawkins Tremayne and John Hearle Tremayne Esq. both of Heligan, in the said county of Cornwall, and William Rashleigh of Kilmarth in the same county or their heirs successors or administrators . . all such estate Term or terms of years and interest as I shall have therein respectively at the time of my demise. Upon trust that they, by mortgage or sale of a competent part of my said real or personal estate (except my dwelling house at Duporth) aforesaid and the lands and fields thereto belonging and called Duporth Farm . . and sell at Interest . . as they may for the payment and discharge of all my just debts . .'[1]

Two letters written immediately following the death of Charles, suggest that the family were not ignorant of the acute financial situation in which they had been left:

'William Rashleigh to Robins, 10 March 1823: We know nothing for certain about Duporth, though we have paid a visit there, nor can we learn whether my poor uncle died in affluent circumstances or not. We believe that Miss Rashleigh (Pattie) is to have Duporth for life.'[2]

Dr. Rodd, according to the Menabilly manuscript, made the following comment to his wife on his return from St. Just, on 14-15 March, 'Harriet has got nothing; Sophia has got nothing and Pattie has got just enough to live on.'

Charles's wish that his 'dwelling house at Duporth' should not be sold to pay off any debts, and Pattie's hopes of being allowed to remain – indeed being able to afford to continue to live there, were shattered, when Joseph Daniel announced that it was to be sold as soon as possible. The date of the sale is unrecorded, lost when the title deeds were stolen, but took place within the year, being purchased by a Dr. Thomas Mein Pattison, mentioned earlier, who was acquainted with the Rashleigh family.[3] Regarding the theft of the title deeds, Dr. Pattison only lived at Duporth until 1828, when he put the property on the market. A Dr. Bull, who was both a qualified doctor and chemist, came down from Bristol accompanied by a friend, making enquiries of Dr. Pattison's solicitor, pretending that he wished to buy Duporth. Left alone in an office to scrutinise the deeds and other documents, both men slipped away taking all the papers with them. Only a week or so later, Bull was arrested in London for the murder of a girl he had misled (incidentally the first person seized by the London police as a result of information communicated by telegram). A portrait of Bull which appeared in the press was recognised by Thomas Coode, the solicitor, who made the journey to London in an attempt to recover the documents, but they were never found. Regarding Duporth, it was purchased from Pattison by Mr. Freeth, Steward to the Duchy of Cornwall.[4] Following Daniel's earlier sale of Duporth to Dr. Pattison, Pattie then went to live in Cuddra House, but in time this became too much of a financial burden for her, and she was forced to move into the adjacent Cuddra cottage, where she remained until her death on the 26 October 1847, aged sixty-six, still a spinster.

Literally the day prior to Charles's will being read, Charlestown's pier suffered considerable storm damage, which required immediate attention. The interesting thing about the following letter is that within only three days of Rashleigh's death, it appears that Crowder and Co. had already agreed to purchase the harbour, which suggests that negotiations were in progress some time before Charles' demise:

'Mr. Wm. Petherick to the Rev. Henry Tremayne, 12 March 1823. The damage done to the pier at Charlestown will cost from £50 to £100 to repair, this expense will of course be borne by the purchaser. Mr. Burnley has sent up a man, formerly in his employ at Pentuan (sic),to look at it. Mr. Crowder saw the weakness of the port that has given way when he was here, and Mr. H. H. Tremayne also saw it, and felt disposed to take it down in the spring. We shall use every exertion to get it repaired.'[5]

The situation must have been a nightmare for the executors of Charles's estate, and sorting out such a large private manor, the many leaseholds, the legal practice, Charlestown, various estates and business share holdings and the debts, took quite some time. In fact, no real changes in the ownership or management of the port took place until 1825, during which time we can only assume that the executors continued to manage the property, since trading certainly continued. The level of debt we shall never know, but we have found no evidence of any large sums owed locally. The principal creditors were William Augustus Crowder, QC. of Bell & Crowder, who had represented Charles in his long legal battle with Joseph Daniel over Duporth House, a William Henry Crowder, either his son or brother; Edward Rose Tunno; James Henry Shears; Thomas Margrave and Edward Sartoris. What role the latter four played in uncertain, possibly bankers, but William Crowder, of Surbiton and 55 Lincolns Inn Field, was certainly a lawyer. How much they were jointly owed is anyone's guess, but it was a considerable sum, well beyond the capital means of Charles's estate. Therefore, as soon as probate was cleared and the will proved, the executors commenced to dispose of saleable assets, which included Rashleigh's shares in various ships, amongst other things:

> 'The West Briton. 16 April 1823. Shares in Vessels. To be Sold by Auction, on Wednesday the 30th day of April instant, at Three o'clock in the Afternoon, at the Hotel, at Charlestown, in the Parish of St. Austell, in such lots as may be then determined on, One-Fourth of the Sloop *DUPORTH*, One-Eighth of the schooner *CHARLES*, five-sixteenths of the Schooner *PHEASANT*, One-Eighth of the *BRILLIANT* and *WATERLOO*, Three-Sixteenths in the smack *PATTY* and One-Sixteenth of the Schooner *SWAN*. All of the Port of Fowey, and regularly employed in the Coasting and Coal Trade, from Charlestown. For further information apply to Messrs. Coode & Sons, Attornies, St. Austell.'

All those vessels were registered at Fowey, many having been built there, only the *Swan* having been launched at Charlestown, in 1822. In May, further Rashleigh assets were disposed of:

> 'To be Sold by Auction, on Saturday the 10th day of May instant, at Four o'clock in the Afternoon, at the Hotel, at Charlestown, a very good MACKEREL SEAN, 160 fathoms long. A GROUND SEAN, 60 fathoms long, Mackerel Sean Boat as Good as new, Follower and other Materials. For viewing the same, apply to Walter Roberts, at Charlestown. Dated 3rd May 1823.'[6]

Two days later, the sale of Duporth Farm stock was being advertised:

> 'CAPITAL FARM STOCK. On Monday the 12th of May next, and following days, an Auction will be held, for SELLING LIVE and DEAD FARM STOCK of Charles Rashleigh, Esq. deceased, on his Farms in St. Austell, viz.

On CHARLESTOWN FARM

A large mow of Hay, A mow of Barley, A mow of Oats, A rick of Hay, 7 good Farm Horses, 4 Mules, 10 Working Oxen, 8 Fat Bullocks, 20 Young Bullocks, 3 Cows, and a Heifer, 1 Bull, 40 Wether Sheep, 41 Ewes and Lambs, 20 Young Sheep, 2 Rams, 11 Pigs, 3 Asses, 20 Hogsheads of Cider, 120 Caps and Posts, Thrashing Machine, 4 Waggons, 6 Horse and 4 Ox carts, Harness, 2 Cart Wains, Tormentor, Ploughs, Harrows, Scuffler, &c. &c.

AND ON DUPORTH FARM,

A mow of Oats, A rick of Hay, 2 good Carriage Horses, with their Harness, A capital Mare, after *Bagatelle*, 2 young Cows, 3 Young Bullocks, 16 Ewes and Lambs, 30 Young Sheep, A Family carriage, Market Cart, &c. &c.
A Number of rare Foreign and Domestic Poultry, consisting of Swans, Pea Fowl, Gold Pheasants, &c. For viewing the Stock,
apply to Thomas Hodge, the Hind, at Charlestown.
The Sheep, Bullocks, Horses, Corn and Hay, will be sold on the first day, and the Husbandry Implements, Cider, &c. on the following days. Each day's Sale to commence precisely at One o'clock.'[7]

At the height of the summer that same year, when the corn was ripe:
'To be sold by Auction on the 12th August at 4 o'clock in the afternoon, at Charlestown Hotel, the CORN, now growing on Duporth, Charlestown and Cuddra Farms.

On Duporth	Cost	Measure
Long Down Field	£7	2R. 16P
Quarry Park, Barley	£3	3R. 13P
Lamb's Close, Barley	£3	1R. 28P
On Charlestown Farm		
Mill Field, wheat	£20	0. 0
Orchard Meadow, barley	£1	1R. 25P
Peter's Close £1 3R. 22P		
Crinnis Middle Field, barley	£3	0. 0
Lower Part of Down Field, oats	£4	0. 0
On Cuddra Farm		
Well Park, barley	£3	3R. 22P
Hollow Burrow, wheat	£3	1R. 18P

Thomas Hodge, the Hind, at Charlestown, will shew the fields, and for further information apply at the office of Messrs. Coode & Sons, St. Austell. 29th July 1823.'[8]

The office of the legal practice in St. Austell was sold to Robins, and Rashleigh's town house went to a Mr. Dunn. The final sale of 1823, which took place on 9 September, was quite extraordinary, being the contents of Charles Rashleigh's well stocked wine cellar at Duporth.

Even for a wealthy land owning gentleman, who entertained well and frequently gave dinner parties, to have 1,860 bottles of port laid up seems an excessive amount of wine, and what about 396 bottles of brandy, or 486 bottles of Madeira!

'The West Briton, 29th August 1823. Superior old Wines and Cordials for Sale. To be sold by auction on 9th September 1823, at Duporth, Saint Austell, the late residence of Charles Rashleigh, Esq. deceased, his well-selected stock of Wines and Spirits, viz:

Old Port	155 dozen	Saluterna	18 dozen
New Port	6 "	Lachryma	22 "
East India Madeira	39 "	Lisbon	2 1/2 "
Malmsey	23 "	White Wine	16 "
Hock	4 1/2 "	Brandy	33 "
Mountain	8 "	Hollands	28 "
Claret	9 "	Rum	6 "
Bucellas	40 "		

Nearly the whole of the above has been from *ten to twenty years* in bottle. The whole will be put up in small lots for the accommodation of purchasers. The sale will commence precisely at Eleven o'clock. St. Austell 18th August 1823.'

One year after Rashleigh's death the remaining contents of Duporth House were sold, but only after the family had taken the pieces they wanted. Pattie probably furnished Cuddra House from the family home, taking heirlooms; other pieces going to Sophia Grylls and Harriet Rodd, particularly the latter, who had children, whereas the other sisters had none. Known items of furniture from Duporth are extant at Menabilly, other pieces, including what is believed to have been Charles's personal desk, survive in St. Mabyn, Cornwall, in Scotland, some even as far away as New Zealand, having been taken there by descendants of the Rodd family when they emigrated. Right up until Duporth House was pulled down in 1988, an original bow-fronted, veneered, double wardrobe remained upstairs in what had been either Charles or Grace Rashleigh's bedroom, simply because it was too large to be removed through the door!

'HOUSEHOLD FURNITURE, Hothouse and Greenhouse Plants. To be SOLD by AUCTION on Wednesday the 31st day of March instant, and following day, at Duporth, in the Parish of *St. Austell*, late the residence of Charles Rashleigh, Esq. deceased, the HOUSEHOLD FURNITURE; Comprising Four-Post, Field, and other Bedsteads; Feather Beds, Mattresses, Counterpanes, Quilts, and Blankets; Bureau, Dressing Tables and Washstands; Mahogany and other Chests of Drawers; Wardrobes; Pier and other Glasses; a large quantity of China, Glass and Earthenware; Fire Irons and Fenders; a large and excellent Turret Clock; large Kitchen Cupboards; a very large Kitchen Table; Kitchen Utensils; a Smoke Jack &c.

About 200 dozen of Black Bottles
Also, the whole of the Hothouse, Greenhouse and Exotic Plants,
Orange and Lemon Trees; the whole in excellent condition. Also,
The Family Carriage,
Which has been recently put in a complete state of repair. The sale
to commence each day at Ten o'clock precisely. The Household
Furniture will be Sold first. March 10th 1824.'[9]

It was said that during the 19th century, there was not a single tin
smelter who was not a banker, which explains why Charles took out
leases from the owner, John Sawle, initially in partnership with Francis
Polkinghorne in 1778, and again in 1815 for a term of sixteen years
with Edward Fox & Co., on the St. Austell Blowing House and works,
on Blowing House Hill.[10] The town works by now consisted of three
premises, the Old, the New and Higher Blowing Houses, but despite
the fact that smelting was a very lucrative business, the former furnace
had been standing idle for some time. Depression was hitting the mining industry following the war with France, and this, coupled with the
fact that the Old Blowing House was in a state of disrepair, was probably the reason for its disuse. In fact, the amount of tin smelted by the
St. Austell works between 1820-1830 was very impressive:
1820 – 1,145 blocks (of 3.5cwt); 1821 – 1,792; 1822 – 1,566; 1823 -3,206;
1824 – 4,137; 1825 – 3,204; 1826 – 3,069; 1827 – 2,707.[11]

In 1825, Williams, of Harvey, Davey, Williams & Co., bought the Old
Blowing House in St. Austell, which by then had stood idle, under
lease to Fox, Rashleigh & Co., since 1821. The new owner repaired the
works and arranged that the Old House would only be used for common tin, the New and Higher Blowing Houses converting all the higher quality grain tin. This revived the disused reverberatory furnaces at
the Old House, utilising it as a smelting works which lasted until 1839.
At this stage, the nearest coinage town was Truro (which became a city
in 1877). This meant that every six weeks numerous tons of tin blocks
or ingots had to be dragged by horse and cart, at considerable expense,
over some fifteen miles of hilly road, for assay and stamping. It then
had to be brought back, if not sold on the spot and, apart from a hated
and inconvenient delay of a month and a half between coinings, it was
uneconomic and time wasting. This led to several towns making application to open a coinage hall, and that for St. Austell was finally granted in 1834. Where exactly the coining took place in the town is
described only as in the 'Cow Market', which may have been the cattle
market off the Mevagissey Road. As a direct result, mines from far
afield began to send their ore to the St. Austell area for both smelting
and coining, since both operations could now be achieved in the one
area, considerably reducing handling and carriage costs.

In point of fact, the smelting business was so good that a new company was formed in 1834, the Charlestown Smelting House Co., set up by
John Taylor & Sons. Taylor, known as the 'Norwich Nipper', had

arrived in Cornwall about 1815, and apart from being the man who later built *Ardanconnel* (179 Charlestown Rd.) for his daughter, had opened the Charlestown United mine in 1819, an amalgamation of several old mines at Boscoppa, Bethel, Boscundle & Holmbush. This new set of furnaces were erected on a site to the 'north-east of the harbour', and should not be confused with the much older Charlestown Blowing House situated alongside Charlestown mill. This was attached to the mill's eastern side, on ground later occupied by the stables and carriage house associated with the large property *Charlestown Hill*, later *The Grove*, which became the Crowder family's country home as its fourth occupants. A letter from H. Lake to Thomas Robins mentions this development:

'Trevarrick. 27th September 1824. I have just received yours of yesterday respecting Mr. Geach, who I understand is about to have a situation in a new blowing house at Charlestown. I must again decline seeing him on this business, as I have before told you, and cannot say anything about the security on Blowing House Hills. It may be wise of Wm. Rashleigh to take it rather than lose the whole. I will deliver your message to Mr. Pedlar when he calls.'

It should be noted that whilst this letter was dated 1824, the new Blowing House did not materialise that year, neither is it shown on the 1825 map of Charlestown, the very first accurate survey and map of the village, but may have been on ground occupied by the shipyard. An outline of what smelting entailed would not be out of place at this point, since an appreciation of the operation brings home not only the costs involved, but also its reliance on suppliers, which in turn reflects trade in the port. Smelting was by now carried out in reverbatory furnaces, which were granite and brick structures, with a furnace separate from its 'charge' of ore. The fuel used was now coal, having previously been charcoal, the heat from which was carried through a shaped flue, across the 'charge' furnace and away up a tall chimney stack. Smelting commenced by lighting the fire, then mixing the 'charge', which consisted of black tin ore, mixed with 20% culm or crushed anthracite, some slaked lime or fluorspar and a quantity of dross or slag from a previous smelting, the whole stirred and damped with water. After some 2-3 hours the charge would become molten, and the whole operation or 'reduction' of the ore charge would be completed in some 6 hours. The older Blowing Houses were much more crude and inefficient, constructed inside rough structures of rock or turf under a thatched roof, which frequently burned down! The large granite furnace was fired by charcoal, it being recorded that the New Blowing House in St. Austell consumed 5,194 packs of this fuel during 1802, at a cost of 2s.6d a pack (£649.2s.6d pa., or £162,000 today). In these older furnaces, the fuel and the ore were layered together, the metal puddling in the bottom of the hearth. In Charlestown, initial purchases of ore from 1834 were from the Polgooth and Charlestown United mines, in which Taylor was both manager and shareholder, but before long ore was being brought to the village all the way from St. Agnes, Poldice, Great Beam and mines in the Tamar valley. For whatever reason, this second smelting venture in Charlestown was never really successful, since during 1835 the number of tin blocks coined in St. Austell from the new house was only 787. A great deal more will be said about Charlestown mines later, when we reach the 1840-50 period. The Crinnis area, adjacent to Charlestown, which gave its name to the Crinnis mine, first saw copper excavated in 1808, and in 1811 was said to be the richest this side of the Dolcoath find; it yielded 10,000 tons the following year. After a decline, it experienced another boom as an extract from the West Briton of 4 April 1823 shows:

'Saturday 29th March. Joshua Rowe, proprietor of the Crinnis Mine, in course of working, a very rich lode or vein of copper ore was discovered which took a westerly direction, through the lands adjoining Crinnis which belonged to the Earl of Mount Edgcumbe. Mr. Rowe agreed for a lease, or set, for working the new mine, with Messrs Rashleigh & Coode, agents for Mount Edgcumbe and commenced working it before the set was executed.

Others who had adventured with Rowe earlier, tried to claim the set, which Rowe has named Wheal Regent. An uncle of Rowe's, later raised money on the lease as if it were his own.'[12]

In the meantime, Charlestown continued to develop and prosper; at the same time the lengthy legal process of determining ownerships and settling outstanding debts had come to an end. As is so often the case, even today, when a business develops over a period of time, the individuals concerned seldom bother with a record of what has been achieved. Everyone will say, 'Oh, we can all remember what happened,' except of course they do not, by which time much information and detail is lost. Such was the situation at Charlestown in 1823 following Rashleigh's death, the executors finding there were no maps of the port or village and only incomplete records as to who was leasing what, and what rents were being paid. Therefore, in 1825 a Falmouth surveyor, Richard Thomas, was engaged to survey the whole of Charlestown and relevant properties owned at Holmbush, Mount Charles and elsewhere. This resulted not only in the first map of the village, but also a complete inventory of the property, with a list of tenants and their rents. This shows a total of 224 fields, houses, barns, cellars, gardens and plots, every one leasehold from Rashleigh. In addition, there were six leasings at Mount Charles, ninety-nine at Treverbyn, six at Benallack, and eighteen associated with Gatty's, Relython and Wood Mills, at Luxulyan.[13]

Crowder, of Slimfield, in Berkshire, and Sartoris, of Bishops Waltham, in Hampshire, had by now agreed to accept all of the leasehold property in Charlestown at valuation, in lieu of the sums owed them. At the same time, their offer to purchase the remainder of the estate was accepted, and they became the new owners of the port sometime in the spring of 1825, trading as Charlestown Estate. The total land area they acquired amounted to 484 acres, 2 rods, 18 poles, of which 333 acres was Charlestown itself, neatly bounded by the sea, Porthpean Road, the Turnpike/Lostwithiel Road and Campdown. At Mount Charles, the property included Parnal's Barn, with two dwellings at the rear, which occupied the corner on the north side, now a branch of the National Westminster Bank. At Holmbush, there were 23 dwellings, which literally made up Holmbush village, all situated on the south side of the Lostwithiel road and most still standing. The new owners were not too happy about the land on which the port had been built:

> 'From Henry Coode, Grays Inn, to Thomas Abbot Esq. Duchy of Cornwall Office, 5th July 1825. An estate has recently been purchased by some clients of ours from the devisces of the late Charles Rashleigh, the title of several portions of which consisting of both freehold and leasehold is derived under the Duchy of Cornwall, and we understand that the evidence of it is alone to be obtained at the office of the Duchy.
>
> In the abstract of title supplied to us, it is stated with reference to about 2 acres of land near the sea, upon which a quay and pier have been since erected, that at an assassion or arrentation for the manor of Tewington held on 30th August 1787, one Nevel Norway (sic) took the above premises of the Comm'rs. to hold till the next assession only under a rent of 3s.4d and 2d(pa) and that by an indenture dated 29th October 1789, Norway sold his interest to Charles Rashleigh for £100. It is further stated that at the assession in October 1794 for the said manor, Charles Rashleigh by grant from the Commissioners took the same premises together with a parcel of beach or strand and a quay or pier erected thereon under the old rents of 3s.4d and 2d(pa) and the increased rent of 40 shillings.
>
> By a copy of Court Roll dated 1st November 1796 or 1790 (?) it appears that a special court for the Manor Mr. Rashleigh surrendered the above premises to the interest that Mr. Cooke should take the same and was therefore admitted Tenant.'[14]

Nine days later, on 14 July 1825, Crowder wrote to Edward Coode:
'The delay in production of the Deeds should not prejudice the Trustees of Mr. Charles Rashleigh by proof proving the purchase.' The sudden change of ownership obviously caused several individuals with ad hoc agreements or arrangements to feel concern for their future. Thomas Carlyon of Tregrehan, appears to have had an arrangement with Rashleigh going back some eighteen years:

> 'Thomas Carlyon Esq., to the Rev. Henry Hawkins Tremayne, clerk; Jon. Hearle Tremayne, both of Heligan; Rev. Edward Rodd, of St. Just-in-Roseland and Martha Rashleigh, of St. Austell, spin-

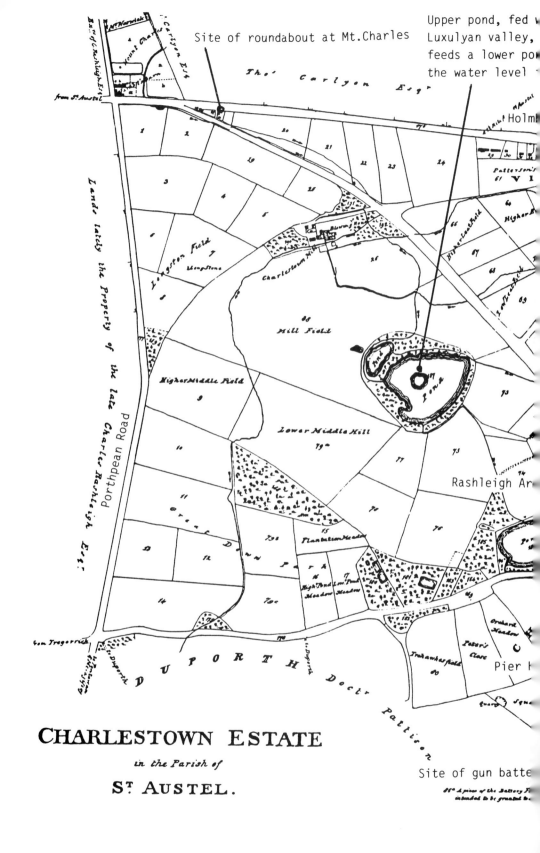

Site of roundabout at Mt.Charles

Upper pond, fed w
Luxulyan valley,
feeds a lower po
the water level

The Carlyon Esqʳ

Holm

Patterson's
VI

Higher

Rashleigh Ar

Site of gun batte

CHARLESTOWN ESTATE

in the Parish of

Sᵗ AUSTEL.

from
urn
aintains
r dock.

This early map of Charlestown dated 1825, was
drawn specifically to determine ownership of
particular properties following the death of
Charles Rashleigh in 1823. Ownership of all
the leasehold land & buildings had passed into
the hands of Augustus Crowder QC, hence this
survey became necessary, and provided future
generations with Charlestown's first accurate
map. A record of all the names associated with
numbered plots & buildings shown is held by
the joint Curator's of the Heritage Centre.

Old access road, prior to railway

aul's church

of childrens play field

Site of Shipwreck & Heritage Centre

ster; devisees on the will of Charles Rashleigh, deceased. Re-lease of Right – Charlestown. Re. an Agreement made on the 10th July 1807 between Charles Rashleigh and Thos. Carlyon concerning liberty for Thos. Carlyon to land on the quay at Mr. Rashleigh's port called Charlestown, coals and other articles of merchandise requisite or desirable for the immediate use or consumption of Thos. Carlyon and his family while resident at Tregrehan, free from quay dues and other charges, also to lodge for up to 10 days goods or coals so landed, but not to interfere with other commerce . . application for release.'

Since Charlestown was to expand considerably under its new owners during the next 75 years, a description of the village as it was at the time of Rashleigh's death in 1823[15] may be of interest. First, none of the smaller roads, lanes or alleys in the village as yet had official names, their local identity probably only emerging when they were officially recorded on the first Ordnance Survey map, therefore, their 20th century identity will be used for clarity. Secondly, all rental sums quoted are annual, and in 'old money' (ie.pounds, shillings and pence). Commencing on the eastern side of the harbour, the property now named *Salamander* (No.1 Quay Road), indisputably the oldest building in the village, was the *Content* pilchard cellar, which was divided into four units, all leased to Matthew Vounder & Co. for £20. Above were four one-roomed dwellings, one leased to Elizabeth Williams, along with a garden plot behind Bark House Lane, for £3.3s The other three rooms, which also had garden plots in the same area, were taken up by Charles Coombe, John and Richard Organ, all paying the same annual rent. No.2 Quay Road (which later was split into two homes, numbered No.1/2, before reverting back to one dwelling and was only known as the Harbour Master's House in the late 1900s, was occupied by a John Webbe, at £12.12s. Nos. 3 & 4 Quay Road were lived in by William Hotten and Grace Lyle respectively, paying £3.3s, No.5 being empty at the time. No.6 was occupied by Elizabeth Rickard, at a rental of £10.10s; No.7 by Elizabeth Melhuish, at £19.19s; No.8 was jointly leased to David & Kennett Banks for £14, and No.9 to Baker Banks at £10, whose garden is now occupied by Ivy House. When built c1845, *Ivy House* was originally named *Marine Villa*, which was in keeping with Marine Terrace, the original name of Quay Road. The other properties in this row, today numbered 10 to 31 Quay Road, did not exist in 1825, being built c1845. The ground on which cottages No.12-17 were later built was then the garden of William P. Banks, the port's shipbuilder, who leased all the shipyard at the head of the dock, along with the large three-storied property now known as *T'Gallants Guest House* (No.6 Charlestown Road, at one time two houses back-to-back) for £42. The same gentleman also had what was called the 'Blocking Shop and yard behind, with Rigging Loft over', known today as the *Long Store*, Duporth Road, the rental then being £4.4s. What today is the Cornish

Smoked Fish Companys premises in Duck Street were dwellings and a barn, divided into four units. Three of these were houses on two floors, only one with a garden, which were leased to John Rundle for £6.6s, the other to William Harris at £3.3s. The remainder of the building was a 'cellar and loft', thought to be the eastern end, which was vacant at the time. This entire building had previously been a granary and probably built as such, almost certainly associated with *Polmear Farm*, subsequently used as a clay cellar in 1900's.

This farm, where the infamous Joseph Dingle had once lived, had no tenant in 1825, hence its rental is not known, but the property was very much as it is today, consisting of a farm house with outhouses, two mowhays and large orchard in front of the house. It also included a wainhouse, Garden Meadow, Sentry Close, and fourteen other named fields or 'parcels' of land. The row of cottages that now extend from *Polmear Farm*, commencing with No.33 Quay Road, through to the Rashleigh Arms, were not all built at the time. No.33, later to become the Custom House, was occupied by a John Bunny, on an annual rental of £12.12s; No.34 by James Phillips for £14, and the last one in the row, now No.35, by Josuah(sic) Melhuish, for £12. From there to the main road, on the site of the present *Rashleigh Arms* and two cottages, stood a long single storey, open fronted china clay cellar, with chamber, loft and garden, occupied by Dickens & Co, 'used by samplers, Edward Rowse'. rent £36.6s.

On the site of the existing Methodist Chapel, on which building was commenced in 1827 but not completed until 1830, once stood a small meeting house, already mentioned in Chapter 2, where the Charlestown Sunday School met, which may well have served as the first village church. The forecourt of the *Harbour Motor Company* was at the time a cobbled ore floor, the area behind, now occupied by garage workshops (a cooperage in the 1900s) was a coal yard, stretching east to the boundary of No.36 Quay Road. At the top of Ropewalk Lane, now occupied by house No.26, stood two china clay cellars, rented to Scredda Adventurers at £12, whilst at the bottom of the lane, on the south side were three gardens, rented to Thomas Rundle, £15, Henry Davey, £11.1s and William Roach, £10.10s, the latter renting the end two cottages (Nos.28 & 30) and gardens for £10.10s. The others (Nos.32 & 34), were taken by William Paynton and Daniel Bond at £3.3s. The cob and granite outhouses and sheds at the bottom of the *Ropewalk* were all in existence before 1825; the Ropewalk itself, a long straight lane with trees on either side, was leased to Matthew Vounder for £24. For that sum Vounder also rented what were then two small two fields lying parallel with the the present-day playing field, the lower of which is shown as having a mine shaft or adit in its centre. Described today as the 'allotments', the small area of land and half of the current playing field was a china-stone yard, the reminder to the north as far as the un-named lane running east-west being a cobbled ore-floor, exactly the same as the car park in front of the Rashleigh Arms. Visitors using this rough surfaced area in front of the Rashleigh, often unaware of the historic nature of the surface, complain that it should be covered over with tarmac, to save wear and tear on their car springs, but that would be unthinkable. It is, in fact, listed as being of historic importance, and is a geologist's delight, since the rounded beach stones with which it is covered can be traced from far and wide. Stone can be identified as originating from Plymouth and Scotland, Scandanavia and France, Germany and Spain, all ballast stones discharged at Charlestown from early sailing ships, brought up from the beach and set in the ground. At the far eastern end of the un-named lane, running across the top of the playing field, right in the entrance drive to the authors' home, *Ropewalk House*, was a mine shaft, now capped. Whilst supposition, presumably the lane was created purely to give access to whatever mining activity took place there. From here north, to the present day Church Road, incorrectly named by a council road sign, and due to be returned to its historically-correct name of Church Lane, was one large pasture known as Ropewalk Field. Devoid of cottages and church, this stretched to the woodland belt of the Ropewalk, with no further development until Holmbush or Mount Charles, apart from an Assay Office, mentioned later. On the west side of the dock there was considerably more development. Almost all the original buildings here of Charles Rashleigh's time survive intact, but only as far as the corner of Duporth Road. The nearest dwelling to the harbour at the time was a house leased to Baker Banks jnr. for £12.12s, which stood at the southern end of a long cob and granite malthouse building. This had been erected parallel with the 'road' leading up to the gun battery, in what is now part of the front gardens of the Coastguard cottages. This malthouse stretched right back to the hotel; the malthouse, hotel, stables, outhouses and three adjacent fields all being leased to John Cory for 14 years, from Christmas 1820, at £320. The malthouse and dwelling remained standing and in use until demolished around 1880, when a violent storm, which destroyed a large section of the outer basin wall, caused the track leading to the gun battery to subside, taking the entire house and centre part of the malthouse with it. Since Rank's store next door to the hotel had yet to be built, there was an open space before reaching the 'pink cottage' (No.21 Charlestown Road), then leased to a Joseph Stephen for £4.4s. Immediately north of this and attached, but long since demolished, was a second cottage and garden, in which John Roberts and Thomas Martyn lived, for £3.3s each. Attached to this cottage, running back into what is known as the Heavy Transport Yard, was the second of Charlestown's fishery buildings, the *Rashleigh* pilchard cellar. Leased to Thomas Rundle & Co. for £20, this formed part of a rectangular complex of two such cellars, the others being *Union* cellar (also Thomas Rundle for £20), now Charlestown Wrought Iron, and *Friend's Endeavour* cellar, the first building in Barkhouse

Lane. The latter has since been altered somewhat, being increased in height, and used up until the early 1980s by John Moore, a well known Mevagissey shipwright, who launched the last Charlestown built vessel into the inner dock. Apart from the actual *Bark House*, which gave Bark House Lane its name, the only other buildings here were the *Killing House* and adjacent *Lairage*. The former was of course the slaughter house, the latter a building in which animals were allowed to rest and calm down overnight, following a stressful journey on foot from some distant farm. The remainder of the lane and high ground behind the stream was leased as vegetable gardens to Thomas Eplett and John Stephens.

The present car park was the very old coal yard going back to 1795 and possibly earlier. This also has a cobbled floor, of which small areas are still visible. Charlestown Gallery, an artist's studio, which has variously been occupied as an ice-cream parlour, chandlery, sport-diving centre and, before that, a Steamer Store, was probably the original coal yard office and store. Known as the Great Coal Yard in 1825, it was vacant at the time when Messrs. Crowder and Co. took ownership. The area at the back of the coal yard, adjoining the *Long Store* and now a secondary coach and car park, was a very large open air timber yard, in which incoming cargo was stored.

Immediately north of the car park lie the original and intact lime kilns, which had a total of five hearths, four of which were back-to-back, now part of a pottery workshop. These were vacant and unleased in 1825, along with the granite two storey, buttressed building between the two kiln areas. At the time this was described only as a cellar, but historically was the 'gun shed', from 1793 for over one hundred years, when the Crinnis Cliff Artillery Volunteers disbanded. This served as a repository for the original four, eighteen pounder, muzzle loading cannon, as well as the larger guns supplied towards the middle of the 1800s, along with their garrison carriages, shot, powder and handling equipment. Now owned by Gilbert & Goode Ltd, the old carpenters workshop on the upper floor is being used as their office. Adjacent, fronting Charlestown Road, are the offices of Stratton Creber, land agents and managers. Whilst now two storied, the upper floor a relatively recent addition, this was in fact the original village Counting House. Equipped with two weighing machines in 1825, their proximity to the kilns suggesting they were used to determine the amounts of limestone handled and burnt in the kilns, this was the financial and administrative hub of Charlestown from 1793 to 1986, when Charlestown Estate Ltd. ceased to own the village. A plot of land, now a private car park adjacent to the Count House was, in 1825, used for the storage of limestone and culm. This area is still overlooked by a row of cottages which back on to Duporth Road, which for some 136 years were double-cottages, back-to-back, known locally as 'front' and 'back' row. Built on to the eastern end of these is a larger property, now

91

occupied by Alan Leather Associates and Anna's Workshop. At the time this was described as a 'dwelling house and Shoemakers Shop, with garden', leased to a Henry Davey for £11.1s. The unfortunate tenants of the 'back-row' of cottages which once fronted Duporth Road, had to cross the highway in order to use their privy closets, which were at the far end of each individual garden. These dwellings, being only one bedroom and very small, were demolished in 1964, in order to make room for the 'Front Row' cottages to have bathrooms built on. These cottages, commencing with 'Back Row', were occupied as follows: No.11 Duporth Rd, William Tremellyn, £7.7s rent (a Second World War air-raid shelter still stands in the garden); Philip Hammer, £4.4s; Catherine Husband, £2.2s; Samuel Williams, £2.2s; William Stephens, £2.2s; George Inch, £2.2s; Andrew Pearce, £2.2s; Samuel Davey, £2.2s; Elizabeth Nancollas, £2.2s; William Hender, £3.3s. The occupants of 'Front Row" again from the western end, were as follows:

No.63, William Warren, £5.5s; No.61, John Hocking, £3.3s; No.59, William Varcoe, £3.3s; No.57, Thomas Eplett, £3.3s; No.55, John Stephens, £3.3s; No.53, Henry Stephens, £4.4s; No.51, John Roberts, £4.4s; No.49, Benjamin Stephens, £3.3s; No.47 Joshua Mitchell, £3.3s; and in an end cottage, probably No.45, Joshua Organ, £3.3s.

North of Anna's Workshop, there were no buildings, only huge ore floors, until you came to the modern School Lane, and what is now called West Polmear and Tewington Farm, No's.91-99. It must be said that neither of these were so named in Rashleigh's time nor even described as farms up until the late 1900's, the names being quite recent additions. That they were occupied by farming people is in no doubt, since No.99 Charlestown Road, described as a 'dwelling house, garden and outhouses' was rented to a Thomas Hodge, at £8.0s, who also had the 'cellar' building attached (No.97), but the 'stable and part of yard' was let to a Mr. Levers. What is now No.95 was another 'cellar', rented to William Crowle, who lived next door (No.93) for £43.0s, but had the addition of a 'outhouse', (No.91), and seven large fields. The large granary in this rectangle of farm buildings, undergoing conversion to a dwelling in 1994, was in vacant possession in 1825.

North of the granary was a small complex of buildings all associated with the farm. What are now cottages, Nos. 103-9 Charlestown Road, were at the time described as 'outhouses', leased to the same William Crowle for a conditional term of seven years, from Lady Day 1824, at £43.0s. The 'conditions' probably related to the change of ownership and landlords. In front of No.109, situated on what is now a pavement area, was another weighing machine, whose function we must assume was to check the loads of china stone, or else copper and tin ore, deposited on the various floors in the area. The lane or alley way running back from No.109 had no name at the time, but was later known officially as *Eleven Doors*, and unofficially as *Chinatown*. It derived its name realistically from the fact that the doors of eleven different dwellings fronted on to it, all tiny cramped cottages huddled together, conversions of original cellar buildings. On one side these were joined to a large granite barn, now owned and occupied by Partech Electronics Ltd, the building later to serve as a crushing plant for china stone, with its own water wheel. *Chinatown* was a reputation rather than a nick-name, since it was here that the sailors visiting the port could find ladies of 'easy virtue'. Most seaports had their complement of prosti-tutes, and Charlestown was no exception.

The yard behind Partech Electronics, now used as a car park was, in 1825, described as a copper ore floor, leased to the Pembroke Mine Adventurers free of charge. This area later became part of a cooperage. From here to Charlestown Mill there were only open fields, the higher pond, with its island, and associated plantation. The mill served to grind corn for the village and surrounds, its waterwheel powered by the flow of leat water, at the time worked and occupied by Thomas Hochen, along with the attached 'mill house, garden and lane', for £100 pa. For this Hochen also had use of all the fields from the top of Charlestown Road to the first cottage at Holmbush, on the south side of the Turnpike, on which he probably grew his own grain crops.

Attached to the mill building itself was the much larger Blowing House, its offices and grounds, which fronted Mill Lane right through to the main Charlestown Road, ground on which *Charlestown Hill* House, or the *Grove*, was later built. The Blowing House was of course, leasehold, being leased to the Blowing House Company for a term of 21 years from 1820, for £31.10s. Today, nothing of this building remains, its granite fabric presumably being utilised elsewhere in Charlestown. In an interview with Lady Florence Crowder at the *Grove* in 1981, she stated that 'a cottage at the back of her house was once connected with silver smelting, brought across from the Silver Mine near Porthpean'. The only other buildings off the Charlestown Road were situated roughly where the roundabout on the A390 now stands, being a house and garden, leased to John Polkinghorne, aged 47, on the lives of his wife Philippa, aged 52, and daughter Philippa Courtney, 13, for £1.0s. Next door, on the very point of the triangle where the two roads met, stood the Assay office, taken by a William Geach for £1.10s. This was a small 'laboratory', where analysis of copper and tin samples was carried out for purity and therefore value. Whilst not connected with building, Rashleigh, or the 1825 survey, the map does mark the position of the Mount Charles Longstone, a Bronze Age menhir, 11.4ft(3.5m) tall. The land on which it stands was formerly known as Gwallon Downs and an extensive cemetary of round barrows, now destroyed, stood close by, on what are now the playing fields for Penrice Secondary School. The Longstone is granite, the nearest source of which is more than a mile away.

There only remained the twenty-two properties fronting the Turnpike Road at Holmbush, on the south side. Access to these from the village was then along Church Road (Church Lane) where, just before the point where the road ended level with the Ropewalk, it forked off left to Holmbush. This track was eventually closed off when the railway embankment was built, probably in 1857-8, the line opening between Plymouth and Truro in May 1859. The occupants of the various cottages at Holmbush were as follows:

No.18 – William Kinver, 36; O.Carlyon, 15; Fred Carlyon, 11; £2
No.20 – Thomas Hancock, 32; wife Elizabeth, 28; daughter Jane,7;14s
No.24 – Nich. Lentern, 45; son John, 18; daughter Mary Ann, 16; 14s
No.24 – James Jenkins, 31; wife Mary, 34; son James, 7; 14s
No.26 – John Jenkin, 43; sister Mary, 32; nephew James, 7; 14s
No.28 – John Richards, 33; wife Gertrude, 40; son William 7; 14s
No.30 – Richard Terrill, 30; wife, 27; daughter Elizabeth, 9; £1
No.32 – Henry Peters, 45; sons Joseph, 23 and John, 11; £1
No.34 – Edward Watts, 29; wife Sarah, 27; son James, 5; £1
No.38 – Thomas Stephens, 30; wife Elizabeth,28; daughter Jane,7; 13s
No.42 – John Wheeler; children Philip,27; John,25; Hannah,20; 10s.6d
No.42 – Will. Trenwith; son William, 26; Will. Ward,11; Thos. Ward,8
No.44 – William Hammer, 36; wife Honor, 37; daughter Jane, 10; 10s.
No.46 – John Clemow; wife Joanna, 59; sons William & Francis; 10s
No.48 – Lydia Kelly; sons John, 27; William, 24; Charles, 23; 10s
No.50 – Nich's. Bursey; daughters Sarah, Rachael & Martha; £1.10s
No.52 – Will. Nettle, 45; wife Elizabeth, 43; son William, 8; £1.10s
No.54 – Elizabeth Williams; children Ann, 21 & John, 17; £1
No.64 – Joshuah Organ, 57 & I. Reynolds, 32; 10s
No.66 – Thomas White, 31; wife Susan, 29; son William, 9; £1.10s
No.68 – Walter Roberts, 34; Jenny Varcoe, 31; son Charles, 15; 10s
No.70 – Matthew Pascoe, 39; wife Jenefer, 38; son Charles, 11; 10s
No.72 – Peter Eddy; Will.Pearce,28; wife Eliz.,29; son John; £1.10s
nb. Nos.36 and 40 Holmbush Road, and Nos.3,4,6,7,11,13 and 15 on Hillside, were all built after 1825.

The building of the port at Pentewan was by now beginning to have some effect on Charlestown. Opened on 17 February 1826, importing coal and exporting china clay, initially business at Pentewan was so good that within a year the approach roads were found to be totally inadequate for the volume of clay transported and the owner proposed a railway line from St. Austell. The terminus was just off West Hill, the system being gravity worked from the higher section, then horse drawn to the port. Constructed during 1828 by Richard Carveth, at a cost of £5732.6s.8d, it was in operation by 1829. Whilst it has been claimed that for most of its career, Pentewan lagged behind its larger, more convenient rivals, in point of fact Pentewan's exports in 1828 had overtaken Charlestown and by 1831 the port was handling one-third of all the clay produced in the area. The potential profits in exporting clay were so promising, that Joseph Thomas Austen Treffry, formerly known as Joseph Thomas Austen, commenced to build Par harbour in 1828. This was yet another competitor for Charlestown, whilst a consortium of adventurers even put forward a proposal to create yet another port at Porthpean, costing £7,000, but fortunately, it came to nothing. However, the trade boom at Pentewan was not to last for long, and by 1838 its exports had dropped to a little over a tenth of the total clay output. The port was put up for sale on 11 August 1843, when it was bought by Messrs. Martin, Martyn & Yelland. The introduction of steamships in the late 1800's, which were unable to enter Pentewan's tiny basin, put even more pressure on the owners, who could not compete. The rail line connection from St. Austell remained unchanged until 1873-4, when its gauge width was reduced from 4ft.6ins. to 2ft.6ins to allow the use of steam locomotives, introduced in an attempt to cut costs, but trade never really picked up again, the line being taken up and scrapped in 1918. Deprived of its lifeline, the port's output dwindled to almost nothing, the last clay shipment leaving Pentewan in 1929, the last trading vessel in 1940.

The next big development in Charlestown was the building of the foundry, but accounts regarding the year of opening are conflicting. Since the 1825 survey map of the village shows nothing of a foundry, the land on which it now stands being the empty Higher Leat Fields, it is difficult to interpret the following letter, written by P. R. Hodge to Thomas Robins, dated St.Austell 14 January 1825:

'Mr. Geach has informed me that he has transferred the premises (which I hold under a lease of 21 years and in which I carry on the business of an Iron Foundry) to Mr. R. I have had it in contemplation for some time past to remove the old building and build a new one, the front wall of which should extend to the road, thereby enclosing a piece of waste ground which is now entirely derelict since the shutting of Mr. Balls Foundry (which is not likely to be used as a foundry again). I am much pressed with business, so much so that I have been obliged to increase the number of my workmen, but my shop is not large enough for them to do their work conveniently. The great increase in my business will not allow me to lay out money in alterations, which otherwise I might have done. My present rent is £13.10s a year. I would gladly give £7.10 a year more if Mr. R. would lay out £100 in altering the premises.'[16]

This conflicts with an account entitled 'One Hundred and Twenty Years of Engineering at Charlestown' which suggests that a James Thomas 'came to St. Austell in 1830 to establish an engineering works and foundry', since a P. R. Hode appears to have had an iron foundry in the village from as early as 1804, Charlestown being a wise choice because of its proximity to the local mines, and the supply of water from the port leat. It was also of great advantage to the harbour.[17] In 1845 Mr. Thomas's venture proved successful and he formed the Charlestown Foundry & Ironworks Co. It would therefore appear that

The western end of the old Charlestown Foundry, the oldest and only non-domestic building in Charlestown still used for the purpose for which it was originally built, now owned by Denver Charlestown.

Mr. Geach's foundry predates that of Mr. James Thomas and his brother William by more than twenty years, with P.R. Hode possibly earlier, but its location in Charlestown is speculative. The lengthy article referred to above goes on to describe the nature of the work undertaken by the foundry. 'Valuable income was earned from the manufacture of main-shaft kibbles, weighing 6-7cwt. Customers appeared to prefer hammered (ie. wrought, as opposed to cast) iron plates and bars for kibbles, piston rods, sweep rods and crankshafts for large engines. Old horse shoes were a popular scrap material, the foundry often having 50 tons in stock. The equipment necessary to produce the wrought iron work was a large coal-fired furnace and a porter, similar in appearance to a garden spade with a long iron handle. Also a crane, in which the porter could be hung and, most important of all, the tilt-hammer. The largest of these in use at the Charlestown foundry were steam driven until 1880, when they were sold, only a smaller set, driven by the water wheel being retained.'

A description of the process to produce a wrought iron object reveals some of the skill involved, apprentices learning their trade the hard way, going through all the different stages in turn.

'To start the heat, the porter plate was covered in layer upon layer of scrap metal until the desired depth was obtained, care being taken to

The last of four waterwheels in Charlestown, this once worked the huge tilt-hammer in the foundry. Driven by leat water, channeled to the village all the way from Luxulyan to maintain the depth in the dock, the stream crossed beneath the Great Charlestown Road as it was known, no less than four times, serving different mills and locations.

close all the hollow spaces. This stack was called the faggot. When this was done, the furnace would be lit, with four 2ins. blast nozzles blowing away at the bottom, until ready to take the faggot, which was placed inside the furnace with just its iron handle projecting. When the faggot had reached the correct temperature, the white hot sparkling mass of metal would be withdrawn, placed between the bitts (sic) of the hammer and lightly hammered as the temperature dropped. The hammer blows then got heavier until full force was reached, the hammerman manipulating the mass into shape. It was customary for the man to pay half of his boy's wages himself. He could then send the boy out to the local inn to fetch him his refreshment.'

The output from Charlestown Foundry was very varied and included machinery for tin dressing, stamps for crushing minerals, Cornish buddles, column pipes, pump rods, buckets, pistons, and tools. Water wheels were also in great demand amongst farmers, and the foundry turned out dozens of them, for sale at home and abroad. The opening of the Wheal Eliza mine locally brought much work to the foundry from 1863, and when other mines were closing down in the 1880's, this one mine alone saved Charlestown Foundry from going out of business. China clay then came into its own and once again the works were busy, making boiler gear and shovels, which will be mentioned at a later date.

An interesting and somewhat obscure business development in the village in 1833 concerned therapeutic baths. The West Briton newspaper for 28 March carried the following advertisement:

'Charlestown Sea Water Baths. The warm and cold seawater baths will be opened on Monday next, 1st July. The benefits derived by invalids in general, from the use of warm sea water baths are well known at the present day, but to sufferers of cutaneous, pulmonary, rheumatic complaints, it is impossible to eulogize their efficacy too highly.'[18]

Similar facilities had been available in Penzance for some years, that business being offered for sale on the 16th June 1825:

'Seawater Baths at Penzance. To be sold by sealed tender, for the remainder of a term of 1000 years at an annual rent of £3, the seawater baths lately erected at Penzance. Together with all the furniture thereto, everything useful for ladies and gentlemens's bathing. The house consists of two excellent warm baths, a cold bath, a pump room and handsome spacious waiting room over the baths, which command a delightful view of Mount's Bay. Built a few years ago at the expense of £600.'[19]

The obvious question is where could these baths have been situated in Charlestown? Obvious requirements were access to salt water, heat to create the 'warm baths', an undercover operation with privacy for the sexes to change and possibly, like its Penzance counterpart, a waiting room with sea views. Only one location could possibly have met these requirements, which was the lime kiln building once located on the *Round House* site, at the mouth of the harbour. Two storied, the upper floor could well have provided all the necessary facilities, utilising heat from the kiln furnaces beneath the building, with easy access to salt water. How long it survived is unknown, as is the date that the lime kiln building was demolished, but is believed to have been around 1875.

Seldom in research does one come across such a gem of correspondence as the following letter, which today may cause us to smile, but at the same time reflects on one aspect of life in 1834, certainly as far as one gentleman saw it.

John Allen, Liskeard, to J.H.Tremayne, Heligan. 30 May 1834.

'Sir, I am aware that much is due from me by way of apology for the liberty I am about to take in addressing thee on a subject of much importance, on which my views differ from those entertained by thyself. I might convey them anonymously or more publickly, but it seems to me more candid to state them plainly and without ambiguity or any breach of confidence.

I therefore venture to remark that having lately been at St. Austell and Charlestown, I was much impressed with the scenes of idleness, dissipation and immorality which I witnessed. The labourers and mechanics neglecting their work, not only losing their ordinary wages, but spending the money required for the support of their families at Beer Shops and Keil Alleys(sic). The sailor staggering home drunk, using the most horrid oaths and an object of terror & pity to all reflecting persons. The shopkeeper and baker unpaid & the money which they ought to have received wasted at public houses in rioting & wickedness. And what is the cause of all this folly? Why, it is the St. Austell Feast and Charlestown Boat races & so on.

But why do not the Gentry of the neighbourhood exert themselves to put a stop to such evil? Ah, strange to say, some of the most respectable encourage & support them. Even J.H. Tremayne Esq, a most excellent Magistrate & Landlord & much interested in the welfare of the community (it is said), subscribes to wrestling matches & encourages them by his presence!'[20]

We were more than fortunate in locating J.H. Tremaynes reply, which reveals another side to the story:

'Sir, Your letter needs no apology. I have been too long in a public situation in this country not to submit with great readiness to any temperate criticism. St. Austell Feast has been celebrated with festivities on the days following Trinity Sunday for generations past, and I could no more put a stop to it than move the town from its base. But I should by no means wish to do so. I by no means agree with you that the poor man can have amusements every day without infringement on their labours.

99

I wish that they should occasionally enjoy these manly & social games which are so congenial to the British character. One reads the history of those times when all sports were forbidden. I saw no drunkeness & witnessed no immorality. What they might have been at a later period in the evening I know not. A large encouragement is given by the law to houses of reception for the purpose of drinking, & to those houses people will resort at the time of the feast. If the police was defective and the houses open at a late hour, I am very sorry for it, but I do not believe drunkenesss was encouraged by the wrestling or any public games.'[21]

Today's Charlestown Regatta festivities stem, of course, from the much older St. Austell Feast week, the residents of the town utilising the port facilities, since it was the nearest place at which swimming and rowing races could be held. Feast week in time became the Charlestown Bay & St. Austell Regatta, until the Second World War called a halt to such activities, after which it was revived as Charlestown Regatta. More will be found on this subject in Chapters 6-8.

Despite the fact Charlestown United was the leading tin mine in the area, described as extremely rich in the 1830's, by 1846 it was in serious financial trouble, having made a loss of £7,846. Bold Venture, Fatwork, Boscoppa, Bucklers and Wheal Virtue sections had all closed, leaving only Boscundle working. Hard hit by a slump in tin prices, 112 shares in Charlestown United, quoted in the West Briton newspaper in January 1842 at £650 each, fell in 18 months to £250, with few takers. A decision to abandon the last sections of this great mine, which despite its name was located in the Holmbush area, was made in October 1849 following an accident. Some old Cuddra workings were holed and flood water drowned three miners, conditions being so dreadful underground in the flooded sections, that it took 14 days to find just one body. Despite an uncertain future, the Appletree mine, overlooking Charlestown, sold off in October 1824 and closed down shortly after, reopened in 1840 amid much speculation. Eleven years later, with workings over half a mile out under the sea, it was in fact the last of the local mines able to turn a profit at the time.

There can be little doubt that the life style of a Cornish miner was not one to be envied, one author's description suggesting that 'a miner's life was miserable, a dangerous, squalid existence. The rent owing occupier of a damp cottage, gaunt on a diet of potatoes and pilchards, and addicted to the local beer-shop.' Several first hand accounts of working conditions in the Charlestown United mine survive, and make for sober reading, particularly when some of those interviewed, both male and female, started work when only 10 and 11 years old.

Richard Thomas, aged 55 years. Examined at Charlestown, April 1841.

'Went to work on the surface at 10 years of age, but went underground almost immediately, and was on the air machine blowing for one year. Considered it a favour to go underground since he

100

got 5s. a week there but only 1s.3d. at grass. Had worked in bad air so bad that men sitting at the place of work with him fell off the place & would have died had they not been removed. He had worked in a mine carried under the sea, with a bed of mud and sand where the air would take fire at times & scorch their clothes. At grass the work was from 6am. to 6pm. with 2 hours for dinner. Has known hundreds drop from poor air & die of a decline. Once knew a man laid up for 5 years due to poor air. Poverty compelled a man to continue.'

Henry George, aged 50, had been in mining for 42 years:

'Started work at 10 years, but was taken to work on his father's back at the age of 8, to a depth of 70 fathoms(420ft), and stayed down till father came up again. Very few accidents at East Crinnis mine, the ladders being short, inclined at 1ft. per fathom. Father paid 6d. a week for each boy of his to attend evening school for several winters. Those employed in the ore crushers would spit stuff "black as ink". Working under the sea at Par, the air very bad, blue flame would issue from the back of the level, singeing his jacket.'

William Rowett, 13 years old when examined:

'Had worked in the buddle for 4 years, starting at 7am. and finishing at 5.30pm. Once or twice a month they worked for as long as they could see, then went home for supper, being given an hour, then worked by candles till 12, then an hour to have a pasty and worked till 2 in the afternoon. Was paid for the day, plus a half.'

Elizabeth Hockin, 17 years & 6 months, stated that:

'Her work is spalling (sic) which she had done 4 years, but was recking (sic) before that. Finds spalling hard work, causes pain in her limbs and back which does not go when she lies down. She gets up at 5.30am, stays up till 9 or 10pm.'

Between 1836-37, the number of children under 13 years of age employed by Charlestown United mine on surface work were 59 boys and 20 girls; those between 13 and 18 years old were 55 boys and 74 girls. The wages paid to all classes of workers at the time were:

Labourers, underground, between   £2.12s. & £3.5s. a month.
Boys, underground . . . . 17s.6d. to £1.0s. a month.
Boys, surface work . . . . £1.0s.7d. a month.
Women & girls, surface work . . . . 16s.3d. a month.

That Charlestown United mine and the village Smelting House had been busy, can be gauged from the volume of tin processed, recorded in the Charlestown Black Tin book:

1840. 26 June to 3 July,   511cwt.2qtrs.20lbs. worth £1344.2s.7d.
1840. 13 July to 25 August,   1622cwt.2qts.15lbs. worth £3,601.16s.8d.

This record of tin sent to the village for smelting contains the names of some 50 local mines, which can be found in the appendix.

A Francis Barrett was employed as one of the principal agents managing Charlestown United mine at the time, and his comments on the working conditions of the local miners reads as follows:

'Men can earn from £2.18s. to £3 a month, after deducting every charge. Ten or fifteen of our boys work one night in a month. We have never had an accident arising from our footways; Christmas Day, Good Friday and St. Austell Feast are the holidays. The boys and girls are employed by a "tributer" who pays them. When they get 30s. a month, they are allowed 10s. in advance for subsistence; a few may get a shilling or two extra by working after time. Food brought to the mine by the children is generally a potato pasty with a little meat, for the most part as often mutton or pork, not much beef. Being pregnant before marriage is very common, subsequent marriage to legitimize the child is the rule. There are few desertions, the feeling amongst the miners being so strong as to drive a man from the district.'

One such recorded desertion in 1870 concerned a Charles Hendra, of Charlestown, described as a Naval Reserve. 'He was brought back to St. Austell from Newcastle by Inspector Marshall of the County Constabulary, arriving on Sunday. The following day, 18 June, Hendra pleaded guilty before Mr. William Luke, to a charge of allowing his wife and three children to be chargeable to the St. Austell Poor Law Union. The prisoner said he was employed at Newcastle in a shot and shell factory, but that he lost time through having a bad hand. He said he was afraid to write to his wife as he might be caught. The magistrate said he had very little mercy for men who ran away from their families and sentenced him to two months hard labour. It appears the prisoner solaced himself at Newcastle by playing the fiddle in public places.'

Finally, as we reach the half century, two events with deep seated village connections. William Pearse Banks, shipbuilder, gave up his shipbuilding yard at the head of the dock in 1840, having built a total of nine vessels (their names and details can be found in the appendix). The yard was then taken over by Anthony Luke, a St. Austell cooper, and his brother William Luke, a wealthy merchant and shipping broker in the village. William was responsible for building the *Beeches* (No.60 Charlestown Road), which remained the family home for some time following his died in 1871. All three of Charles Rashleigh's daughters were to die within a 13 year period, the first being Martha, or 'Pattie', who passed away in Cuddra Cottage on 26 October 1847, aged 66. Much loved in Charlestown, the last reference to her we found was a letter dated June 1836, 'I am very glad that Col. Carlyon has thought right to remove the engine house outside my garden. It is now levelled with the ground and he has taken the roof, but has left the stones.'

Chapter 5   Reference Sources

No	Source
1	Crowder family papers (copy will in CCC. CRO)
2	Menabilly papers mss.
3	CCC. CRO. DDR.5317
4	Menabilly papers mss.
5	CCC. CRO. DDT/2735A
6	West Brition
7	ibid
8	ibid
9	ibid
10	CCC. CRO. DD.CF.1853
11	CCC. CRO. DDX/363/4
12	West Briton, 4.4.1823
13	Charlestown Estate 1825 Survey map & inventory
14	Coode collection, CCC. CRO.
15	Charlestown Estate 1825 Survey map & inventory
16	CCC. CRO. DDR.5317
17	120 Years of Engineering at Charlestown. CCC. CRO.AD.448
18	West Briton, 28.6.1833
19	ibid
20	CCC. CRO. DDT/2794
21	ibid

CHAPTER 6

George Augustus George. 1851 – 1880

The Easter week of 1850 saw bad weather that caused much excitement in Charlestown, when a vessel was wrecked within the confines of the harbour, in front of hundreds of onlookers. The *John & Henry*, a wooden schooner registered at Ipswich, left Falmouth on 29 March with a pilot on board, in ballast for Charlestown to load china clay. Despite the wind blowing hard from the south-east, and the black-ball displayed at the yardarm of the entrance mast, warning ship's captains it was not safe to enter, the schooner continued for the harbour. Realising that both captain and pilot were obviously unaware of the danger, and that despite it being high water, it was impossible to open the dock gates due to the swell, the harbour master ordered out the hobbler boat, to warn them they should make for the shelter of Par or Fowey. Somehow the pilot persuaded the captain otherwise, and the *John & Henry* went alongside in the outer basin at Charlestown and tied up. That night the wind increased and by morning was blowing with hurricane force. The ship's crew, assisted by the dock porters, did all they could to save her, but a heavy ground sea in the basin caused the schooner to be thrown violently against the harbour wall with every wave; the decision was taken to scuttle her, but she refused to fill in the heavy swell and was slowly smashed to pieces where she lay.[1]

Shipwrecks at Charlestown or within St. Austell Bay were in fact infrequent, there being only some eight in seventy-five years, but with many more strandings where vessels were later refloated and saved. These were mostly schooners and the *Providence*, of Par, was typical. Caught in a sudden gale on 26 August 1826, she drove onto the rocks at Polkerris, where her crew were thrown into the sea. The local Coastguards saved all the men, after putting to sea in their their rowing galley, which acted as an unofficial lifeboat. A similar fate befell the *Diligence* and her crew in 1829, the senior officers in the Coastguard rescue teams receiving Gold and Silver medals respectively. The 410 ton schooner *Ann*, foundered just outside Charlestown harbour during heavy weather in 1835, whilst on 31 October 1853 the 39 ton *Lady Eleanor*, drove ashore near Pentewan. On passage from Peterhead to Alloa in ballast with a three-man crew, she had taken shelter under the high cliffs but dragged her anchors when the wind changed. She was later refloated and saved. A much publicised case of wrecking in the district concerning a Charlestown man, was heard before the magistrates at the Bodmin Quarter Sessions at Michaelmas 1838. William Houghton, described as 'a respectable looking man', was charged with having stolen ten pieces of wreck timber on 10 July. The prisoner and his brother had salvaged the timber, found floating out in the bay, landing it from their boat at Charlestown Quay. Mr. Colenso, the Agent for the Duchy of Cornwall, on reading of it in the West Briton newspaper, immediately went to the quay and branded it with a broad-arrow mark, claiming it for the Queen, as Lady of the Manor of Tewington. He then instructed Mr. Hoare, the agent for the village, that it was not to be taken away for a year and a day. Houghton, determined not be be deprived of his salvage, then sold the timber to a Mr. Hancock, of Canna Carra, for 5s, which was the offence for which he was standing trial. The jury decided that the landing of it on the manor did not give Colenso the power to claim and brand it, consequently Houghton was found not guilty and discharged.[2]

The 90 ton *Heir of Madron*, of Pwllheli, sailing from Plymouth to Charlestown, struck the outer arm of Charlestown harbour on 2 January 1854 so violently whilst trying to enter port in a force ten, south-east severe gale, that she became a total wreck in the shallows.[3] That same year, the small brigantine *Meridian*, with a crew of four, had only just left Par harbour on 21 November, when high winds drove her onto Par beach. Fortunately, her crew were saved, as was her cargo of copper ore when she was refloated some days later. Another rescue by the Polkerris Coastguards, which earned three of their number RNLI Silver Medals on 6 May 1856, brought about the installation of the first of four successive lifeboats at Polkerris, after the authorities had received details of how a boat had been lowered 200ft. down a cliff to save one man. It was the Coastguard cliff patrol that raised the alarm, calling out their Polkerris based six-oared galley. This managed to reach Gribbin Head, but was unable to round the Little Gribbin in gale force winds to reach Polridmouth, the scene of the wreck, so was forced to return empty handed. A small boat and long lengths of rope were then sent for, but by the time they arrived across some three miles of wind-swept headland the vessel had gone to pieces. Her crew of three got ashore but were left stranded on the rocks beneath sheer cliffs, and before help arrived two were washed off and drowned. The small boat was then lowed 200ft to the sea, Captain George Norcock RN, Coastguard Thomas Henwood and Seaman Richard Johns, sliding down the ropes to man the boat and save the sole survivor, a quite amazing rescue.[4]

The first of the Polkerris lifeboats was the 30ft six-oared RNLI *Catherine Rashleigh*, placed on station in November 1859 and paid for out of the William Rashleigh RNLI Fund, to which many locals subscribed. This boat was found to have dry rot in her double diagonal construction within two years, and was replaced by the larger 10-oared *Rochdale & Catherine Rashleigh* in 1866.[5]

Other local wrecks included the *Beatitude*, a 177 ton brig with a six man crew, of whom four were lost on 16 September 1858, when she became stranded on Swellers Point in a force six, south-easterly gale.[6] An unidentified vessel also foundered in St. Austell Bay in the same year, its figurehead and other wreckage floating in on Porthpean beach on New Year's Eve. The figurehead, some 8ft tall and painted white, of a female holding a cornucopia in rich gilt, was handed to the Deputy Receiver of Wreck at Charlestown. What became of it is unrecorded. Another south-easterly gale created havoc amongst shipping in Charlestown on 9 May 1862, causing the *Margaret*, of Fowey; *Robert & Henry*, of Looe; the smack *Hound*, and schooners *Breton* and *Katie Darling*, to either strike the outer pier or collide with each other, all five ending up on Charlestown beach, the former with her stern-post knocked completely out. Much to the surprise of those living at Porthpean, they awoke on 20 February 1872 to find a very dilapidated hulk of a vessel lying on the beach. Unidentified, it was thought to be that of an English trader sunk in the bay some eighty years earlier, which rough weather had disturbed on the seabed and washed ashore. A bonus for the locals, it was said to have had 'a fine assortment of oak and other wood on board'.

What building went on in Charlestown following Rashleigh's death is a matter of conjecture, since there is no record. A general yardstick enabling us to differentiate between older and post-1825 building is the method of construction, since that of the Rashleigh era was predominantly granite walls to the first floor level, then cob up to the roof line (a mixture of clay, chopped straw and dung). Only *T'Gallants*, and the *Pier House Hotel*, whose size dictated an all granite construction, plus the old Estate Office (once the Count House and built of brick), and a couple of original houses close to the sea, are different in structure. Nos.73,75 and 77 Charlestown Road, all granite houses, were built around 1833 by the Werry family, on a ninety-nine year lease, the properties reverting to Charlestown Estate Ltd. in 1932. These were the first of a number of properties privately funded, which eventually fell into the ownership of the Estate. One room of No.75, facing the road, was once a shop, first a butchers, run by the Werry & Hodge families, who also had a dairy and creamery at the back. Later, thought to be around 1920, this became a sweet shop and dairy, surviving until about 1950, when it became a lock-up for the other village shop. In 1966, in order to give their large family more room, the shop area was incorporated fully into the house by Mrs and Mrs. Sidney Averill. Other additions to the village included the *Rashleigh Arms*, built on the site of an old clay cellar; St. Paul's church, the shipbuilder Luke's house (named successively over a period of time as *The Villa*, *The Lawns* and *The Beeches*), *Marine Villa* (now *Ivy House*), *Pond House* (also known as *Bulteel's House*) and additional cottages on Quay and Charlestown Roads. The *Rashleigh Arms* is believed to have been built in 1851, taking over from the *Pier House Hotel*, which then became a farm, housing two families. The previous year Judge George Augustus Crowder, QC. and E.J.

St. Paul's church, Charlestown, as it appeared for almost 120 years, prior to its spire being added. Although planned for the original construction in 1851, funds ran out and a spire was not added until the mid 1970s.

Sartoris had donated a piece of land fronting what is now Church Road (Lane), on which construction of St. Paul's Church commenced.[7] Designed by E.G. Street and built by Christopher Earl(e), it was consecrated by the Bishop of Truro in 1851, although parish registers date from 1846. It appears that whilst designed to have a spire, there was insufficient funds available for this feature to be added, so that instead of a peal of bells, the church authorities had to settle for two single bells, one hung within a stone arch, with another in a small wooden tower. It was not until 1971 that a spire was finally added, housing a peal of six bells, each donated by individuals. One of these was the famous actor Noel Coward, who had been a frequent visitor to Charlestown, staying at *Pond House*, and who knew St. Paul's church well. Constructed of fibreglass, the spire was lowered intact into place by means of a crane, although many still claim that a helicopter performed the task. Another feature of the church worth mentioning, is its organ. It is well documented that Charles Rashleigh greatly enjoyed listening to and playing the organ, and that Duporth Manor housed such an instrument. This was located on the ground floor, in the first room leading off the entrance hall on the left. In correspondence of the period, visitors to Duporth often commented on their being greeted with great waves of music flooding the main entrance on arrival. The instrument in St. Paul's Church is believed to be that same organ once belonging to Charles Rashleigh, donated by the Session's family when they bought Duporth in 1925. If the reader should be wondering why a new church was thought desirable at this late stage in the development of Charlestown, perhaps it had something to do with the fact the population of the village had reached the remarkable figure of 2,871 by 1852.[8] Amongst the residents at that time was a Joseph Dingle, aged 29, described as a 'mariner', he and his wife Mary, aged 27, living at No.97 Charlestown Road.[9] Whilst a common name in the district, one cannot but wonder if he was a relative of his infamous namesake?

The managing director of Charlestown Estate was by now, another George Augustus Crowder (1843-1924), of Orton-on-the-Hill, Atherstone, Warwickshire, elder son of the previous George Augustus (1799-1873), now retired. Crowder, Snr. incidently, acquired a considerable reputation in London as a man 'for the ladies', being described as 'the biggest Roger in town'. He also achieved a degree of notoriety, when he accused a man of cheating at a gaming table, stabbing him through the hand with a knife. Great confusion arose with two directors of Charlestown Estate having identical names, so the son, preferring Augustus, changed the order of his Christian names, from George Augustus to Augustus George. This went some way towards solving the problem, but continued to cause great confusion even after George Augustus, Snr. died.

The fact that Pentewan, utilising its railway, continued to handle large quantities of china clay, and that Par docks, built originally only to handle the copper ore output of local mines, was now also shipping clay, caused George Augustus Crowder and his fellow directors to consider a railway into Charlestown as early as 1846. No doubt the Railway Bill of 1835, for a line from Exeter to Falmouth, initially passed by the Commons but repealed by the House of Lords, was seen as a potential boost for the clay trade. Although extended from Exeter to Plymouth in the 1840's, a line linking Plymouth and Truro was not opened until May 1859, but in anticipation, Charlestown Estate's directors, Edward Rose Turner, Richard Budsten Crowder, Frederick Robert Crowder and George Augustus Crowder, entered into an agreement with the Cornish Railway Company, at an early stage in its history:

'In consideration of the said parties hereto of the second part, abstaining to the above mentioned Bill, it is hereby agreed that in the event of the passing of the said Bill, into Law, the said parties of the second part shall be at liberty to construct at their own expense, a junction railway, on any part of the Charlestown Estate to a convenient part on the Cornish Railway line on the said estate, and that the said Company shall at their own expense and at all convenient speed thereafter, construct and lay down the necessary sidings, and other works at the point of junctioning and shall give the said parties all facilities for joining and using the said railway. The second party may work their own locomotives on the said railway, or if the atmospheric shall be adopted, the

108

Until the advent of the motor lorry and the piping of clay slurry direct from Carclaze to dries in Charlestown, the movement of china clay from the pits above St. Austell to the port was carried out by horse drawn wagons such as this. For almost 140 years clay wagons had to pass through Fore Street, the main thoroughfare in St. Austell.

Company shall give the second party all necessary facilities to use the railway. That the traffic passing from the main line to the junction line shall not be subject to the six mile traffic clause, but shall be charged at a rateable mileage toll.'[10]

Appreciating in advance that the gradient leading down to Charlestown's dock was probably too steep for conventional steam engines, the directors were obviously considering the alternatives. 'If the atmospheric shall be adopted', an expression used in the agreement, referred to a new experimental alternative to locomotives, which was Brunel's patented Atmospheric Railway, in use on a stretch of line at Dawlish, in Devon. Other options included a stationary locomotive fitted with winding gear, taking trucks up and down on wire cables; a locomotive that pulled itself and trucks along by means of cables, or a 'rack and pinion' system, as used on mountain railways. Despite a part of the agreement that specified 'all convenient speed thereafter', nothing came of the agreement, but the issue of a rail link was revived eighteen years later, in 1864. It was to the son, Augustus George, that Mr. Rosser, Civil Engineer, addressed his estimate of costs for the enlargement of Charlestown harbour, and again in 1874, his comments on the proposed rail link. Why the improvements to the dock and rail link were not made is uncertain, particularly since the volume of exported clay grew steadily year by year, offering almost guaranteed profits. Perhaps the necessary investment capital was not available, or the directors disagreed that it was necessary or financially viable?

'1864 – Estimate of cost of enlarging and deepening the harbour of Charlestown, and the construction of a branch railway, to connect the same harbour with the Cornwall Railway. Prepared by Mr. M. Rosser, Civil Engineer, Llanelly, South Wales.

1.	Removal of earthwork from Dock, 47,329 cub.yds. @ 1s.6d per yard	£3549.13s.6d
2.	Masonry work, 962 cub.yds. @ 10s. per yard	481. 0s.0d
3.	Railway, earthwork, 7692 cub.yds. @ 1s.6d	576.18s.0d
4.	Ballast, 2889 cub.yds. @ 2s. per yard	263.18s.0d
5.	Rails, 113 tons.10cwt. @ £7 a ton	794.10s.0d
6.	Fishplates and bolts, @ 28 tons	105. 2s.8d
7.	Nails, 1380lbs @ 1 1/2 per lb	10.12s.6d
8.	Sleepers, 1815 in no. @ 2s.6d each	226.17s.6d
9.	Fencing, 1170yds. @ 1s.0d per.yard	58.10s.0d
10.	Drains, 1000yds. @ 1s10d. per.yard	50. 0s.0d
11.	A masonry bridge under the road to the harbour, 549 cub.yds. @ 10s	274. 0s.0d
12.	Coping, 17 cub.yds. @ 15s. per.yard	12.15s.0d
13.	A bridge over the Parish Road, 352cub.yds. @ 10s	176. 0s.0d
14.	Coping, 17 cub.yds. @ 15s. per. yard	*12.15s.0d*

Total: *£6121.12s.10d*

Additional items, to include a beam engine drum	700. 0s.0d
Wire rope	85. 0s.0d
Four turntables for the engines	400. 0s.0d
Wrought iron girders and a bridge over the Parish Road	132. 0s.0d
Revolving capstans	100. 0s.0d
Sleeves and paynes near incline	35. 0s.0d
Timber for the road bridge	40. 0s.0d[11]

Laying and backing	*50. 0s.0d*

Overall total cost: *£8691.12s.10d*'

The engineer's letter of 8 September 1874 read:

'Dear Sir, I am very sorry not to have replied to your communication earlier. When the Cornwall Railway Company were in Parliament your late father secured an Agreement giving a right of siding at Mount Charles, and in the construction of the line, a level piece was put in to facilitate such a junction. Soon after I had anything to do with Charlestown, the matter was again looked into, and it was found desirable on account of the length of time that had elapsed to have a new Agreement, and this was brought about through Mr. Green, acting under your late father's directions. This last Agreement, if not amongst your father's papers will no doubt be with Mr. Green, who can give you every information about the same. I remember he took a great deal of trouble in the matter. I expect that whenever the railway is made it will have to be in the same hands as the Dock Company. I should say that the Proprietors of Charlestown will have to make the work branch through their own property. It cannot now be long before the Cornwall Railway will become a narrow gauge, I think I saw this referred to at the Great Western Company's last meeting. Is not a connection with the Cornwall Mineral Railway as important, if not more important as a connection with a broad gauge line? I expect the mineral railway touches numerous ironstone mines and clay producing points, then it is worth considering as to whether a very narrow, cheap line between Charlestown and the clay and iron producing points, with a connection to a siding on the Cornwall line at Mount Charles would not be best? Truly yours, M. Rosser.'[12]

Events over the next sixteen years, from 1854 to 1870, included the re-opening of the Crinnis copper mine under the name *Great Crinnis Consols*. The old *Rashleigh* tin mine on Brick Hill (Duporth Road), situated in the corner of a field near the entrance to Duporth Manor was also reopened, given the new name of *South Polmear & Dalley's mine*, working lead, zinc and arsenic under the overall management of the Polmear Mine Co. On 17 May 1855, Rashleigh's eldest daughter Harriet died at Trebartha Hall, near Launceston, aged 76, and two years later, on 10 November 1857, the Charlestown Naptha Works was put up for sale. Very little is known of this enterprise, which appears to have been in business some twenty years, other than that it was located on the site of the present tennis courts and coppice at Penrice School. As with the Blowing House, the Naptha Works made use of the port leat to drive yet other water wheels, and the lay-out of the stream suggests it fronted Mill Lane. Naptha or napthalene, was derived from coal-tar, an inflammable liquid, which when crystallised, was used for killing moths. It was also used in what were called 'naptha-flares', to provide artificial light.

'Sale of Charlestown Naptha Works, Mr. John Nicholls to Messrs. Sampson & Lanyon. Draft Bill of Sale, 10th November 1857; Coode Shilson & Co. This indenture between John Nicholls of Charlestown Naptha Manufactury on the one part, and Benjamin Sampson & Richard Lanyon (trading under the firm Kennall Gunpowder), all that mill, shells, condensing pipes, mills, water wheels, machinery, apparatus, plant etc. under the building erections called the Naptha Works at Charlestown and also all stock-in-trade, goods, wares, merchandize, live farm stock, household and office furniture, plate, linen, china and all the estate, benefit, property, claim . . . Benjamin Sampson & Richard Lanyon to pay all costs and expenses, the sum of £200 with interest thereon of the rate of £5 per annum.

The schedule above referred to consists of:

5 cast iron retorts with stays complete; 6 cast iron condensing pipes; 2 cast iron condensing shells; 3 copper shells, taps & heads complete; 5 copper condensing pipes. 2 cast iron dry floors; 2 cast iron cake oven doors; 5 iron fire doors & bare shells; 2 cast wrought iron receivers; 1 cast iron vapourising pan and frame; 8 wrought iron shifting cannisters; 156 bags; 18 casks and 5 horses for the same; 12 brass taps, and 11 large taps; 2 ladders and 3 wooden steps. 3 four wheel carriages; 4 wheel barrows, and 2 hand barrows; 1 Acitate Bruiser, and Frame; 1 small Crabb winch, and 14 tails; 4 beam scales, and 19 iron weights; 1 copper. and 3 iron seives. Various cross cutting and hand saws, 2 hatchets, 10 shovels, 2 trowels, 4 hand dishes, 3 lanterns, 1 cwt. iron tools of various descriptions, 15 glass carboys, 12 stone jars, 8 tin cans, 26 baskets, water-wheel, charcoal mill, 3 chairs, 1 desk, 4 Hydrometers, 1000 new fire bricks, 1 ton of Founders dust, 60 tons of wood, 7 tons of charcoal, 100 tons of Newcastle coal, 10 tons of Newport coal, 80 tons of coke, 20 gallons of Naptha, 10cwt. of Acitite(sic) lime, 20 dozen spokes, 1 grinding stone. Farm Stock: 1 cow, 2 horses, Trick Hay, Trick Straw, 1 field of turnips, 2 waggons, 2 carts, 1 plough, 1 harrow, 1 roller, 3 sets of harness.

HOUSE FURNITURE: 5 beds, 3 wash-stands, 3 chest of drawers, 3 bedside stools, 4 cooking glasses, 4 toilet sets, 8 tables, 16 chairs, 4 kitchen chairs, 1 clock, 3 maps, 40 volumes of books, 6 carpets, 2 hearth rugs, 3 fire sets, 1 pair plated candlesticks, 1 plated snuffers, 1 stand, sundry glass, china, earthernware, bed linen, cooking, dairy and washing utensils.'[13]

In the same period, Charles Rashleigh's youngest and last remaining daughter, Sophia Grylls, also died, aged 71, on 5 March 1860, at the home of her in-laws near Helston. She willed that she should be buried in Luxulyan churchyard, and she was laid to rest next to her husband in a double grave, close to the church on the north side, bringing to an end that branch of the Rashleigh family.[14]

The Charlestown or Crinnis Cliff gun battery and its Volunteers continued, surprisingly, almost to the end of the century, despite the fact that the original French threat had long since evaporated, and there was no real justification for their existence. The only recorded instance of the battery ever supposedly firing its guns in anger, is said to have taken place in the early 19th century. One Sunday afternoon a large frigate under full sail entered the bay with no flag flying. The officer in charge of the battery ordered a round-shot fired across her bow, where-upon up went the Union Jack, and a gig with the First Lieutenant aboard came ashore to bear the compliments of the commander of the frigate to the officer for his good look-out. The officer incidentally was a local man, the father of R.G. Lakes, of Trevarrick, St. Austell. The battery was, of course, very much a part of the community, the local men proud of their uniforms and of being accepted into the Corps. A vivid description of a practice shoot using the 'big-guns' as they were described, in August 1868, offers an insight into their activities:

'Cornwall Artillery Volunteers, No.4 Battery. On 8 August at 4pm the members of this battery assembled at the armoury (the Gun Shed, located between the lime-kilns), and headed by the brass band of the corps, marched to the battery to compete for the prizes given by the County Association. The officers present were Captain W.T. Banks; Lieuts. Kernick and Williams, and seventy non-commissioned men and gunners. The target was moored at a distance of 1,400 yards (1,280m) and fifty-five rounds of shot were fired. The practice was exceeding good, never better since the formation of the corps, now seven and a half years old. Captain & Adjutant Edyvean complemented them on the working of the guns and the exceeding good practice. Corporal Warne won 1st. Prize; Gunner Sgt.Trudgeon, 2nd; Sgt. Inch, 3rd; Gunner Ferris, 4th; Gunner Walkey, 5th; Gunner Thomas Inch, 6th. The weather was fine, and a number of spectators appeared to enjoy the manoeuvres.'[15]

The reference to the corps being formed only seven and a half years, was the change in organisation from the old Crinnis Cliff Volunteers to a more formal county artillery corps, with a number of full-time profes-sional Royal Artillery sergeants seconded for training recruits and maintaining safety standards. Its members went once a year to the Raglan Barracks, Devonport, for training courses and drill. No.4 Battery (Charlestown) was first formed on 10 January 1861, and on 4 October the same year, the competition for the county prizes was held at Charlestown, with the Lord Lieutenant and a large number of spec-tators present. Similarly, on 2 July 1863, when the competition took place at Hayle, two of the Charlestown officers took part, Lt. Kernick winning 1st. prize. In 1865, No.4 Battery also formed part of the Guard of Honour at Fowey, when their Royal Highnesses the Prince and Princess of Wales visited the town.

Originally equipped with four 18pdr. cannon, the Charlestown Battery exchanged these for 24pdr's. in 1860, which were the guns used for the August 1868 competition.[16] Members of the corps were not only trained in gunnery, but also in the use of carbines. One month after the above competition, they were assembled for an inspection:

'18 September 1868. The members of the Corps assembled for inspection on Friday last, under the command of Captain W. Tonkin Banks. After going through carbine drill and general inspection, they were put through the big gun drill, and a few shot and shell were fired, after which they were warmly congratulated by Col. Godby on their efficiency.'[17]

By the time the Charlestown unit was inspected on 26 July 1884, the battery was equipped with a single 32pdr. gun, essentially a 24pdr. barrel bored to a larger diameter, sitting on a garrison carriage weighing some 1.5 tons. Colonel Newman, Royal Artillery, the inspecting officer remarked:

'The men were very clean and smart. Saw practice (six rounds from the 32pdr.); gun drill very good. Repository exercise well performed. Average attendance of men at drill very satisfactory'.

No wonder the people of Charlestown were proud of their battery and volunteers; it must have been a considerable blow to the community when the corps disbanded in 1898. The reference in the inspection report to 'repository drill' is worth some elaboration, since it answers a number of questions concerning the handling of the guns. The limitations of sailing ships regarding weather, meant that there was little likelihood of an invasion attempt or serious coast raid by the French taking place in winter. Hence iron cannon in volunteer batteries such as Charlestown, were removed from about October until April and placed under cover, in this case, in the Gun Shed. The wooden garrison gun carriages may or may not have been left in place, only the barrels being taken away, or possibly both. Lifting the early 18pdr. cannon barrels, which were probably 7ft.6ins (2.43m) long, weighing 1.7 tons (1727kg) from their carriages, then getting them into position beneath a 'dilly', was known as 'repository drill'. In action, a gun might topple over, break its breeching rope, or if hit by enemy shot, could be dislodged from its carriage, so this exercise was practised frequently. A 'dilly' was a four-wheeled vehicle, essentially with no floor or sides, only a heavy wooden beam running its length, with very strong axles, drawn by four to six horses. Positioned over a gun barrel lying on the ground, the cannon was raised using levers and lots of man power and lashed to the beam with rope, when it was then ready to be transported. The only entrance into Charlestown's gun-battery is now only about 3ft.9ins (1m) wide, but a glance at the brick and stone work suggests that this was once probably 6ft. (1.8m). If so, then a 'dilly' could easily have been backed in before loading for the return journey down the steep cliff path (then much wider and properly made up), with 'drags' fitted to the wheels, the volunteers and gunners hanging on to dragropes to prevent the carriage and gun over-running the horses. The 24pdr. guns issued in the 1860's, between 8ft.4ins.(2.5m) and 9ft.(2.7m) long, weighed from 1.8 and 2.4 tons, whilst the 32pdr. 'great-gun' which replaced the others in the 1870's. weighed about the same; they were all handled in a similar manner, to and from the gun-shed as required.

One aspect of life in Charlestown that was in serious decline by now was the pilchard industry. During the early 1800's the southcoast fishery was the most important in Cornwall, but by 1872 had disappeared entirely between Cawsand, in Plymouth Sound, and Mevagissey. The disappearance of the huge shoals of fish that once frequented the shallow bays was probably due to over fishing, although the seine fishermen of the time refused to accept this, blaming the new drift netting industry. Certainly, by 1920, a seine catch had become a thing of the past. In a remarkably few years, this pilchard seining industry died out completely with all its centuries-old tradition and folk-lore, its romance, excitement and skill, its financial speculation and its hard work. Within Charlestown, reference has already been made to the names of early seine cellars, which took what ever name the owner chose to give them. Most such enterprises, when they came up for sale, intact or by shares, were auctioned off at the Charlestown Hotel (Pier House), and many such transactions took place there. In April 1804, shares in the *Charlestown* and *Three Sisters* seine, owned by John Parnall, were sold. The *Charlestown* seine was on the market again in 1811, 'the boats and nets in a good state of repair, and well found in materials.' It changed hands again in 1813, when Joseph Dingle became bankrupt, together with the *Porthmeor* and *Three Sisters*, part shares in the *Friends' Endeavour* and *Parr* seine. On the death of Charles Rashleigh in 1823, a mackerel seine was up for sale on 10 May, which whilst un-named was probably the *Rashleigh* seine, which was put up again, along with the *Content* on 24 September 1825; at that same sale the *Lamb*, of Polkerris, the *Bee*, at Trenarren and the *Harmony*, of Porthpean, all changed hands. As the industry declined in the 1860s, catches becoming smaller every year, so it became harder to find a buyer for a seine. The *Charlestown* seine net and gear was offered in the Western Morning News on 8 May, repeated on the 10th, then alternate days through to the 25th, nine advertisments in total. When the *Polkerris* seine went on the market in 1867, the owner spent 19s. on handbills, 15s. on advertisments in the West Briton, and similar amounts with the Cornwall Gazette, Western Morning News, and Sherbourne Mercury, before a sale was achieved, fetching £213.13s.3d.

Other events of the period included the transportation of a huge 14 ton block of granite from Luxulyan quarry to Charlestown, for shipment to London. Reported on 16 October 1868 as having been moved to the port the previous week, 'the weight was so great that it could only be brought a short distance the first day, then with sixteen horses was taken to this place. In passing the bridges at Luxulyan, the Rev.C.E. Hosken directed the driver to go quickly over. This was attended to but even then, two of the bridges broke down, though the wagon, with the stone, in consequence of the speed passed over safely first.'[18] For what purpose the granite was destined is not recorded, but it may have been a sarcophagus, perhaps a smaller version of the 70 ton block of Luxulianite chosen for the Duke of Wellington, when he died in 1852. Excavated, sawn and polished on site at the Treffry workings at

Lanescott, the task took two whole years, at a cost of £1,100. The granite then found its way to the crypt of St. Paul's by sea, probably via Par, bearing in mind the Treffry connection in the quarry and port.[19]

On 20 November 1869, the St. Austell Weekly newspaper carried the following announcement, 'A Reading Room and Library has been established at Charlestown. In connection with the Reading Room, there is an evening school conducted by the vicar. On Tuesday a selection of music and reading was given by Mr. Brown, who presided at the piano.'[20] Belonging to St. Paul's church, this referred to the small, two storey stone building fronting Church Road (Church Lane), generally known as the old Church Sunday School and Scouts Hall, and now used as an infants pre-school playgroup. Only a month or so earlier, the same paper announced, 'to encourage shipwright apprentices in boat building and learning to skilfully propel them, the 1st Prize for 1869 was awarded to young Trudgeon's boat at Charlestown, 2nd Prize to a mackerel boat, and 3rd Prize of 5s. to Ferris's boat.'[21]

Other everyday matters recorded during 1870-1 included a debt incurred by a mining company regarding coal, which was probably a sign of the times. 'To, the Robert Hooper Coal Co. 24 August 1870. In the matter of the Companies Act of 1862 and of the Wheal Polmear Mining Company, previous to the receipt of your letter of the 29th, a claim for £15.10s.4d has been made by Mr. Charles Pidwellon on behalf of the Charlestown Coal Company . . at present I am unable to state when payment will be made.'[22] Wheal Polmear was in the process of being liquidated at the time, selling off its assets, '7 March 1870, boiler for sale, in good condition as new, made in Glasgow of thick plate, 17 years old, weight 10 tons.'[23] A letter from a Frederick Marshall to Richard Miners dated 17 March stated, ' the engine and boilers are the only things which you are not to allow to be removed without a written order from me, the other materials not being in your charge. You must not intefere with the removal thereof.'[24]

The engine and boiler were obviously valuable assets, still not sold by November, 'Letter from Z. Williams to Liskeard Iron Works. I cannot accept your tender of £180 for the engine and boiler, as I have already refused £240, but I will accept £250 on the following terms; £50 to be paid at once, the balance in 3 months.'[25] Newspaper advertisments winding up the Company were posted in three west country newspapers over 27-29 January 1870. Meanwhile, amongst other events, the St. Austell News of 8 April 1871 reported, 'Indecency. Joseph Walkey of Charlestown, aged 60, was on Saturday charged before Mr. R.G.Lakes, with behaving indecently to a girl of 15 years of age. He was found guilty and sent to prison 14 days.'[26]

The launch of a new ship in the village always caused much excitement, an event being reported in the St. Austell Weekly News and Advertiser, dated 29 January 1870:

'On Tuesday morning great excitement prevailed upon the quay

The port once boasted three cooperages, where barrels were originally made for both 'wet' and 'dry' commodities, which included beer, salt meat, pilchards, herring and china clay. During the 1800s and as recently as the 1940s, the finer grades of clay were still being packed by hand and shipped in 2cwt (224lbs/101kg) casks as shown in this photograph.

here which has been unusually quiet for some time, on account of the launch of a vessel from Mr. William Luke's yard. The vessel has been prepared for a start for some days, and on Tuesday a team of stout horses having been harnessed to her, she was soon on her way down the docks, and after the usual pulling and hauling, shouting and screaming, she was successfully launched. She looked a very nice craft.'[27]

Presumably launched without the formality of a naming ceremony, since none is mentioned, we can reasonably assume this was the smack *Little Fred*, since the schooner *Challenge*, also being built at the same time, was not ready for launching until August. The 43-ton *Little Fred*, named after William Luke's eldest son, was 'built 40ft above sea level and put down the road into the dock on wheels'. Luke then traded her himself across the Bay of Biscay to Spain and Portugal, carrying herring. The name *Little Fred*, in fact gave John Stephens the idea of starting his own fleet of ships all with the same prefix, which, in time, included the *Little Wonder, Little Mystery, Little Pet* etc.[28] John Stephens, was the eldest son of Thomas Stephens, landlord of the Rashleigh Arms from 1851 (probably its first tenant from new) to 1873. John was also a cooper, as was his eldest son, who in 1862 was listed in Kelly's Directory as a 'Cooper and Shipbroker'. His love of ships and shipbuilding may have come from his mother, who was born a Banks, but

117

what relation she was to William Pearse Banks, who built ten ships in Charlestown between 1816-1836 is uncertain. The *Challenge* was launched during the week ending 27 August 1870, coincident with the Charlestown Annual Regatta, still part of St. Austell Feast week:

'The vessels were dressed with bunting. Small boats not exceeding 18ft long, for which the 1st Prize is £1; 2nd, 10s; and 3rd, 5s. Rowing skiffs not exceeding 17ft long. The 3rd prize went to Thomas John, Charlestown. At 5 o'clock the launching of a vessel took place by the name of *Challenge*, by Mrs.F. Higman. This was watched by hundreds of spectators. The vessel was built by Mr. Luke of Charlestown, and will carry 180 tons. Her keel is 75ft beam 20.5ft.'[29]

William Luke's death on 16 December 1871, was a shock to the village:

'Sudden death of William Luke. This gentleman died suddenly from disease of the heart. Mr. Luke was a large employer of labour and his loss will be greatly felt throughout the neighbourhood. The funeral took place on Sunday morning at the family church, of which he was a church-warden.'[30]

The Lukes had traded ships between Plymouth and Charlestown as early as 1826 when John Luke, a Plymouth shopkeeper, owned the 33-ton *St. Austle Packet*, built for him at Fowey that year. By 1840 Anthony Luke, mariner turned merchant, was thoroughly established in Charlestown, trading in china clay and stone, rope and tar. He employed William Pearse Banks, the Charlestown shipbuilder, to build a number of vessels for him, the last being the *Busy* in 1836, and when the yard became available in 1840, Luke took up the lease, adding ship-building to his business interests. As already mentioned, Anthony died in 1856, having added at least five vessels to the list of Charlestown-built ships. His son William died, aged 48, at his home known as *The Villa* (now *The Beeches*). He and Stephens had got on well together, so much so that they became partners in the brigantine *Jane*. When William died, leaving a widow and infants, Stephens was only 35 years old, and it was to him that Elizabeth turned for advice regarding her late husband's many businesses. Stephens at the time was employing 72 men and 5 boys, probably in the cooperage behind the *Rashleigh Arms*, his home being in Hotel Row, the row of cottages between the inn and Polmear Farm, now known as Quay Road. When Luke died there was an unfinished brigantine on the slipway. Stephens supervised her completion, and on being launched, when she was named *Pride of the Channel*, Stephens acquired all 64 shares in her from the widow.[31] The father's death was by no means the end of the Luke family in Charlestown. The china clay and stone marketing business was continued by Alfred Luke, and the hemp, tar, and rope business by William Henry Luke, the widow continuing to live in *The Villa*.

On application to Charlestown Estate to lease the shipbuilding yard in place of Luke, Stephens was stunned to hear that the owners intended to double the size of the dock, by digging away the shipyard and cliff, and that the *Pride of the Channel* was certainly the last vessel to be built in the village, as far as they were concerned. Possibly there was a greater income to be made from loading china clay into ships, than that received for leasing the shipyard. Stephens was left with a stock of timber, tools and employees who included skilled shipwrights, in particular Peter Ferris II, who was a brilliant shipbuilder. His son, Peter Ferris III, worked with him in the trade, which he had learnt whilst employed by Luke. In order to keep the men in employment, Stephens obtained permission to build just one craft, a modest fishing boat, for a John Pearce of St. Austell. This was completed on the level ground by the weighbridge, but with the boatyard at Fowey he wanted still unavailable, Stephens then resorted to the time honoured practice of building his next ship on the beach at Charlestown, on the western side, where others had been built in the 1790's. He must have been desperate, since just one severe south-easterly gale could destroy any unfinished vessel so close to the sea. The only advantage it seems was the fact he could not be charged rent; exactly why is uncertain, since the Crowders leased the two beaches from the Duchy of Cornwall, and owned the land over which the work- men and materials had to pass. The day of the launch arrived:

'On Monday last, large crowds gathered to watch the launch of a schooner belonging to and built by John Stephens of Charlestown and Fowey, built on the beach to the right of the pier, a launch site a long way from the water. At 7am she slid down, but the baulks gave way and she was thrown on her side, and they could not refloat her. Mr. Stephens then entertained his workmen and friends, some 120 of them, to a supper at the Rashleigh Arms. The band of the Charlestown Artillery Volunteers played several selections in the afternoon and evening. On Tuesday morning, the men excavated around her, she was righted and refloated, and with the aid of a steam tug helped out of her difficulty and towed to Fowey.'[32]

How long it took for the dock to be extended to its present size is not recorded. Bearing in mind that the excavation work was undertaken by hand, using pick and shovel, with probably the occasional charge of gunpowder to break up the rock, a whole year is a reasonable estimate, so that it was probably completed in 1873. The cost overall was £3,011.11s.10d, paid for directly by Edward Sartoris and Augustus Crowder, who at the time were receiving director's fees from the Estate of £750 pa. each. The total number of vessels using the port in the year 1872, prior to the enlargement, was 293, with 343 in 1873 and 331 in 1874, after the improvements. Exactly how profitable Charlestown was for the owners over the years has never been revealed, but on the port account alone the income for February 1872 was £35.10s, plus a further £70 from rented properties, with an annual turnover of £2,207.13s.7d

A busy scene in Charlestown dock c1910, with some seven sailing ships in port, horse-drawn carts on the west (left) side full of incoming coal, others loaded with outgoing clay to the east. The chimney stacks of both Lovering clay dries can be seen in the background.

for that year.[33] As a comparison, the gross income for 1852 had been £1,454.19s. This picture of booming employment at Charlestown was short lived, since in 1873 the tin-market collapsed, leaving over 1,000 workers in the area idle, despite there having been an increase in the price of Cornish tin only three years earlier, brought about by troubles in Malaya. It was the boom of 1870 that caused the *Appletree* mine to be re-opened, *Charlestown United* being pushed deeper and deeper until it reached 225 fathoms, a quarter mile below adit. The decline in 1873 happened at a time when the population of the village had reached an all time high of 3,236, and the consequences of unemployment locally were very hard. There had been a steady decline in mining since the collapse of copper prices between 1862-65, with the forecast for tin equally as bleak. In 1869, the 21 year lease on the Charlestown Smelting House expired, and Enthoven decided to move his centre of operation to London, where he refined imported ores and Derbyshire lead at Rotherhithe. The lease of the Smelting House, the term Blowing House not having been used for some 30 years, was then taken up by Williams, Harvey, Bolitho and Daubuz in one-third shares, and despite tin prices being at an all time low and mines closing, continued to find local ore to smelt. The account book for the Charlestown Smelting House Company reveals the following summary of business:

'At the account for 12 months ending 31 Dec.1869, black tin handled = 460 tons, 4cwt. Value = £6,304.3s.3d.'

For the same period in 1870, the amount handled on behalf of Charlestown United mine alone was 708 tons, 14cwt; value = £9,410.3s.4d, with the following years of 1872, 192 tons; 1873, 206 tons; 1874, 130 tons, and finally on 9 October 1874, 6 tons 6cwt, the very last output from this consortium, the mine closing that October for good, having been worked almost continually since 1819.

Bolitho's Smelting Works continued, handling 752 tons, 11cwt in 1876; 799 tons, 19cwt in 1877, from a total of ten mines still in production; and in 1878, 1035 tons, 16cwt of which 722 tons was ore imported through the port.[34] By 1882, the smelters could only scratch together 364 tons, 17cwt, from a total of 31 mines, clay and stream works, the last entry in the account books being for 1883, the Charlestown Smelting Company closing down completely in 1884. The clay trade took some of the unemployed men, the only hope for the remainder being to seek work abroad, but few could afford to take their families with them. Those left behind were half starved, dependent on uncertain remittances sent home, and charity from the county and individual parish distress funds. Consequently, many local families split up, never to be united again. As a complete aside, readers may be interested to learn that on 8 June 1871, it was officially recorded that one of Charlestown's residents was the oldest Methodist in the world! It was admitted on proof of birth, that Mrs. Eliza Shaw (n'ee Flamank), born in 1772, who had joined the church on 3 January 1785, and was now aged 99, had been a Methodist for 86 years.[35]

Chapter 6   Reference Sources

No.	Source
1	Royal Cornwall Gazette, 5.4.1850
2	" " " 19.10.1838
3	" " " 13.1.1854 and Lloyd's List 6.1.54
4	Wreck & Rescue, Vol. III, Noall. C & Farr. G, 1965 p166
5	" " " " " " p173
6	Royal Cornwall Gazette, 24.9.1858
7	Charlestown Estate Letter Books
8	Kelly's Business Directory, 1852
9	Census Return, 1851
10	Crowder family papers
11	ibid
12	ibid
13	CCC. CRO. DD.CF.4053
14	Menabilly papers mss.
15	Royal Cornwall Gazette, 13.8.1868
16	Historical Record of 1st. Cornwall Artillery Vol's. p136-9
17	Royal Cornwall Gazette, 22.9.1868
18	" " " 16.10.1868
19	A Short History of Luxulyan Parish, Rowe. Dr. John
20	St. Austell Weekly News & Advertiser, 20.11.1869
21	" " " " " 21.8.1869
22	CCC. CRO. DD1.CF.742 p21
23	" " STA/202
24	ibid
25	ibid
26	St. Austell Weekly News & Advertiser, 8.4.1871
27	" " " " " 29.1.1870
28	Ships & Shipbuilders of a Westcountry Seaport, Ward-Jackson, C.H. 1986. p52,64
29	St. Austell Weekly News & Advertiser, 29.8.1870
30	" " " " " 16.12.1871
31	Ships & Shipbuilders of a West Country Seaport, p105
32	West Briton, 7.5.1874
33	Charlestown Estate Letter Books
34	Charlestown Smelting House, Tin Account Book, CCC. CRO. DD/RG/56
35	West Briton, 8.6.1871

CHAPTER 7

Everyday Charlestown. 1881 – 1890.

An insight into the many aspects of trade associated with Charlestown generally, and in particular the foundry, can be found in the St. Austell Railway Books, which record the delivery or collection of goods by horse-drawn vehicles between the port and station. Taking 1884 as typical of the period, we find that the following items were transported:

Date	Reason for visit and goods transported.	Charge
16/01	To 2 cases of herring from station.	12s.0d
08/02	To 2 loads of 2 tons of tinplate from station.	18s.0d
15/02	To 2 loads of 2 tons of tinplate from station.	18s.0d
13/03	To 10 cases to Moir & Sons.	5s.0d
04/04	To 12 cases to Messrs. Jenkyn & Son.	
28/04	To 10 cases to Moir & Sons.	5s.0d
17/05	To two horses, two men and wagons after presses.	14s.0d
"	To station with dies.	4s.6d
"	To 4.5 tons of coal from station.	£2.0s.6d
"	To Charlestown to collect ingots.	4s.6d
19/05	To 1 ton of tinplate from station.	9s.0d
01/06	To R. Warne, for lead.	4s.6d
02/06	To 1 ton of tinplate from station.	9s.0d
05/06	To Charlestown to collect ingots.	4s.6d
06/06	To station for oil from St. Ives (1 ton).	4s.6d
	To station for oil from Bristol (10 cwt).	4s.6d
18/06	To 2 tons of tin from St. Austell station.	18s.0d
	To station for large cutting shears.	4s.0d
20/06	To 25 cases to station, Fenwick & Co.	
21/06	1 ton of tin from station.	9s.0d
28/06	To Charlestown to collect ingots.	4s.6d
28/06	To St. Austell Station for furnace and grills.	9s.0d
8/08	To station for lead and grills.	4s.6d
	To station for oil.	9s.0d
14/08	To Charlestown for tin.	5s.0d
	To carriage of fish to factory on 11/08	10s.3d
17/08	To 40 thousand @ 2d.	6s.8d
22/08	To carriage of 5 tons of tin from Pentewan.	£1.10s.0d
"	To carriage of lead, 1 ton.	9s.0d
25/08	To 36 thousand to factory @ 2d.	6s.0d
30/08	To 1 ton, 1cwt. oil from station.	10s.0d

24 & 29	By Lamps Craggs, Bone Box	£1.2s.0d
31/08	To 25 thousand to factory @ 2d.	4s.2d
07/09	To 25 thousand to factory @ 2d.	4s.2d
11/09	To carriage of grills, 150	4s.6d
"	To wood for 600 cases from the quay.	5s.0d

The items carried to and fro tended to follow the same pattern, with only the occasional 'spice from Plymouth', 'labels from France', 'latten brass from Birmingham', 'nails from Plymouth', etc. What exactly '25 thousand @ 2d.' or '40 thousand @ 2d.'referred to is uncertain, but at a rate of 2d. for 1,000, so that 25 x 2d = 4s.2d for example, they were probably barrel staves, one of the few commodities which would have been shipped in such quantity.[1]

In 1881, three years before Charlestown Foundry changed hands, the management converted what was described as a 'Boiler Wagon', which had been used in the foundry for many years, into what was probably the first mechanically drawn steam road vehicle in the area. Described as 'a massive piece of rolling stock, capable of carrying anything by the standards of the day, it could be hired for £1.1s.(a guinea) for eight hours. Equipped with double horse-shafts, the original unloaded wagon needed two good horses to pull it, but when loaded with 30 tons, a team of 24 horses was often required. On arrival of the Road Locomotive, the shafts were removed and a draw-bar fitted.' It is probably true to say this was the beginning of heavy road haulage using steam in east Cornwall. In 1885, the Foundry changed hands, being bought out by Thomas Martin of Lee Moor, Devon, in partnership with John Stephens, George Hawke, John Barratt and Richard Williams. The boiler shop was now equipped with modern machinery and, in addition to boiler-making, the company went in for building railway bridges, amongst which were some for India. Their largest single contract of the 1880's was probably that for the Holsworthy-Bude railway line, which required nine bridges, built at a cost of £12.2s a ton. Contracts were also obtained for steel work for station buildings at Plymouth and Kingsbridge, as well as waterwork equipment at Torquay, Brixham and other west country locations. During the same period, both Charlestown and the foundry benefitted greatly as a result of frequent breakdowns on the Pentewan railway system, the port shipping extra clay, the iron works repairing defective equipment. A growing demand for clay crushing and grinding mills also brought Charlestown extra business, as did Walter Hicks' St. Austell Brewery. Tin streamers were also at work in the 1890's at Pembroke mine on Par Moor and at Crinnis, and required shovels and stamping gear.[2] The *St. Austell Gazette and Mid-Cornwall Advertiser* reported on 21 November 1895 that, 'The foundry has received an order from Messrs. Garton & King, of Exeter, for a replacement boiler for the St. Austell Workhouse (the site of the Sedgemoor Centre of St. Austell College), used for cooking and other purposes. A short time ago, they built a 10-ton Lancashire boiler for Little Treviscoe Clay Works, at St. Stephens.'

The administration of Charlestown Estate continued through an Agent, who received his instructions by post from Mr. A.G. Crowder, then living at 65 Portland Place, London. He in turn, more often than not, required confirmation of any particular course of action or expenditure from his fellow director and co-owner, Mr. E.J. Sartoris, of 1 South Villas, Campden Hill Road, London. The Estate Letter Books for the late 1800's are full of fascinating glimpses of life in Charlestown, showing that Mr. Crowder was firm but fair in his dealings, but also compassionate when necessary. It also shows that running Charlestown Estate and the port was never easy, neither of the directors receiving the financial return one would expect from such an investment. A.G. Crowder's letters show that he took an active interest in all aspects of Charlestown life, despite being an absentee landlord, being instrumental in many changes in the village, including possibly the eventual building of a Charlestown School:

> '9 Nov. 1885. To: R.H.Williams, Cuddra House. *Miss Vivian's inefficient school at Mt. Charles.* Miss Vivian (now married I believe) keeps a school, I understand, in a cottage since she gave up the Chapel Sunday School Room (at Charlestown). About 13 children were found a short time ago being taught in a room 8ft. square. It seems to me that the matter might well be brought under the notice of the Sanitary Authorities that such a state of things is injurious to health. May I ask whether you would take the matter up?[3]

Presumably Mr. Williams took no action, prompting Augustus Crowder to write direct to the authorities concerned:

> '16 Dec. 1885. William Coode Esq, Clerk to the Guardians. *Mrs. Prior's school at Mount Charles.* May I venture to draw the attention of the St. Austell Sanitary authority to the overcrowding at Mrs. Prior's little school at Mount Charles? I am informed that the room in which the children are taught is about 10ft. square by 6ft. in height & that as many as 17 children have been seen there, several of them between the years of 12 and 14. The room in question belongs, as I understand, to Mrs. Prior's mother who, being a pauper, in receipt of relief from the St. Austell Union, is under the control of the Guardians. Several Charlestown children attend Mrs. Prior's school and I believe the overcrowding is likely to prejudice their health.'

> '25 Nov. 1885. To Mr. Sartoris. *Re.Jenkyn's House.*' (*nb* Jenkyn was the Agent, living in *Pond House*, who wished to retire, hence he sought to lease his house for the remainder of his term). 'His lease has 12 years to run. He asks £10 a year, running the remainder of his term to recoup him for his improvements. As far as I can judge, I should think this was probably about fair. Will you agree

to give it? He has put on a new roof, built a W.C (right up from the ground) to be used from inside the house (with water laid on), built a large wash house and two privies, laid down a brick causeway along the back of the house and built a high wall along one side of the garden.'

Mr. Henry J. Bulteel was by now the new Charlestown Estate land agent, who had been recruited by Augustus Crowder personally as of 21 November 1885 to replace Mr. Jenkyn, the previous agent, he having written to Augustus on 3 October stating that he wished to leave Charlestown, having served seven years in the position. Regarding Henry Bulteel, Crowder wrote to Sartoris (his fellow proprietor, then living in France) saying:

'I have fixed on a Mr. Bulteel who has accepted an offer of £150 a year, rising by fixed increments to £250, with a house or its equivalent in additional salary (ie. about the same, rather less on account of the house not being worth £50 a year even with repairs etc. as we arranged for with Jenkyns, who has lately been having £300 and no house). B. has been for several years a sort of resident sub-agent on a large estate in Somerset. B. acquired a knowledge of accounting and business by 8 years training in his cousin's bank at Plymouth. He is keen about the sea, keen on yachting and likes Cornwall. He was born at Plymouth and most of his relatives live near there. Although an Eton man his private means are very small and I am assured privately that he is simple and economical in his views and not a bit above our work.

W.H. Crowder thought he appeared sensible, energetic and business like, and likely to suit us and stay with us. His age is 32 and he is married. His wife is daughter of a commander in the navy and she also likes Cornwall and found the climate agrees with her better than any other. B. has been down to see Charlestown, but his missis (sic) couldn't go as she expects to be confined next month. I had applications from men with more varied experience but feel they would have used our agency as a stepping stone and changes are bad for us and the place.'

Henry Bulteel was a most respected man and served Charlestown Estate and the Crowder family faithfully, living in *Pond House* (which was always known simply as *Bulteel's House*), until his death on 30 October 1924, when the position of agent was taken over by his son Walter.

'26 Feb. 1886. To James Stephens, Charlestown. I much regret to find you are still employing William Lobb as limeburner, that his incivility to customers is driving away the trade. Thus the value of our property & dues as well as your business is being injuriously affected . . I consider myself bound to take action in the matter. No one knows better than yourself how difficult it is to recover trade when once it has been lost.'

127

'23 July 1886. To Messrs. J. Lovering. *Erection of Clay Dries* etc. Referring to what has passed between you & Mr. Jenkins & Mr. Bulteel, the Prop's. of Charlestown would much prefer to let to you the ground required at a moderate rent and that you should conduct the dries yourselves. It seems somewhat outside the province of a landlord to find money for any trade or business and I would much rather avoid doing so. We quite appreciate that the scheme is likely to suceed and that it would be of great advantage to the Port.'

Lovering's proposal to build clay dries in Charlestown, resulted from the realisation that the transportation of clay could be speeded up, with less mess, loss of clay and reduced costs, if clay slurry – literally liquid clay, could be piped overland, from the pits direct to clay dries. Many such dries were built alongside sidings, in the ever growing railway network, thus eliminating road transport, but in the case of Charlestown, which had no railway, clay slurry was piped direct to the village from Carclaze. The difference in height between the two areas meant that the slurry flowed by gravity, with no pumping being necessary. Two huge dries were built in Charlestown, one north of Church Road (Lane) on ground now occupied by Denver (Charlestown) (Charlestown Foundry), the other which still survives, close to Polmear Farm. These were erected during 1906-7 by John Lovering, the upper-dry as it was called, having its fireboxes at the Charlestown Road or west end, its huge chimney to the east. This building was pulled down just after World War 2, when E.C.C. purchased Charlestown Foundry, and expanded the workshop area. Both clay works were capable of drying 450 tons a week, some 900 tons between the two at Charlestown, which resulted in 250-300 less horse drawn wagons carrying clay through Fore Street, St. Austell each week, much to the relief of the town's people. The lower dry, which could transport dried clay in 'trams' under cover, direct to ships in the Charlestown dock via a narrow gauge 'tram-way' at several levels, continued until 1968, after which clay was once again brought to the port by road, this time in lorries.

Although an absentee landlord, visiting Charlestown only two or three times a year, Augustus Crowder was quick to pick up any possible source of trouble in Charlestown, even the local policeman:

'26 Sept.1886. To: Col. Gilbert, Bodmin. I have good grounds for believing that it would be to the interest both of Charlestown and of P.C. Deacon himself that he should have a change. It appears that he has got connected with undesirable people there and that in consequence he is not so efficient as he was. I have no definite complaint to make and I only venture to ask you to consider whether you are able to see your way to take an opportunity of removing him in such a manner as to imply no censure ?

In 1886, E.J. Sartoris expressed an interest in selling his sharehold-

ing to Augustus Crowder, which was the subject of much correspondence between the directors:

'17 Nov. To Mr. Sartoris. I am afraid that I regard the Charlestown
property as subject to too great risks to make me desire to acquire
your share and besides being so troublesome to manage the
returns on the capital invested are as you know very small considering the commercial nature of the return.'

'14 June 1887. To Mr. Isaac Watts. *Queen's Jubilee.* You may reckon
on receiving £10 from Mr. Sartoris & me jointly, for the feasting of
the old people & children of St. Austell parish.'

'15 June 1887. To Mr. Sartoris. *Jubilee Feast.* All the old people and
children in the parish of St. Austell, which includes Charlestown
are to be regaled (sic) on Jubilee Day & we are asked to subscribe.
What do you say to £5 each? *Death of Thomas Penhall.* This excellent man died suddenly a short time ago. He was such a faithful
servant to us that I should like to put up on the outer pier wall a
plain slab to his memory. I find the cost would be about £7. Do
you care to join me? *Sale of Charlestown.* Since you suggested that
the dual ownership was not a very satisfactory thing, I have been
thinking the matter over . . you might possibly like to buy my
shares?'

The memorial to which Mr. Crowder referred can still be seen, mounted half way along the outer pier, consisting of a granite slab, inset with
lead lettering which reads, 'In memory of Thomas Penhall, for 45 years
the conscientious and devoted servant of the Proprietors of
Charlestown. Died 20th April 1887.' In what capacity Penhall served
the estate is obscure. Born in 1821, he died at the age of 66, hence must
have spent his entire working life at Charlestown. We do know that his
son Joseph was the leat-man, who in turn died of cancer in 1889 (see
letter of 12 Aug 1889).

'24 June 1887. To Mr. Sartoris. *John Hockin.* Late carpenter at
Charlestown. He has been with us a great many years & though
not particularly quick took an interest in his work and did it well.
His conduct has always been good. He is now past work through
age and infirmity. His wife keeps a small shop. Bulteel asks me
about a pension. What do you say to 1s. a day? *Midsummer treat to
those employed at Charlestown.* You may remember that we give
either dinner or tea, with rowing, games etc. at Charlestown or an
excursion. Bulteel tells me that the employees are giving something extra this Jubilee year & he proposed that we should charter
the Fowey steamer and give them a day at Falmouth or Plymouth
with dinner and tea. His letter only reached me this morning and
he wants to arrange for Tuesday on account of the dock being
pretty empty & asks for an answer by return.'

Charlestown Estate employees, dressed in their best clothes, probably for the annual outing, pose for a group photograph on the ore floor in front of the Rashleigh Arms, with what is now the Cornish Smoked Fish building in the background.

'29 June 1887. To Mr. Sartoris. *Charlestown bonfire & fireworks.* The deficit amounts to only £1.16s.8d. Bulteel says that he should have suggested 2 gns each but that of course is now not necessary. He adds that they have this year a deficiency of between £2 & £3 in their Regatta Fund & that he thinks it would give general satisfaction if we were willing to help them with that. We already subscribe 3 gns a year to the Regatta. Perhaps we might pay off the deficit as it is Jubilee year. What do you think?'

'27 July 1887. To Mr. Sartoris. You will be glad to hear that we won the lawsuit at Bodmin in regard to damage to the schooner *Catherine* at Charlestown. There can be no appeal as the case was decided on the facts and not on points of law. Of course we shall have to pay our own law costs – the defendant only pays taxed costs. The drought is about to cause us expense I am sorry to say. We have practically no water and must hire an engine to pump up sea water into the dock.'

'11 Nov 1887. To Mr. Sartoris. The cost of pumping up sea water into the dock during the late drought will be heavy. Both engine and pump had to be hired from London. I find Bulteel a capable man in action and determination. He carries out work promptly and throughly but I do not think him economical. The older the house property gets the more repairs have to be done & as Bulteel makes a good job of all such work, I feel sure that our dividend will suffer. I have done what I can to impress on him the necessity of economy consistently with doing justice to the tenants. It would be a good thing if you were to pay Charlestown a visit after the winter and stir up matters a bit. It would not be well I think for you to say anything to Bulteel about your desire to sell as it would unsettle him.'

'14 Nov 1887. To Mr. Jenkins. I am glad to say that I have arranged not to appoint *Joseph Walkey* as porter. Am I not right in believing that, in J.P's opinion *Phil. Hammer* was a "light-fingered" gentleman as well as lazy? The immediate cause of his being dismissed from the portering was his immorality with somebody else's wife, I think? *Jane Coombs, the old woman who was never married.* I see from your notes on out-door paupers that she was a bad character in her young days & that all her children are illegitimate. Do you mean that she had illegitimate children by different men? *Lime Kiln.* I should much like your opinion as to this. I find that Jas. Stephens has discontinued burning and that we are having to fetch lime from Par. Jas. S. quits at Xmas. B. has advertised but did not receive a single offer. You know no doubt that there is a limekiln in (or near) St. Austell? I have instructed B. to advertise again but failing offers I want to be prepared with a course to take. I don't like taking the thing up ourselves, as I believe it would involve a man to burn and a boy in the office, and now that the trade has been lost, I feel pretty sure that this would not anything like pay. The result would probably be that the man and boy would be set to other work for most of their time, & become a permanent addition to our staff. Charlestown is an isolated place on the road to no where and as there are kilns at Par and St. Austell, it seems to me that we should get hardly any customers.'

'13 Jan 1888. To Mr Sartoris. *Mrs Hockin*, widow of our late carpenter, is an invalid & keeps a little shop in Charlestown. She has a struggle to get along I believe. Will you agree to a gift of £5, to be repeated each Xmas? She is about 70 and her husband worked for us for a great many years. *Profits*, I sent £475 to your bank on 21st Dec. The amount for the year is a good bit short but there has been extra expenditure especially as to pumping sea water into the dock.'

'1 Feb 1888. To Mr. Jenkins. Can you kindly answer the following questions about Charlestown?

1. Estimate of cost of the ordinary Dock cleaning?
2. Do.   Do.   Pond cleaning?
3. Was the Dock cleaned annually during your agency? If not what years did you miss?
4. Were the Ponds (or one of them) cleaned out in alternate years during your agency? If not, what alternate years did you miss?'

The routine cleaning of the dock, entrance, ponds and leat were an unfortunate but necessary expense on the Estate. During the late 1800's and apart from World War 1, right up until World War 2, the Estate employed a work force of some 33 men. This comprised an administration staff consisting of the Agent or Steward, the chief clerk, an office boy and part time female assistant on rent days. The others were the Harbour Master, Dock Master, foreman (who was always a carpenter), two other carpenters and an apprentice, two stone masons, a black-smith, painter, two labourers, a leat-man and a rubbish-man. The latter drove a horse and cart around the village, collecting household, office, shop and ship waste, then carting it off to the dump where it was burnt. In addition, certainly up until World War 1, sixteen dock porters were also full-time employees.[4]

The leat-man had the important but lonely task of keeping the water course from Luxulyan viaduct to Charlestown in good repair, and clear of leaves, twigs and other rubbish. This included the banks, crossings, tunnels, sluices and weirs, since the flow of water was controlled by shuttering-boards at several points. These allowed the flow to be diverted to or from the foundry, flour-mill, smelting house, naptha works, china-clay crushing mill, clay settling lakes around the upper pond, or the upper and lower ponds themselves, finally down Bark House Lane into the dock via two sluice outlets. Once a year, in the weeks after Christmas, gangs of men, four in each, would be employed in a 'spring-clean' of the water system, from end to end. Starting at Luxulyan, they would clean and tar the wooden boarding near the aquaduct, working their way back to Charlestown, putting in new shut-tering and weirs, repairing bridges, rebuilding the banks and cutting back the undergrowth. For the actual leat-man, the job was particularly dangerous, since his work often took him underground, into disused mine shafts, tunnels and adits, about which more will be said later. On reaching the top pond, the gangs would drag grapnels systematically across its width, pulling out branches, mud, china-clay and leaves, then clean the lower pond in the same manner. On completion, the dock would be filled to its highest level, so that when the gate sluices were opened close to low tide, two great columns of water roared out, wash-ing away the accumulated silt and sand in the outer harbour, revealing a man made cut granite floor, hence maintaining the depth of water for shipping. The dock itself was then drained and the gates opened so that they could be tarred, the hinge pins greased and the sluices cleaned, any necessary repairs being carried out at the same time.[5]

High sided 'wedge' shaped iron plates were placed end on end on the dock floor to form channels, men shovelling away the mud and silt, helped by water pouring in from the ponds. Horse drawn carts were then able to enter the dock at low water, by going round the head of the quay, taking away rocks and mud. When new wooden gates were fitted in 1890, identical to the original set, their height was such that the internal water level could be brought right up, within feet of the dock walls. This allowed a tremendous head of water to be built up, which when released to flush out the outer basin, took away all the sand and mud. Deliberately or otherwise, when the new steel folding gate was installed in 1971, it was built some 6ft.shorter in height than its predecessors, preventing anything like the same head of water being created, so that sluicing the outer basin could never again be as efficient as it was in the old days.

'24 Feb 1888. To Mr. Jenkin. We are in a mess about Charlestown. Can you manage to come to the rescue? Bulteel, poor fellow, is a good deal worse & has been suffering a lot of pain. The stone, he feels sure has descended into the bladder. His uncle at Plymouth has his wife laid up with pleurisy. If you could help us by going down to Charlestown till B. is able to work again, I would endeavour to lighten correspondence between you & myself.'

'11 Aug 1888. To Mr. Sartoris. *Mrs. Annear.* The above is the widow of an old labourer of many years service. She had an affection (sic) of the eye & I begged Bulteel to send her to the the eye infirmary at Plymouth & obtain a report. The surgeon is trying to put it right by lotion, failing that a small operation will be necessary. In that case she will have to remain in the infirmary for a short time at a charge of 9d a day for board, lodging & treatment. Are you agreeable that the cost of getting the old lady cured should should be borne by the Estate?'[6]

The only reference we have found to the death of one of the co-owners and directors is the following letter:

'7 Dec 1888. To Herbert Sartoris & Evans Gordon Esq. *Charlestown Estate.* I shall be happy to carry on the management of the Charlestown property for the present, exactly as I have been accustomed to do during the lifetime of the late Mr. Edward John Sartoris.'

'12 Aug 1889. To Evans Gordon. I find that our leat-man Joseph Penhall has been pronounced incurable by the hospital people. The doctor says he c'ant (sic) live long. I am afraid he has internal cancer. Do you agree that we continue the weekly allowance to him of 10s for the present?'

'15 Aug 1889. To Evans Gordon. I enclose a letter from Bulteel who recommends an allowance of 14s a week to Joseph Penhall, what do you think? It seems to me that if we help at all we should do so adequately. There are eight mouths to feed. The only alternative is to leave them to apply to the Parish. As Penhall's father served us so well for so many years, I think we should agree to Bulteel's suggestion.'

Joseph Penhall died within a month, the directors then behaving in a totally uncharacteristic manner towards the widow, who they knew had eight mouths to feed, especially since the directors had previously appeared to think so much of Joseph's father, Thomas Penhall, whose memorial plaque is on Charlestown pier:

'20 Sept 1889. To Edward Stocker, Elmsleigh Villa, St. Austell. The decision that Mrs. Joseph Penhall must give up the house and land held by her late husband has been arrived at after full consideration of all the circumstances & I regret to say that it is final.'

Charlestown Estate always shunned publicity and, with almost all its residents in rented or leased property owned by the Crowders', there was always the very real risk of tenants being evicted if an individual went 'against the stream', by airing their views through the press. Hence, the years 1889-91 were exceptional in that Charlestown was mentioned almost weekly in the St. Austell Star newspaper, possibly due to a reporter with Charlestown connections. The first of these concerned Mr. Nepho, Chief Coastguard Boatman at Charlestown, reported on 5 April as having been 'promoted to the rank of 1st. Class Officer, who is about to take up control of a station in West Cornwall. His friends in Charlestown will be sorry to lose him. They are pleased at his promotion as it will be of considerable monetary advantage to him.'[7] Exactly where the Coastguards were living in Charlestown in 1889 is uncertain, since Coastguard terrace is believed not to have been built until 1892/3. At the same time, 'the shipping trade of the port has been brisk during the last few weeks. The Dock is full at the present time, and the prospects for the future appear to be good.'[8] Perhaps it was this that prompted the Agent to announce that Charlestown Harbour dues were being increased to 2d. a ton; that the fee for opening or closing the dock gates was now 7s. and that ballast could be supplied at 3d. a ton.[9] Another item concerned the Methodists, 'The Wesleyans have decided to re-seat their chapel and erect a new rostrum. Preparations are being made to carry out this work forthwith.' Their *Band of Hope* was also busy: 'A public tea was held on Good-Friday. Tea was provided for the members (about 150) at 4pm. A tea for visitors and friends was also on table at 5pm, of which a good number partook. At seven, the chapel was full, to listen to the service and sing "Father Come Home", rendered by the choir in a very credible manner, especially the solos and duets by Miss Knight, Wedlake, Mathews and Elliott. The connective readings were rendered in a very impressive manner by Mr. J. Pascoe of St. Austell. There was a collection taken at the close in aid of the Band of Hope Fund, but was very large considering the number of people present.'[10]

Reference to the Charlestown Sunday School was made in the press in both April and May:

'At the Weslyan Sunday School on Sunday afternoon (26 April), Mr. Philip Hore, who is leaving the neighbourhood, was presented with a very nice bible by the teachers of the school, for valued services as a teacher in the past. In responding, Mr. Hore said he should greatly prize this gift and often think of the contributors when he was far away.'[11]

Another bible went to a Mr. William Hewett of Charlestown on 31 May, who was leaving the country for South Africa.

'He was presented with a handsomely bound bible, the gift of teachers and children as a token of respect. Mr. Hewett has been a teacher for some years, and has associated with the school from boyhood. He has always been a willing helper and his leaving will be felt by all.'

A headline of 19 April reported on an entirely different topic,

'Horse Seriously Injured. Last week, a horse belonging to Mr. Richard Jolliffe, whilst being driven from Holmbush to Charlestown, suddenly bolted and rushed through Church Lane at a furious speed until it reached Mr. Breen's workshop, where its legs became entangled in the drawing chains, causing it to fall to the ground, breaking one of his legs so that it had to be shot.'[12]

The workshop was of course the old blacksmith's shop facing onto Charlestown Road, just above *Pond House*. Another incident concerning an animal belonging to the same owner was news on 31 May under the headline, 'Found at Last'. The St. Austell Star, published on Fridays, told the story in detail:

'A valuable bullock was missed from the farm of Richard Jolliffe of Charlestown, on Saturday evening, 25 May. Much sympathy was felt for the owner, as he had only recently lost a valuable horse. After a long and careful search, about 2 o'clock the following day, Sunday, an old mine shaft that had been boarded over was found to be caved in. Mr. James Frost of Charlestown volunteered to be lowered to the bottom by rope and he discovered the bullock, apparently alive and well. The shaft being about 30ft (9.5m) deep, ropes and ladders were procured from the Charlestown Proprietors stores and a son of Mr. Jolliffe, assisted by William Lucking, of Charlestown, descended the shaft and securely slung the bullock. A good many willing hands seized the rope and "with a long pull, a strong pull, and a pull together", the imprisoned bullock was safely landed on the surface. It barely waited to be liberated from the ropes by which it was bound before it scampered off with a lively run to join its comrades in an adjoining field, much to the joy of the owner and to the satisfaction of the onlookers who had assembled in large numbers.'

135

Whether or not prior news of a pending court case in London between a music hall artiste and Augustus George Crowder reached Charlestown, we shall never know, but it probably made interesting reading for the residents of Charlestown when it finally reached the St. Austell newspapers:

'29 May 1889. At the Queen's Bench Division of the High Court, before Mr. Justice Manistry and a special jury. Miss Bessie Bellwood, a music hall artiste, sued Augustus George Crowder, a magistrate, for alleged libel, viz. that in a letter addressed to the Manager of the Canterbury Music Hall, Crowder had written, "Sir, Complaints having been made to me of the indecent performances on the part of Miss Bellwood, I might add that she has been dismissed from the Royal, the Cambridge and Pavilion Music Halls . ." The outcome was a verdict and judgement by consent for the plaintiff for £5 and costs. In addition £2 paid into Court, and £45 to cover solicitors and clients costs. Miss Bellwood stated that it was necessary for her to vindicate her reputation. Mr. Crowder expressed regret that he had acted on information which had since turned out to be erroneous.'[13]

Looking back, we can only guess at the true circumstances that brought that case to court.

Saturday 11 May, saw the Charlestown Artillery Volunteers on parade:

'They mustered in strong force and headed by their excellent band under the conductorship of Bandmaster Brooks, marched to St. Austell and back. On their return march, a halt was made, and the men partook of refreshments provided by the officers, Captain Lovering and Lt. Bale. The men greatly appreciated the kindness shown them by their officers.'[14]

The next news item was more serious, concerning a fire in the grounds of Charlestown Mill. The fire started on 22 May:

'Fire near Mount Charles. On Wednesday, about 1 o'clock, a fire broke out in the yard adjoining the Charlestown Mills, and before it could be got under nearly £10 worth of hay, the property of Lake & Son was destroyed by the fire and the water which was used to extinguish it. The cause of the fire is unknown, but very strong suspicion rests on a boy who had absented himself from school and was seen loitering about the place previous to the outbreak.'[15]

Following the earlier work carried out on the Wesleyan Chapel that April, by September the Trustees had agreed that the building should have a complete restoration and, 'to accept the tender of Mr. Blamey of Veryan for £170, the contract has been signed, and work should be completed by 8 December 1889.'[16] Under the title 'All are Welcome', a committee of volunteers in conjunction with the Weslyan Sunday School made arrangements that September for a series of classes,

' . . for educating the young men belonging to Charlestown &

Dressed in their Sunday best, suggesting it was either a Sunday or Regatta Day, sightseers crowd the jetty in their hundreds to watch the first steamship enter Charlestown, c1905. This was the 108ft long Iron Duke, *of Cardiff, built in 1857, powered by a 38hp. 2 cylinder compound engine, which brought in Welsh coal.*

Holmbush this winter. It is hoped that very many will embrace the opportunity to get instruction in reading & writing etc.' That October they held a public meeting in the Sunday School Room: 'a stirring address was given by J. Knight, CC. and Captain Tregaskis, with readings by W. Watts. The choir gave a selection of duets and choruses. R. Williams, FRS. of Cuddra House presided and gave an excellent and instructive address listened to with rapt attention. A collection was made, the meeting a thorough success. It was hoped that a great number will embrace the opportunity to improve and benefit themselves by attending the next meeting.'[17]

The annual Regatta took place as it did every year in June, the date depending on the tide being suitable at Charlestown on a Monday afternoon. The event was then a combined affair between St. Austell and Charlestown, with a joint committee, and entertainment spread between four districts over four days. Events commenced on the Sunday at Charlestown with the Sunday School Anniversary celebrations, the children attending in their best clothes, for a service, bible readings and then a special tea. At the same time either Anderton & Rowlands, or else Whitelegs fairground people would be setting up their roundabouts and stalls on the lime kiln ground, opposite the Rashleigh Arms, and side shows where the public telephone box now stands, once both village church services were over, but never before, ready for the Monday, which was Charlestown Regatta Day. Everyone worked until noon as normal, the dock porters commencing at 4 am in order to get a full days pay before the Regatta commenced, events being held in the basin and a small field alongside the Ropewalk, which later was the site of the Skinner family's tennis court, near which is a very old capped mine shaft. On Tuesday the Charlestown and Mount Charles Weslyan Sunday Schools combined to hold a sports day, with bands, marching and childrens races, the fairground people moving overnight from place to place. Wednesday was the St. Austell Feast, when similar events took place in and around the town, and Thursday, the last day, was Trethurgy Feast Day, similar to St. Austell's. The St. Austell Star's report of the 1889 regatta (21 June) events makes interesting reading:

'Charlestown & St. Austell Bay Regatta and swimming matches took place on Monday afternoon, the arrangements being carried out by a committee consisting of Messrs. J.Hammer; W.H. Lake; D.McIntyre; W.T. Lovering and J.G. Blight, together with Mr. H.J. Bulteel, Hon. treasurer, and Simon Truscott, Hon. Sec. The weather was very fine, and the event was made quite a holiday, large numbers attending from St. Austell and adjoining places. A finer place for a regatta could hardly be imagined, there being so many places, at various altitudes, from which a splendid view of the bay is obtainable. Absence of wind, however, prevented the two sailing events being carried out.

The other items, consisting of rowing, swimming, diving etc. were watched with keen interest. The SS. *Gallant*, from Fowey, was announced to arrive and run trips in the bay, but unfortunately met with an accident. She left her moorings to convey a large number of people who were waiting on the pier at Fowey to Charlestown when she broke down, it being reported that one of her cylinders had burst. The accident caused great disappointment. During the afternoon Charlestown brass band played a selection of music, and thus considerably enlivened the proceedings. Charlestown itself presented the appearance of a fair. The results of the regatta are appended:-

Two-oared boats – 1. Pet; 2. Annie; 3. Why Not
Punts – 1. P. Williams; 2. T. Short
Four-oared boats – 1. Hind; 2. Bonz; 3. Watch
Two-oared boats, extra – 1. Jubilee; 2. Petrel; 3. Little Harry
Four-oared ships' boats – 1. Nelly; 2. Elizabeth Hampton; 3. Pride-of-the-West. Swimming matches:
310 yards – 1. H. Chesterfield, Mount Charles; 2. H. Knight, Lostwithiel; 3. R.Brenton, Mount Charles
Boys, 18 years of age, 200 yards – 1. J. Rowse, Charlestown; 2. G. Knight, Lostwithiel; 3. W. Robins, Porthpean

Boys under 15 years of age – Eleven started. A present was made to some of the younger competitors.

Diving for plates from the Pier by John Pash, coastguard, gave great satisfaction. Walking the greasy pole and wheelbarrow race for men and boys were very amusing. The two sailing matches will take place on July 4th.'

It is perhaps worth noting that the original fife and drum band associated with the Artillery Volunteers had by now developed into a full-blown Charlestown Brass Band, which was soon to merge with that of Mount Charles.

The huge tonnage of china clay being shipped out through Charlestown annually, now greater than ever, led to many more ships in the dock at any one time, which in turn brought its own problems, not least of all, seamen falling into the dock at night, some of whom drowned. Whilst the boating tragedy of 1889 was not connected with the dock, the victims were all Charlestown lads and it was the forerunner of a series of accidents which eventually forced the directors of Charlestown reluctantly to install initially oil lamps and later gas around the harbour. On 25 August 1889, three young men, Joseph Pappin, a cooper; Robert Harvey, a hostler at the Charlestown Hotel, employed by a Mr. Coad, and John Williams, a lime burner, left the port in a small sailing boat for a cruise. They reached Mevagissey about 8pm, stayed ashore for about an hour, then left to return to Charlestown, but were never seen alive again. Their upturned boat was found off the Grippen Head (sic), but it was two weeks before the first body came ashore, at Hallane beach. A woman bather accidently stepped on John Williams' corpse in the shallows, her screams bringing PC. Noy and a coastguard to the scene. Pappin's father offered a reward of 20s. for the recovery of his son's body or that of Harvey, the former eventually being found at Pentewan. Being a member of the Charlestown Artillery Corps he was buried with full military honours at Charlestown churchyard, where 'thousands attended' according to a St. Austell Star reporter.[18] Thirty years earlier, on 11 September 1859, a similar accident claimed the lives of four other young men of Charlestown, John Cocking, Richard Coumbe, James Hobba and Joseph Nettle, whilst crossing from Mevagissey to Charlestown in similar circumstances.

On 28 August 1889, the Rashleigh family was well represented on the bench at the Tywardreath Petty Sessions, when James Hammer of Charlestown appeared before them charged with assault. Sir Coleman Rashleigh, Bart; Messrs. C. B. Rashleigh and E. W. Rashleigh, JP's; and Lord Robarte, found Hammer guilty of catching William Daniels of Par by the throat, striking him in the face and otherwise assaulting him, the defendant stating that 'words had passed', he was fined 30s.

A number of drownings in the dock and basin at this time included the master of the schooner *Richard Cobden*, of Belfast. Captain George

139

Powell had retired to his bed early in the afternoon of 26 November, but at 7 pm woke and asked his son to fetch him some whisky. Absent for only fifteen minutes whilst he went up to the Rashleigh Arms, on his return his father could not be found anywhere. At 9 am his body was discovered floating in the dock. It was supposed that in the son's absence the Captain went on deck, struck his head on something and fell overboard.[19] Feelings locally ran high when on 13 February 1890, Henry Arthur Rigby, a lad on board the schooner *Livingstone*, also drowned at night after falling in the dock. The headline of 21 February in the local paper read:

'Supposed drowning in Charlestown Dock. A lad belonging to the vessel *Livingstone*, lying in Charlestown Dock, had in darkness on Thursday night walked into the water and been drowned. His cap was found in the morning floating in the Docks; every effort has been made to recover the body but has not been found. He went ashore to make a small purchase and in returning met his accident. Great excitement prevails at Charlestown in consequence of the frequency of these fatal accidents. His body was found three days later at the bottom of the Dock.'

The inquiry was reported in the St. Austell Star at length:

'Sad Drowning at Charlestown. Adjourned inquest.

The jury had been selected with great care in consequence of the strong feelings aroused in the neighbourhood. Several of the members were summoned from St. Austell, and Mr. A. Luke of Eastleigh, was the foreman. The evidence previously taken seemed to show that the accident occurred in consequence of the unprotected and unlighted state of the docks. Similar fatalities having occurred previously, the jury expressed the opinion that it was necessary to have an interview with Mr. A.G. Crowder (of London), the managing proprietor, and the coroner was requested to summon him to attend at the adjourned inquiry. As the docks were private property, the proprietors could not be compelled to light them. Consequently, the coroner deemed it advisable to communicate with Mr. Crowder prior to steps being taken to bring him down. The following correspondence was laid before the jury on Saturday:- Bodmin, February 24th. 1890

Sir, A man having just met with his death by falling over the quay at Charlestown, I, on Saturday last, opened an inquiry into the circumstances, when it transpired that the occurrence was due to the want of some kind of fence and to the absence of artificial light on the quays which were stated to be your property; the inquest was adjourned to admit to my communication with you on the subject. Several deaths have resulted from the extremely dangerous condition of these quays within the last eighteen months, and the coroner's juries have more than once, through me, directed your agent's attention to the subject, and urged that proper precautions should be taken to prevent a reoccurence (sic) of such accidents; but notwithstanding their repeated warnings, I regret to say that nothing has been done; and the jury requests me therefore to urge upon you most strongly the necessity of proper fences and light being supplied without further delay. I shall be glad to receive from you by return of post a letter such as I can submit at the adjourned inquest to satisfy the jury that the matter is receiving proper attention at your hands, Yours faithfully, E. Hamley, Coroner.'[20]

The Directors responded by return:

'A.G. Crowder Esq, 65 Portland Place. 27th February, 1890 Sir, I hope you received my telegram yesterday . . I have already been in communication with Mr. Bulteel, our agent at Charlestown, in regard to to the sad accident you mention. I shall not fail in conjunction with the other proprietors of the port, carefully to consider what can be done to render the quays more secure at night, and with that object I shall proceed to inquire what means are used at other small ports. On the other hand it seems to me that if the crews of vessels lying in the dock are allowed to sleep on board and to pass to and fro between the vessels and the quays at all times of the night, as I believe is the case at Charlestown, the captains should properly light their vessels and provide the crews with lanterns. It is difficult to see how the quays could be effectively lighted, except at very high cost, unless the local Authority could be induced to light the Charlestown main roads by gas or electricity, in which case the proprietors of the port could no doubt easily arrange for the quays to be lighted also. I should be much obliged if you could tell me of any small ports that are fenced and lighted in a satisfactory manner. The quays at Charlestown have, I believe, been as they now are, since the port was constructed.

I am sir, yours faithfully, A.G. Crowder.'[21]

Recommendations of previous juries, notwithstanding the frequency of similar accidents, having been quite disregarded, the jury did not consider Mr. Crowder's reply satisfactory, and the coroner was asked if they could return a verdict of man-slaughter, seeing that the promise made after the last inquest of lighting the docks had not been carried out. The Coroner, however, advised differently, and the following verdict was then agreed to, the coroner being requested to forward a copy to Mr. Crowder:-

'That the said Henry Arthur Rigby was found drowned in the Charlestown Basin, and in the opinion of the jury the proprietors of the Charlestown Docks, after the repeated warnings of the danger arising from the want of artificial light on the quay, are responsible for such death, and censurable for disregarding the recommendations of former juries. We request the coroner to communicate with the Board of Trade, or other authorities, as will speedily compel the proprietors to effectively light the docks, to enable seamen to go to and fro from their vessels in safety, and so prevent further fatal accidents.'

Another local paper reported the inquest in greater detail:

'Complaint against the Dock authorities. Mr. E.G. Hamley, County Coroner, held an inquest on Saturday into the death of a Henry Arthur Rigby, aged 15 years, a boy belonging to the schooner *Livingstone*, was drowned in the Docks. Mr. Alfred Luke was the foreman of the jury. Mr. S.H. Libby, auctioneer of Blackpool, identified the body. The Coroner reported that two lives have been lost in the docks within the past 3 months and 3 within a short time. Lights should be placed at the Docks and seeing that the Proprietors of Charlestown receive a large revenue from the Docks, he could not understand why these lights were not erected. It appeared that the sole reason why these lives were lost was the absence of lights. Witnesses were called, Mrs. Adams, shopkeeper at Charlestown, deposing that the deceased came to her shop at about 8 o'clock in the evening and bought half a pound of biscuits and a packet of cocoa and after a short conversation, he left to return to his ship. Next morning his cap was found floating in the Docks; it was supposed that he was trying to get on board his vessel he stumbled in the darkness and fell into the Docks. John Shaw, porter of Charlestown, related how efforts had been made to recover the body but in vain until Friday at noon, when the body was recovered. After considering the matter the Coroner adjourned and summoned Mr. Crowder to attend.'[22]

In fact Mr. Crowder never did attend, but communicated in writing, at the same clarifying the legal positions of the three principals of Charlestown, Augustus Crowder stating:

'Me. Herbert Sartoris, of Kettering, Northamptonshire, Esq, Mr. Frederick Crowder, Scremby Hall, Spilsbury, Lincs, Esq, and myself. The two first named are Proprietors of one undivided moiety of the Estate by virtue of being trustees of the estate of the late Mr. Edward John Sartoris, late of Warsash House, Fareham, Hampshire, Esquire. The two last named are Proprietors of the remaining undivided moiety in equal shares.'[23]

Whilst attempts were made to pressure the Directors into lighting the Dock area through the Board of Trade, they could, since it was private property, only make recommendations. A decision to go ahead with lighting was made public on 27 March 1890 in the press:

'It is stated on good grounds that Charlestown Docks will shortly be lit with oil lamps. One would think this is a good opportunity for the St. Austell Gas Co. to build a new works at this port (not being able to obtain a renewal of their lease from Sir C. Sawle) and supply light from thence to the town. For local government purposes the local district should include the large villages of Mount Charles, Holmbush and Charlestown, which with St. Austell are practically one town.'

The 'Star' of 9 January reported:

'Oil lamps have been placed round the dock at Charlestown. They were first lit on 1st. January and are to be lit every evening. Lamps have also been placed on the piers to light the outer basin, but would'nt be lit except when required by vessels arriving or sailing after dark. The lamps give a good light and are a vast improvement as well as a great convenience to those who have to go to and fro from the dock at night.'

There was very nearly another drowning accident, reported on 26 June under the heading, 'The Use of a Knife. Two foreigners quarrelled at Charlestown on Monday, when knives were drawn. One man leapt ashore but his pursuer, in attempting to follow, fell into the dock and was only with great difficulty rescued from being drowned. The Coastguard took possession of the vessel to prevent any further fighting.'[24] Another incident saw a Fred Jones, merchant seaman, brought before Messrs Coode & Veale, magistrates, at St. Austell Town Hall court, charged with being drunk and disorderly at Charlestown; he was fined 12s including costs.

1890 was of course the year that the dock gates were replaced, the old ones having been in service for 91 years:

'3rd Jan. 1890. To Evans Gordon Esq. *Charlestown – new Dock Gates*. I have been obliged to take a line engineers opinion as to the present gates. I went into the matter with Bulteel on the spot in October. I enclose a letter from Bulteel dated 30th. ult.(see No.5 paragraph), I also enclose Mr. Inglis' report of the 24th. I agree that we had better have new gates, but before giving orders for them I write to ask your approval as the expenditure will probably be over £800!'[25]

The question of new gates rumbled on into April, the cost of their replacement being the deciding factor:

'23 April 1890. To H. Evans Gordon. *New Dock Gates*. I regret to say that the two tenders received are very high. The lowest is £1,300. Bulteel, in consultation with Mr. Inglis Esq. has advertised in the local papers. The two tenders above mentioned were received by application to four good firms. As every day is of importance because of interference with trade and the time of season when calm weather prevails, I should be glad to have your approval of the course I propose to pursue, viz: To instruct Bulteel to accept the tender that he and Mr. Inglis agree upon as the cheapest consistent with efficiency?'

New gates were ordered that month, built by Messrs Hall & Lester, of London & Plymouth,[26] delivered to Charlestown by sea on 4 June and unloaded by the huge sheer-leg crane which once stood on the lower dock wall opposite the Pier House Hotel. The dock was closed for five weeks whilst the old gates were removed, new hinges and gates fitted and the necessary masonry work completed, the dock re-opening on Thursday night, 21 August 1890. It was reported that 'several vessels entered at once.' Within two months it was found that the new gates did not fit properly and Augustus made it quite clear that the contractor was responsible. Because the winter was then upon them, it was decided to work the gates as they were until the following spring.[27]

The Church Reading Room and Library, opened in 1869, came to the attention of W.T. Lovering in 1890, probably because he found it little used, whereupon he wrote to Augustus Crowder, who replied:

'21 July 1890. I symphathise much with the object you have in view but I confess that I do not feel very sanguine as to your success. I have contributed rather largely to several efforts to induce the Charlestown people to maintain and take an interest in the Reading Room & Library, but these efforts have ended in failure. Even in St. Austell the Reading Room etc. has I believe disappointed the promoters.

My experience both in London and in small places leads me to think that working people are best left either to their own resources in these matters, or to the operation of the Public Libraries Act, & I would cheerfully pay my share of a public rate towards a permanent institution managed by Commissioners under the Local Authority. You are quite welcome to take the table and chairs on loan – if they can be found. As to books, I am afraid I should not much like to interfere with the management of those I have put in circulation. There are none now left in Charlestown itself, I believe.'[28]

The last of the Dockmasters at Charlestown was John Moore, the position not being continued after his retirement in the early 1900's. Moore unfortunately found himself in trouble with the law in October 1890:

'To H. Evans Gordon Esq. *John Moore, our Dockmaster* – a very good man – has been summonsed with the Proprietors by the man Holman, the man who met with an accident to his hand some little time ago through, as Bulteel thought, his own carelessness. You agreed to allow Holman 10s a week for some few weeks, in spite of which he summonsed us and Moore. The County Court Judge at once dismissed with costs the case brought against the Proprietors, but after taking a day to consider the evidence, fined John Moore £15 and costs (several pounds no doubt) for carelessness. Bulteel thinks the judge wrong and if he describes the case accurately I certainly agree with him. Moore is really an excellent person and in my opinion we ought not to allow him to suffer but pay the £15 costs ourselves. Do you agree on the part of the Sartoris Trustees? Bulteel tells me he considers Moore's present wages of 30s a week inadequate, and he is shortly going to ask us

'Johnnie' Moore, aged about 82, the last Charlestown Dockmaster, who was solely responsible for the movement of ships within the dock once the gates were closed, as well as the loading and unloading of cargo. He retired around 1910, after which the position was not continued, the Harbour Master assuming his responsibilities.

to pay him some percentage in proportion to the trade.'

It has already been shown that the proprietors were willing to dispose of their shares in Charlestown, at the same time probably making it discreetly known to others. It therefore comes as no surprise that a potential buyer appeared in November 1890, the first of many such offers over the next few years, when Charlestown was at its absolute peak of trading:

'To: H. Evans Gordon Esq. I enclose a letter from a Mr. Fletcher Pagen dated 30th October, about the sale of Charlestown, also a letter from Bulteel received today in which he speaks of Mr. Pagen's reputation. I should be much obliged if you would deal with the matter. I am no use at negotiations of this kind. If you want to know more about Mr. Pagen, I think my cousin, our solicitor (W.H. Crowder, 55 Lincoln's Inn Fields, WC) would make private enquiries for us at Plymouth.'

The outcome is summed up nicely in Augustus Crowder's letter of 4 April 1892, in which he wrote, 'Thank you for telling me of the not unexpected results of your enquiry concerning Mr. Pagen through W.H.C.'

The landlord of the Rashleigh Arms in 1890 was James Stephens, who owned the cooperage behind the Methodist Chapel and numerous shares in local ships. He was almost certainly the same Stephens who had the lease on the Charlestown lime kiln, who had upset not only his customers by his rudeness, but also Augustus Crowder for the loss to Charlestown of the local lime burning trade. Stephens died in November 1890, his business and shares being sold at auction:

'Messrs. Hancock & Son sold by auction at the Rashleigh Arms, Charlestown, on Tuesday the 21st, the undermentioned leasehold property and shares in ships, of the late Mr. James Stephens. There was a good attendance and very fair prices were in most cases realised. The following are the lots, together with the buyers and prices:

Lot 1. A cooperage, store and stall, situated in Charlestown, were bought in, on account of the bids not reaching reserve price. Mr. Bale started at £25 and the bidding reached £110.

Lot 2. Fifty-four shares in the schooner *Devant*, of Brixham, purchased by Mr. Phillips at £8.5s per share.

Lot 3. Three sixty-fourths in the *Emmerline Jervis*, of Fowey, to Mr. Tregaskis of Par, £20 a share. Mr. Kelly bought in at £13 per share, two sixty-fourths in the *Bessie Stephens*, of Fowey. Mr. Hockin of Polruan, £30.10s per share, one sixty-fourth in the barquentine *Ko-in-Nor*, of Fowey. Mr. Luke bought in at £29 per share in one sixty-fourth in the barquentine *Ocean Spray*, of Fowey.'[29]

The last inspection of the year for No.4 Charlestown Battery, 1st. Cornwall Artillery Volunteers took place towards the end of 1890.

'Captain Lovering was in command, also present were Lt. Bale

Employees of Charlestown Estate were recruited as Cliff Rescue Volunteers. Trained and led by the village Coastguards, serving uniformed naval officers and ratings, they manned the Rocket Cart and breeches-buoy on the right. The Pier House Hotel stands in the background.

and H. Lovering, with a muster of 67, besides the Hon. Chaplain, the Rev. A. Ferris and Surgeon Mason, only four members being unavoidably absent. The inspecting officer Col. Parlby was served with a general salute, after which a minute inspection of arms and clothing took place. The Battery marched past and performed a few company movements. Also the manual and firing exercises after which the men marched to the new Drill Hall at Mount Charles, where gun-drill took place with the sergeants. Sgt. Higham next performed the Repository Drill, which considering the detachment, most of whom were recruits, had worked together only once before, was very well done. After thoroughly inspecting the battery books, the Colonel left for Par. In the evening the battery marched to St. Austell, where an excellent supper was presented at the Queen's Head Hotel.'[30]

147

Chapter 7. Reference sources

No.	Source
1	St. Austell Railway Books, CCC. CRO. DD.CF/4054/1 & 2
2	120 Years of Engineering at Charlestown. CCC. CRO.
3	Charlestown Estate Letter Books
4	Transcript of interview with A. Hosegood, 1993
5	Transcript of interview with Hedley Mitchell, by R. Powell, 1971
6	Charlestown Estate Letter Books
7	St. Austell Star, 5.4.1889
8	" " " 5.4.1889
9	Public notice displayed in Harbour Roundhouse (authors)
10	St. Austell Star, 26.4.1889
11	ibid
12	St. Austell Star, 19.4.1889
13	" " " 10.5.1889
14	" " " 17.5.1889
15	ibid
16	St. Austell Star 6.9.1889
17	" " " 20.9.1889
18	" " " 13.9.1889
19	" " " 29.11.1889
20	Royal Cornwall Gazette, 27.2.1890
21	Charlestown Estate Letter books
22	St. Austell Star, 28.2.1890
23	Charlestown Letter books
24	Royal Cornwall Gazette, 26.6.1890
25	Charlestown Letter books
26	Royal Cornwall Gazette, 8.5.1890
27	Charlestown Letter books
28	ibid
29	St. Austell Star, 21.11.1890
30	" " " 26.9.1890

CHAPTER 8

Peaks and Troughs. 1891 – 1984

A prize shooting contest using muskets then took place on Crinnis Beach on Saturday 16 January 1891, everyone having their eye on a beautiful new silver cup recently donated by Mr. Francis Barnett C.C. 'The Company marched from Charlestown to the beach, but the weather was extremely cold, the wind making conditions unfavourable for good shooting'. The men fired five shots each at a range of 200 and then 300 yards, the men not winning prizes being paid a day's work each.'[1] The cold weather persisted, heralding what became known as the Great Blizzard of '91, bringing sub-zero temperatures, blizzard conditions and over six feet of snow across the whole of Cornwall, with drifts recorded up to 40ft. At Charlestown it commenced snowing at noon on Monday 9 March and fell continually for over 24 hours. All work on the dock ceased and Charlestown Road became impassable to vehicle traffic for almost a week. During the easterly hurricane of Monday night, some 300 ft of Mevagissey breakwater collapsed, the repair of which cost over £30,000,[2] but Charlestown suffered only minor damage.

Fortunately, the Old Folks Tea Party had already taken place in the Sunday school room some weeks earlier. This was the eighth such successive event, when between 50-60 people attended. The vicar entertained them with scenes from:

'The Life of Our Lord and the story of Jane Conquest, illustrated by lantern slides, hymns and carols. The old folks were waited on by fifteen ladies. On the following evening, a tea and social gathering was held at Tregrehan Mills, being part of the parish too far away for the inhabitants to attend the Charlestown gathering. An address was made by the vicar, Mr. W. Turner, and carols and hymns were sung.'[3]

The chapel Sunday school-room was very much the centre of village life in those days and still is, with some event every week, a concert being held there on 21 April:

'Those who took part were Mrs. Murray & Mrs. Truscott; the Misses Luke (2); A. Stephens; L. Coles and E. Coade. Mrs. Murray was accompanied on the piano and sang two songs, "I May or May Not" and "On the Zuider Zee".'

The 87th anniversary of the Charlestown Weslyan Sunday School was celebrated on 24 May, Mr. Higham of Roche preaching in the morning and evening, a Mr. Pascoe in the afternoon. A public meeting took place the following day, Monday, and on Tuesday there was a meeting for scholars and friends in the school room.

'Afterwards there was an enjoyable evening in a field lent by Mr. Ellery, where innocent games, singing et cetera were greatly enjoyed. Kind friends gave a supply of sweets and nuts and to the great delight of young and old. The band was under the direction of Mr. S. Rowe, RA, bandmaster, and a selection of music suitable for a large gathering was played.'

That same week the annual Regatta took place, 'there was cold weather and showers of rain. The Great Western Railway steamer *Sir Richard Grenville* carried a large party from Plymouth, Looe and Fowey, and during the afternoon made a well patronised trip in the bay.'

The employees on the quay and their wives had their annual outing on Saturday 11 July:

'. . . through the kind liberality of Messrs. Crowder and Sartoris jnr, the proprietors. They were treated to a trip by rail to Plymouth where they were well entertained, the outing most enjoyable. Good catches of mackerel were made here over the past week.'

On 23 July, the boys and girls in the St. Austell Workhouse were entertained by Mrs. Bulteel at her residence: 'The children were fetched in wagonnettes & enjoyed themselves to their hearts content & will not soon forget the kindness of Mrs. Bulteel in this thinking of them, & throwing a gleam of sunshine into their little lives.'[4]

Other events that summer included a visit to Charlestown of what was known as the 'Union Jack Van', which went to the Drill Hall, now the first floor offices of Partech (Electronics) Ltd:

'A meeting was called at which Mr. Boggis gave an address and exhibited his magic lantern views. There was a good attendance and the hall was well filled. The Chair was taken by the vicar, the Rev. A.H. Ferris, who said he took it as a vicar, not a politician. He wanted that clearly understood, as he did not mix up in politics and hardly knew what his were. There followed a discussion on Gladstone, Irish Home Rule and a debate with a Mr. Ray, who afterwards briefly addressed an audience in the open air.'[5]

The owners of the Foundry held a reception for its staff on 30 August to celebrate the wedding of Mr. Edwards, their general manager.

'This was held in the erection shed and the meal was of beef, bread etc. and there were pipes of tobacco. The chair was taken by Mr. W. Jewell, assistant manager, with Mr. Sheers snr. in the vice-chair. Songs were sung and a recitation given by Mr. Fisher entitled "The Charge of the Light Brigade". Thanks were given to Mrs. Richards for preparing the dinner, and to Mr. T. York, the foreman fitter of the boiler yard, for table decorations.'[6]

October 1891 was remembered for two events, the cooper's strike and what was described in the press as a 'Curious find at Charlestown'. A local boy named Osborne was playing in Cliff Park, the first field to the east of the village, leading up to Carlyon Bay, when in the bushes he found a white duck canvas bag. Inside he found a man's jacket, vest, trousers, cap and two flannel shirts, all nearly new, plus two knives and forks. Taking his find home to his mother, on closer examination she found a loaded revolver, apparently of American manufacture, in the trouser pocket, and eighteen rounds of ammunition, but no one ever enquired after the bag and contents.[7] As for the cooper's strike, which affected both Charlestown and Mount Charles, it was short lived. On Friday 2 October, the men presented a formal request to their masters for an advance of one penny per half-ton cask and a half-penny on the cask heads. The owners met that evening to discuss the matter and, following a further meeting on Saturday agreed to pay them the extra amount, provided they resumed work on the 5th, with the increased amount payable from the 12th. This was accepted and everyone went back, the strike, if one could call it that, lasting just 48 hours. The cause of the dispute went back several months, when a ship load of timber arrived in Charlestown, part of which was damaged in some way. Mr. Inch, who owned a cooperage in Ranelagh Road, Mount Charles, refused to accept the damaged wood, but despite his protest some three or four loads were delivered to his old Naptha Works yard, and the men struck because they wanted more money to work with the timber.[8]

Charlestown was said to be 'seething with excitement' on 26 November 1891 with the promise of a wreck on their doorstep. The ketch *Katie* of Falmouth, on passage from St. Mawes to Charlestown with stone, was seen to be in distress off the Blackhead. The Coastguard rocket-apparatus cart was hauled out from its shed, three horses attached, the men summoned and in less than 12 minutes was on its way under the direction of Mr. McIntyre, Chief Officer. Before they reached Blackhead the two man crew had abandoned ship in their own boat, managing to reach Porthpean beach. The vessel, abandoned in Ropehorn Roads, was later towed safely into the port.

1892 saw over six inches of snow fall on 9 January, leaving the village covered, followed by hard frosts.[9] On the 22nd an entertainment of tableaux was given in the Sunday school-room in aid of the church heating fund, this presumably being St. Paul's, in Church Lane. The evenings programme included 'Saved', rendered by Mesdames Bulteel and Lovering, followed by 'Oh, you Dirty Boy', by Master Lovering.[10] During the week ending 26 February, severe gales from the south-east closed the port completely, battering the outer quay and harbour, finally bringing down a considerable length of granite wall on the west side in front of the old malt-house.[11] With it went part of the road leading to the pier, the subsidence causing the complete collapse of the dwelling at the southern end of the malt-house and half the malthouse itself. Damage was also inflicted to the wall of the outer basin on the opposite side. Whilst repairs cost over £1,000 and occupied the tradesmen well

The outer basin showing extensive storm damage suffered in 1895, which caused the end part of the old malt house attached to the Pier House to collapse. The terrace of Coastguard houses had yet to be built in the field above.

into 1893, it is strange that Augustus Crowder did not mention it to his partner Evans Gordon until 13 May, particularly since the initial estimate for repairs almost equalled the cost of replacing the dock gates, which was for them a major investment:

'To: H. Evans Gordon. *Breach in Wall of Outer Pier.* I forget whether I told you of this. A gale did the damage. Bulteel says it is likely to be a very expensive matter & that it will probably cost at least £800 & that we might have additional expenses if a heavy sea should come on during the progress of the repairs.'

'24 March 1893. To: H. Evans Gordon. I think that Mr. Bulteel had better be entrusted with the carrying out of repairs to the wall on the west side of the entrance to the dock. Especially as the work must be done intermittently, according to tides. Men living on the spot could be employed just when they were required.'[12]

The duration of the repairs can be judged from the fact that Bulteel felt it necessary to either purchase a pulseometer (a vacuum pump that draws in water by condensation of steam in two chambers alternately) for '£119 & £5 carriage from London, or to hire one at £12 a month for the 5 or 6 months it will be required.' The tight financial rein that the Crowder's kept on the village included Bulteel, their agent, to whom one would have thought they would give more licence, particularly since he was so poorly paid, being forced by circumstances to be the agent for the Penrice Estate and others, as well as Charlestown:

'28 July 1893. Bulteel has by his father's death lost a considerable part of his income & on this account asks to be allowed to take in one or two lodging pupils. I do not object on the part of my mother. Do you consent on behalf of the Sartoris Trustees?'[13]

The Artillery Volunteer Corps at Charlestown reached its peak on 5 November 1892, when they took delivery of a new gun and carriage, a massive 68 pounder howitzer, which when added to the two 32 pounder guns they already had, made for a formidable battery if used in anger. The new gun duly arrived at St. Austell on a Saturday, most probably on a flat-bed railway wagon, and, drawn by six horses, was accompanied by the corps to Charlestown. Of a new low velocity type, 5ft long, mounted on a howitzer field carriage, it fired an explosive shell 8ins in diameter.[14] At the time, more frequent use was being made by the Volunteers of the Mount Charles Drill Hall, probably because the village had no suitable building of its own at ground level, into which the guns could be taken for drill. What is surprising is that the authorities allowed the Charlestown Corps to continue for so long, since that at Mevagissey had been disbanded in 1877, when a single blank charge was fired from the last remaining gun to celebrate Queen Victoria's Golden Jubilee. The six small cannon from the battery north of the town were subsequently set into the quay as mooring bollards. Similarly, one small obsolescent cannon was set into the quay at Charlestown.

Two weeks after the 'big' gun arrived, 'a prize giving and concert were held and during the evening gun detachments belonging to the battery competed for prizes. The price of admission was 3d, ladies were admitted and smoking allowed. Tickets could be purchsed from Colour Sgt. Major Squire; Sgt. Highman or Cpl. Shepherd.'

Christmas at Charlestown was always marked by festivities which embraced all the residents, regardless of age or creed, generously supported by either the Proprietors or local organisations, a practice which happily continues to this day. In 1892, a Christmas entertainment was given by the Charlestown C.E.T.S (what those initials stood for is uncertain):

'An entertainment was given in the Weslyan Sunday school-room on Thursday 8 December consisting of Tableaux Vivants, interposed with vocal and instrumental music. The following ladies and gentlemen volunteered their services and all well acquitted themselves. Misses Luke, Brooks, Daniel, Brown and Mallalue(2), Sanders, Coade, Giles(2), Endean, Inch, Curgenven, Dunstone, Broad and Palmer. Messrs. Pyatt, Harris, Gunnell, Inch and Miners. Vocalists were Misses Gale, Jewell and Dunstone, Mr W. Jewell assisted by a string band, consisting of Messrs. Hocking,

Wilkinson and Rowse. Master Reggie Lovering ably acquitted himself on two violin solos. The chair was taken by the Rev. A.H. Ferris, who in his opening remarks stated, that if the affair was a failure, it rested not with him, as Miss Luke was the prime mover. The entertainment was a decided success, which is attributed to the energy of the young people.'[15]

The elderly were catered for during the afternoon of 5 January 1893, at a gathering in the same building:

'The Vicar and his wife had made ample preparations and a goodly spread was provided and about 70 sat down to tea. As soon as the tables had been cleared, a few lantern pictures were shown, which caused great amusement. The church choir accompanied by Miss Pearce, who very kindly gave her services, sang some Christmas carols, which were appreciated. The Vicar gave a very practical and useful address, with a notice for the New Year and, after singing hymn no.27, the old folk dispersed, those travelling a distance being sent in carriages. The following ladies presided at the tea tables, Mrs. Ferris, Melhuish, Lovering, Bulteel, Daniel, Coade, with Miss Daniel and Miss Brookes.'[16]

The Loverings', wealthy clay-pit owners, always made a point of entertaining the Charlestown 'trades people' as they were described, along with their own estate employees, just after New Year.[17] This took place at *The Grove*, the big house which they had built, at the top of Charlestown Road, subsequently the home of the McDougal family, then the Bakers', World War 2 evacuees, Sir John and Lady Florence Crowder and finally Mrs Smythe Osborne, their daughter, and her husband, Major Smythe Osborne. In 1893, 'Mr & Mrs W.T. Lovering, who have been making alterations at their residence, *The Grove*, entertained their people to dinner on Thursday evening.'

Charlestown was now literally in its prime, with great changes and developments proposed. The dock was advertised as having space for 18 coasting vessels of 400 tons, with a maximum draught of 15ft allowed. The permanent crane (sheer-legs in fact, with a swivelling boom, located on the dock opposite the Pier House Hotel), was capable of lifting 15 tons, but the only export trade mentioned was china-clay. Imports included, coal, timber, limestone, iron and coffee. In April 1893, after a very dry spell, followed by heavy rain and easterly gales, a huge section of the cliff edge in Cliff Park collapsed, some 4 to 6,000 tons of earth and rock falling onto the eastern beach. According to the local press, some of the boulders weighed 30 tons, but fortunately no one was hurt.[18]

Charlestown was also about to have its very own school building, as well as a new vicarage, the old vicarage by Charlestown Mill being no longer available. Messrs. Lovering were also about to take a lease on two plots on which to build their clay-dries. Negotiations commenced with correspondence early in 1894:

The inside of the lower Charlestown clay dry, one of two built by the Lovering's just after 1900. On the right, men are pouring clay slurry over the drying floor or 'pan', from a 'tram' on a wheeled gantry, whilst in the foreground a clay worker is about to shovel a block of dried clay into the 'linney', bottom left.

'13 January '94. A.G. Crowder, to H. Evans Gordon Esq. *Site for a Board School.* Will you agree to offering our approval by me and Bulteel @ £10 rent per annum for 99 years? The St. Austell School Board have approached Bulteel on the subject. I understand that they have compulsory powers to acquire the freehold, but Bulteel recommends as above, if the School Board will agree. *Site for a new Vicarage.* A highly spoken of successor to Mr. Ferris, a Mr. Williams, late curate of St. Austell, has been appointed to Charlestown. The house in which Mr. Ferris lived belongs to his father-in-law (under building lease) who has let it to his own son. Mr. Williams has had to take temporarily a house abutting on the Dock which appears to be unsuitable. It certainly cannot continue. Will you and your co-trustees agree to giving a small site upon which to build a vicarage in a position approved by me provided the estimated sum required is first obtained? Do you and Mr. Sartoris (jnr) possess power to give the fee-simple, or do you prefer granting a 99 building lease at a nominal rent?'[19]

The matter of the school was completely settled by November, the plot of land on which it was to be built during 1894/5 being purchased out-right by the School Board. The Charlestown Infants School opened in 1895, with Mrs Mary Moore as head mistress, who was followed by Miss M. Bice. Considerable expansion took place in 1901, after which it could accommodate 135 mixed infants, remaining in use until Friday 11 October 1974, when the new Charlestown School was opened in Beach Road, Carlyon Bay. The old school then stood empty for a while until utilised by Gordon Rogers, previously an apprentice carpenter with Charlestown Estate Ltd, as a joinery workshop, soon to be converted into three dwellings. It was also November 1894 before agreement could be reached regarding a site for the vicarage:

'7 Nov '94. A.G. Crowder to Messrs. H. Rawden & Co, Sol's, 150 Leadenhall St, London. At last a site has been decided upon, viz: about a quarter of an acre in a field numbered 219a. on the Estate plan. You will observe that the plot is situated on that portion of the Estate which is held from Lord Edgcumbe for 1,000 years, but the vicar thinks his Committee will have no difficulty in acquiring Lord Edgcumbe's permission.'[20]

In fact the vicarage site was extended to one third of an acre in 1911, taking in an area of mine waste and part of an old mine building, which the Estate considered of no value to them. Many of the properties in the village were of course held on maintaining leases, which were not always honoured, dwellings falling into a bad state of repair, as witness a property known as *Eastern House*:

'To the Representatives of the late William Hammer, deceased. Notice requiring remedying of Breach of Covenant to repair. Lease dated 1st January 1837, between Edward Rose Tunno, Richard Budden Crowder, Frederick Robert Crowder and George Augustus Crowder of the one part and the said William Hammer of the other part . . whereby you have committed a breach of the covenant by not keeping it in good and sufficient repair, we also require you to pay £22.13s and also the sum of £3.9s. 8d, being the costs & expenses incurred by them for surveyers fees & charges, in respect of the said breach at *Eastern House*: Parlour: Two panes of glass, scarf window frames, new skirting, repair plastering to walls, repair woodwork & cupboards, new handle to cupboard. Passage: Repair front door & fittings, repair back door. Sitting Room: Two panes of glass, repair floor. Kitchen: Repair & renew skirting, repair floor, re-build back wall from ground to roof, two panes of glass. Wash House: Carry chimney of furnace to original height. Bedroom: Repair & fix mantlepiece, two panes of glass, repair window, repair cupboard. Roof: Re-point chimneys, repair roof and fit new crease. Outside: Repair front wall, replace railings and gate, repair and re-fix door to outhouse. Repair Jambe, repair walls, rebuild back boundary wall. Repair and refelt closet.'[21]

The Hammer family also occupied what was known as *Western*

*House,*which required even more work, and it takes little imagination to conjure up a mental picture as to what state the property must have been in to warrant such legal action.

The year 1895 saw the Proprietors offered the opportunity to purchase the entire foreshore area of Charlestown, which until then had remained the property of the Duchy of Cornwall. A.G. Crowder advised 'that we had better buy. If you agree I should propose to offer £45, but should be glad if you would give me a limit, that is of course, if you agree? In fact the Duchy would not settle for less than £70, which was duly paid in January 1896, along with £3 costs.[22] By March great concern was expressed that the churchyard of St. Paul's church was becoming full and there was need for a cemetary. The matter was put before the St. Austell Parish Council, of which a Charlestown man, Joseph Henry Walkey was a committee member, which selected a piece of ground at Camp Downs as suitable. Close to the vicarage, the field chosen belonged to Lord Edgcumbe, and negotiations were certainly protracted, since the 2.5 acre site, purchased for £800, on which two mortuary chapels were built, was not ready for use until 1901.[23]

In keeping with the rest of the country and probably the whole Empire, 26 June 1897 was a public holiday to celebrate Queen Victoria's Diamond Jubilee. In Charlestown, 240 children and teachers met in Church Lane at 3.15 pm and marched through the village, led by the Artillery fife & drum band. Their route took them down to the dock, through a large floral arch erected between the Rashleigh Arms and the Post Office, round the Cask Bank and back, each child being presented with a jubilee mug. Afterwards, 300 adults and all the sailors in the port, sat down to what was described as a 'meat tea'.[24] That summer saw the last annual inspection of the Artillery Volunteers at Charlestown, and it is likely they were disbanded by the end of the year, bringing to an end 104 years of training, drill and dedication. They assembled on 26 June for inspection, 74 rank and file on parade before Lt. Col. Lane, RA, Field Commander of the Brigade. The parade over, Major Lovering lead them in a march to the Battery, where they fired eight rounds at a moving target 1,300 yards offshore.[25] The last reference to the corps in the local newspapers is dated Saturday 24 July:

> 'The 4th DCAV Volunteers assembled in the Drill Hall and headed by the band, marched to the Battery at 6 o'clock in the evening. There followed some extraordinary shooting at the big gun practice when 27 rounds were fired, 16 at fixed targets, a further 11 at drifting targets. Several came close to the fixed, but at the 15th shot, Corporal Shepherd carried it away.'[26]

The near drowning of a local boy in August and winter damage to the pier occupied the resident's minds according to the St. Austell Star. On 6 August Robert Hosegood, a ten year old lad, fell into the outer basin and would have drowned had not a William Hewett, described as a local, recently returned to Charlestown, jumped in and saved him.[27]

157

Gales further damaged the harbour, 'On 1 November, heavy seas caused extensive damage to the eastern side of the outer pier wall, which can not be repaired at this time due to bad weather.'[28] The same series of storms caused a cliff fall on the eastern beach which killed a young boy. Charles Tiller, aged 14 years, staying with relatives in Charlestown, having been sent to England from America to regain his health, was playing on the beach, collecting driftwood and wreckage with others on 10 November. One boy went into a small cave in the cliff, Charles remaining at the mouth holding a bag. Without warning a large quantity of rock fell some 200ft, striking the boy on the head, killing him instantly.[29]

Twelve days later there was almost a wreck in the outer basin. The brigantine *Malpas Belle* of Truro, on passage from Charlestown to Rouen with clay, went aground and became fast. A tug was sent from Fowey but failed to refloat her, parting two towing hawsers in the attempt. Early next morning, before high water, most of her cargo was thrown overboard into the basin, but with the tide unsuitable to re-enter the dock by the time she was afloat again, she proceeded to Rouen with what little cargo remained in her hold.[30]

Following the turn of the century, things at Charlestown were very quiet. The Proprietors continued to discuss the merits of a branch of the G.W.R. railway to the port, whilst the Loverings sought an acceptable lease for land on which to construct their proposed clay dries. In the meantime the state of Charlestown Road continued to give problems concerning its surface and dust. The road at that time did not have the consistent steady slope it has today, but was distinctly 'stepped' in three places. Leading off from the St. Austell Turnpike, there was a short, steep gradient opposite what is now the foundry car park before it levelled off again. This was repeated just below *The Beeches*, and again just past the Estate Office, which now bore the name plate of Charlestown Estate Ltd, the company being of limited liability from 1905. As more commercial use was found for china clay, so the number of carts using the road increased, reaching 150 a day, their iron 'drags' attached to the wheels to act as brakes tearing up the road surface, particularly on the steep sections. This would be temporarily remedied by a steam-roller, towing a water cart, which visited Charlestown twice a year. The machine would first break up the surface with pointed steel bars, then with liberal sprinklings of water, roll in granite chippings to give a flat surface, a ritual that ceased only when the road was graded and surfaced with tarmac in the mid 1920's.

On 17 December 1903, Mrs. Sarah Crowder, Augustus Crowder's mother, who held the moiety of Charlestown Estate and controlled most of the purse strings, died at 65 Portland Place, London, where she lived with her son Augustus. To him and his brother Frederick, of 110 Banbury Road, Oxford, went her interest in Charlestown in equal shares, Augustus continuing to act as managing secretary.

Whilst mentioned briefly in the 1890's, the possibility of a gas-holder for the St. Austell Gas Co. being sited in Charlestown now became a very real possibility. Negotiations commenced in December 1905, with the Gas company wanting an option to purchase land kept open for 15 years, which the Crowder's would not accept, suggesting that three years was more realistic. The proposed site is unrecorded, described only as 'out of the way, up a side road, on a plot of land of half an acre leased to W.J. Lovering'. The Gas Co.refused to accept less than a 10 year agreement, the Crowder's finally asking for that amount of rental in advance as a lump sum, plus expenses. At the same time an 'Electrical Syndicate Scheme' was seeking to rent land in the village, but Augustus Crowder's reply was quite positive, 'I shall of course be ready to deal with them, but any scheme having for its object the lighting of the Dock or village by electricity & meaning outlay on the part of the Company, I am afraid I should not look upon with favour.'[31] The Electrical Syndicate then opted to purchase the entire village and port, no doubt with the same idea in mind as the Gas Company, of establishing a generating plant in Charlestown, as close as possible to the only port ideally situated for bringing in the necessary coal. The Crowder's opened with an asking price of £70,000, the Electrical Syndicate suggesting £55,000, until on 27 July 1907, agreement was reached at £65,000, in cash, but as with previous offers, nothing came of it.[32]

At the Foundry, business was bad due to the decline in mining, and did not pick up again, apart from armament contracts during World War 1, when they made mortar bomb casings and marine engines, until the 1930's. It was about 1910 when the works received a welcome order from the Goonbarrow mine for a Cornish beam engine with a 36ins cylinder and 10ft stroke. Such orders were now so rare that there was no one at Charlestown capable of the design work, so drawings were prepared by Nicholas Trestrail of Redruth. Neither was the Foundry capable of casting the main beam, so a laminated steel plate beam was built instead. Whilst no one could have known at the time, this was in fact the very last such beam engine to be built in Cornwall.[33] The Foundry's problems were then compounded by a disastrous fire, which gutted the whole of the pattern shop and store, destroying a large proportion of the original wooden patterns used for making gears, valves, tools and machine casting, representing 50 years work. The fire was first seen by Benjamin Tregonning, a labourer in the village. It took the St. Austell fire-brigade 30 minutes to reach the Foundry, by which time the roof had collapsed and the building was gutted. Fortunately, Hayle Foundry still had a large stock of similar if not identical patterns, which were lent to Charlestown so that copies could be made, additional staff to the normal 60 men being recruited specially.[34]

Until now, Brick Hill or Duporth Road, which was still privately owned by Charlestown Estate Ltd, was only a narrow unmade track, originally built to give Charles Rashleigh and his workers easy access to

Duporth manor, Porthpean Road and the cottages adjacent to Brick Hill. The St. Austell Rural District Council wrote to the directors early in 1913, offering to adopt the road, widening it to 26ft 6ins, and surfacing as necessary. In accepting the offer, the directors considered this not only a great improvement, but an advantage in that it relieved them of all future maintenance costs.[35] Widening the road deprived each of the *Back Row* cottages of a considerable amount of garden, so that their outside doors now fronted directly on to the pavement. These cottages were unbelievably small, with just two rooms, one a bedroom, the other a general kitchen cum living-room, their earth closet toilets at the far end of each individual garden, on the other side of the road! Built entirely of cob, *Back Row* was pulled down in 1967, in order to make room for bathroom extensions to the *Front Row* cottages, which are more substantial being built of granite lined with cob.

Initially, World War 1 had little effect on Charlestown. Sailing vessels and an increasing proportion of steam ships continued to load clay for the continent and UK ports, until German submarines turned their full attention to merchant shipping, sinking everything in sight, whether it was a 200 ton sailing schooner carrying china clay, or a liner. The demand for army recruits reduced the work force on the dock to a mere skeleton staff, until the port almost closed down completely. This had near disastrous financial implications for the owners, exasperated by Bulteel's prolonged illness, which eventually forced him to take his 27 year old son Walter into partnership to help run the Estate. Many vessels proceeding to or from the port were sunk by submarines, small clay boats usually being sent to the bottom by explosive scuttling charges rather than by expensive torpedoes, and at least three Charlestown captain's lost their ships to the enemy. Captain Charles Deacon, a Devonian by birth, who married Sarah Lucking, a Charlestown girl, in 1885, making the village his home, lost the 195 ton brigantine *Ocean Swell* to a U-Boat on 5 July 1917, 15 miles south-east of Start Point, whilst carrying wooden barrel hoops from Granville to Fowey, after commanding her for 18 years.[36] A true story concerning this sinking involved Charles Deacon's watch. After ordering the English crew to abandon ship, Captain Deacon asked the German commander if he could go below and get his watch. Suspecting a trick, the enemy officer examined the timepiece, then asked what was so special about it? Deacon explained that his grandson had cut his first tooth on it, showing the mark to prove the point! A year later Captain Deacon was in command of the 119 ton *Bessie Stephens* 10 miles west of Lundy Island, carrying clay from Fowey to Preston, when he was again ordered to stop by a U-Boat.[37] To his astonishment he found its commanding officer to be the same man who had sunk his previous ship. Laughing at the coincidence, the German asked 'Got your watch this time'! Captain George Beynon, who had married Eliza Lucking, sister of Captain Deacon's wife, also settled in Charlestown and lost a ship to the enemy. He was in command of the 182 ton schooner *Martha Edmunds*, when she was sunk by a U-Boat off Ushant on 20 August 1915, with a cargo of silversand from Rouen to Seville.[38]

Following the end of World War 1 the clay trade was so slack that none of the Charlestown directors received a dividend until 1923. Local men returning from the war were offered only part-time work, and there seemed little prospect of an upturn for many years. The biggest event in the village was the extension of the gas main from Mount Charles around 1920, which was laid right down to the dock. This enabled those that could afford it to have indoor gas lighting, instead of oil lamps, but it was many years before every home took up the option, since the owners refused to pay the installation charges. Gas lighting around the dock was installed, as were street lamps, which meant that it provided work for a village lamp-lighter. A Mr. Calf was given the job, and he would start at the top of Charlestown Road, opposite the Foundry, lighting the lamps as he worked his way downhill, finishing off with the dock, regularly followed by a crowd of village children. In the morning the reverse procedure took place, commencing with the dock lamps, and if anyone wanted a wake-up call on his rounds, he would knock on their bedroom windows with his staff.

Why the Hon. F. Hatch Jones, of 1130 Lake Shore Drive, Chicago, USA, should be sent share holding details of the Estate on 8 September 1920 is uncertain, not unless he was a potential buyer:

'Charlestown Estate is situated about a mile from St. Austell, Cornwall. The share capital is £20,000 divided into 2,000 shares of £10 each, all ordinary. The property consists of a small sea port on St. Austell Bay, chiefly used for the export of china clay (the Co. owns none), and the import of coal for drying the clay.

The income of the port is derived from Quay dues on vessels & cargoes. The remainder of the property consists of small houses, cottages, stores & small agricultural holdings & a couple of china clay dries, the ground on which they constructed having been let on a long lease to China Clay Merchants. The Company own the fee simple, ie. the freehold of the property except a portion which is held by them on a 999 year lease from Lord Mt. Edgcumbe at a nominal rent.

The Sartoris family own half the shares & my brother & I the other half between us. I hope the above information is what you desire? Yours faithfully, Augustus G. Crowder.'[39]

A Charlestown family named Stark suffered an awful blow in 1921, when their seven year old son Fernleigh John, nicknamed 'Jackie' was drowned in the dock. Worse still, the same family lost a second son, aged 10 in almost identical circumstances in the dock 11 years later. Young 'Jackie', whose father was a Petty Officer Stoker in the Royal Navy, stationed in the Black Sea at the time, was skylarking around the dock with a boy named Walkey from Brick Hill, jumping in and out of a boat in the dock. It was not tied up tight to the quay and drifted around, consequently the lad jumped and fell in on the west side and drowned. The other Stark boy, Alfred James, was lost on 25 August 1932 on the east side. He was walking along a narrow board on the edge of the dock, when a friend high up on the gantry called to him; looking up quickly, he lost his balance and went in on the east side and drowned. His father, who had left the navy in 1930 as a Chief Petty Officer, was working in the hold of the *Waterwitch* as a docker, unloading coal, joined the search but was unaware it was his own son they were looking for until an hour later. A man in bathing trunks dived in to try and find the boy, the body finally being located by William Hendra, the Harbour Master at 5.40 pm. The Stark family were unlucky, out of five brothers, two were drowned, the third, Robert, an Able Seaman on board HMS. *Lapwing*, was electrocuted when she went down off Murmansk when part of a Russian convoy, on 20 March 1945. The Starks' also had a nephew who drowned in Australia.[40]

By early 1924 Henry James Bulteel was a very sick man, his son Walter having taken over some of his duties, accompanying Augustus Crowder during his bi-annual visits when he made a point of looking at every property in Charlestown. In an almost feudal manner, reminiscent of the 18th century, Augustus and one of the Bulteel's would look at every garden and house, telling the occupier in no uncertain terms if repairs were needed or the grass needed cutting, and woe betide any tenant who neglected their instructions. Walter Bulteel was respected every bit as much as his father, the villagers making discreet fun of his long cigarette holder and the white silk handkerchief that always showed beneath one cuff. In a letter to the other directors, Augustus said of him:

'. . he is about 27 & is one of the assistant valuers in Cornwall under the Finance Act 1910. He has been well educated & qualified for land agency by certificates. He is a bachelor & lives at home (Pond House). I consider him well suited for our work & is a quiet young man with good manners & I have never heard a word against his moral character. He is I believe engaged to be married. Ours is a troublesome Property to manage in many ways as the Directors are aware. It would be difficult to get another local man I fear, whom one could trust and who would come up to our standard socially.'[41]

Called up during World War 1, Walter served as a captain in the Coldstream Guards. His father, Henry Bulteel died on 28 October 1924, aged 71, having been the Agent for the Estate for almost 40 years. Combining two newspaper accounts of the period, the press had this to say of him:

'Born at Plymouth, grandson of the Rev. Bulteel, he was educated at Eton and the Royal Agricultural College, Cirencester. During his long tenure at Charlestown he did much to encourage trade to

PORT OF CHARLESTOWN, CORNWALL.

SIGNALS.

BY DAY. (a) BLACK BALL hoisted on Flag-staff near entrance of Harbour denote Vessels cannot enter.

(b) RED ENSIGN denotes doubtful, but stand by.

BY NIGHT. IF WORKING TIDE, Red Light on South Pier and Green Light on North Pier.

IF DOUBTFUL, Green Light only but stand by.

Hobblers will go off to Vessels when they can enter, and under no circumstances must Vessel run into outer Harbour without Orders.

W. G. BULTEEL,

Manager.

Dated CHARLESTOWN,
November 20th, 1925.

Instructions regarding signals to be shown on the port flagstaff, controlling the entry of vessels into the harbour.

the port, and it was due to his efforts that the lighting scheme was brought into the village. He was connected for over 20 years with Penrice Estate as Agent to Sir Charles Sawle. Closely identified with Charlestown church, he was a regular attendant, fond of all forms of sport, a keen chess player and loved sailing. His memorial service was held at St. Paul's on 6 November, where there was a

Charlestown dock c1914, with the SS. Westdale *and a second steamship astern, both loading china clay from the 'tram-way' gantry, with one topsail schooner loaded and others waiting, probably first having brought in coal or timber.*

large assembly, conducted by the Rev. J.H. Beechcroft. Admiral Sir Charles Graves-Sawle RN, wrote regretting his inability to attend due to ill-health. Mr.C. Coombes represented Charlestown Estate Co, amongst whom were W. Hendra, deputy dock-master, Cyril Rowse at the organ. The funeral took place the same afternoon at Bridgetown, Totnes, Devon, where there was a large attendance.'[42]

Duporth Manor, once Rashleigh's home, lost to Joseph Daniel, bought by Dr. Pattison, then sold to the Steward of the Duchy of Cornwall, Mr. Freeth, passed into the hands of his daughter Mrs. Henry Hodge in 1916, following her father's death. On 21 October 1924 the entire estate was put up for auction at the Lecture Hall, St. Austell, by Messrs.Viner, Carew & Co. Their auction advertisment read:

'The very attractive small country estate known as Duporth, situated within 1.5 miles of St. Austell and adjacent to a coastline of unparalleled beauty with important Sea frontages and Private beach, including a unique Old Georgian residence. Standing in magnificently timbered Grounds and Gardens of rare beauty and overlooking the sea, containing 5 reception rooms, spacious organ room, 10 bed and dressing rooms, 3 servant's rooms, bathroom, hot and cold water supplies, ample offices, main water supply, good drainage, garage, stabling and Lodge. Together with Excellent Home Farm comprising, good farm house with capital range of outbuildings, the whole extending to about 94 acres. Particulars, plans and conditions of sale from the offices of the solicitors, Coodes and Giffard, St. Austell. Cornwall.'

Possibly due to the recession, bidding commenced at only £4,500 and the property was withdrawn at £7,750, but later purchased by a Mr. William Sessions of St. Breward for £8,250.[43] The St. Austell News of 1 September 1925 (which incidently cost 1d), continued the story:

'It is understood that Mr. Sessions, who recently acquired the Duporth Estate, intends to convert the house into a private residential club. There will be extensive alterations and the beautiful organ, also purchased by Mr. Sessions, will remain and a billiard room will be added, with accommodation for hunters and motor cars. He intends to lay out the grounds overlooking the sea for the erection of villas, but land on the Brick Hill side and Pentewan Road will not be built on at present. The residents will be able to enjoy the priviledges of the private beach.'[44]

That was of course the beginning of what is now Duporth Holiday Park, owned by Haven Holidays, having previously belonged to both the Butlins and Rank Organisations. It was not until 13 November 1933 that the land was sold on which Duporth Housing Estate was built, the notice of sale advising:

'Cornwall, south coast, about 30 acres of delightful coasting land for sale at Duporth, St. Austell, Cornwall. Large and small quantities, excellent roads, private and public beaches, uninterrupted views.'[45]

The 56 employees of Rowse's cooperage in Charlestown, c1920, run by the brothers Jack and Arthur. During the Second World War, the premises were taken over as an Admiralty marine store. The young boys in the front row are apprentices. Reading from top left, in five rows, their names were:

Row 1 – *J. Radcliffe; N. Trudgeon; E. Roberts; Geo. Hammet*

Row 2 – *Not known; Ern. Harris; C. Roberts; Jim Kendall;B. Little; Geo.Milford; G. Kingswell: D. Harper; J. Holesworthy; not known; 'Babs' White; B. White.*

Row 3 – *Jim ?; W. Walkey; George ?; 'Sham' Matthews; D. Pascoe; J. Walkey; Herb Rollings; A. Wilson; M. White; J. Deere; H. Kendall; C. Pyatt; G. Marks; J. Shepherd; T. Kendall; D. Bawden; D. Pascoe; J. Hewett.*

Row 4 – *Phil Rowse; J. Rowse; J. West; J. Walkey (jnr); S. Rowings; T. Crocker; J. Lenhall; not known; B. Rooke; not known; B. Pyatt; C. Milford; C. Wilson.*

Row 5 – *Broant; W. Wilson; J. Stark; Jack Richards; Barbary; Harper; H. Tregonning; A. Woolcocks; B. Carter.*

That winter a serious wreck incident was narrowly averted within the outer basin at Charlestown, the last such incident involving a sailing ship. The incident happened on Sunday 9 November, when in heavy weather, the steel schooner *Trio*, from the Baltic with staves for Rowse's cooperage, attempted to beat the tide. With insufficient water under their keel, she grounded on the granite blocks outside the eastern arm and was in considerable danger of being wrecked. Only after a struggle, assisted by the Charlestown dock porters, was she refloated and got into port. Her master, Captain Loopman, had his ribs badly damaged whilst attempting to lower a boat. His comments to the St. Austell News reporter were: 'I did not appreciate the laughing and carrying on of spectators on the pier; I did my best, and was running and shouting first from the bow, then the stern, because my crew were mixed Danes and Germans who were, to a great extent, inexperienced.'[46]

It was many years before the clay trade revived and there was a degree of prosperity again in the village. The late Charlie Walkie, (nicknamed Dayer or Saltwater), born 1905, who was brought up in one half of *Pier House*, one of a family of twelve, was typical of many young men in the village. Sent to sea by his father, Jack Walkie, at the age of 14 on board the *Elizabeth Bennett*, he was put ashore in the late 1920's when the vessel was laid up, and was out of work for 10 years along with other men, until World War 2. Given work as a docker, wages were better at Charlestown than elsewhere, £3 a week instead of the average £2.10s. One of his many recollections was the vertical greasy-pole set up outside the Rashleigh Arms on Charlestown & St. Austell Bay Regatta Day. The landlord would set a leg of lamb or mutton on top as a prize, and the young men would attempt to climb up and get it, usually defeated by the liberal coating of grease. Since there were no rules, a docker named Harry Larcombe got the idea of using what is called a Spanish windlass, a rope strop with a wooden pin, which when twisted, tightened round the pole and gave a good grip. To the delight of the onlookers, using this technique, he had the joint of meat in no time at all – and that was the end of any future greasy pole contests![47] Possibly the best story to come out of Charlestown in the early 1930's concerned Reg Skinner, who lived with his wife and five sons in *Ivy House*, on Quay Road. The Skinner family ran a china clay crushing plant in what is now Partech (Electronics) engineering workshop, and in fact the deep pit which held the crusher is still there, now safely boarded over. The business was in considerable financial difficulties when Reg, with a 10s ticket, drew a horse in the Irish sweepstake named *Miracle*, owned by Lord Rosebury. He sold half the ticket to the owner for £2,000 and thinking he had achieved a good deal, retired to his back lawn on the day of the race, to listen to the radio commentary. The horse came in 3rd, and to his astonishment, he won £7,000, an incredible amount of money at that time, something like 44 years salary to a working man, plus of course the other £2,000. The shock was so great he fainted, but when revived shouted to his wife, 'Mary, Mary, we've been saved'. After collecting his winnings, he put £20 behind the bar in the Rashleigh, for all the village men to have a drink. Did he use the money to advantage you are probably asking? He certainly did, he bought some model 'T' Ford steam driven Centinal lorries, which had solid tyres, started the Western Express Haulage Company and eventually took his business to

The one and only visit by a member of the Royal family to Charlestown. HRH The Prince of Wales, at the top of the harbour steps, wearing RAF uniform, arrived by seaplane on 1 July 1931.

The first steam driven, solid tyre Foden lorry belonging to the Heavy Transport Company c1920, started by Charles Hudson, based in Charlestown, in the yard now utilised by Square Sail Shipyard Ltd. The driver was Leonard Hawkey, the fireman Charlie Mutton, Gerald Mutton's father, who had just come ashore after a spell at sea on the Waterwitch.

Par docks, where there was more work.[48]

Whereas the 1914-18 war had no direct impact on Charlestown, World War 2 was the complete opposite. The Foundry, which was sold to Jones, Curtis & Co. Ltd in 1926, who introduced a new type of centrifugal pump, and sold again in 1935/6 to English China Clays,[49] was given orders to make gun barrel straightening machines, gun mountings, tank brakes and brackets, armoured car turret rings, shell fuse discs, cast iron practice shot, miniature practice firing ranges and a component for the Mulberry floating harbour landing stage units, an all welded construction which called for precision engineering, great skill and specialised measuring equipment. Work went on day and night, with men recruited from the now almost idle clay works, as well as women and youths, all of whom had to be trained in engineering skills. Two concrete pill boxes were built overlooking the port entrance,

Wooden barrel staves from the Baltic being unloaded into four of Norman May's fleet of lorries. The introduction of large diesel driven trucks, discharging direct into the holds of ships, made barrels and cooperages redundant in the late 1940s.

and the beach and approaches covered with barbed wire and concrete tank traps. The Grove was requisitioned for evacuee children, the first of whom arrived on 4 September, as was the Carlyon Bay Hotel and other large premises, and a Royal Indian Army Service Corps unit, complete with dozens of mules, took over Duporth. Air raid shelters were dug and stocked, and sleepy little Charlestown suddenly found itself at war. The annual Charlestown & St. Austell Bay Regatta was discontinued of course and not revived until 1946. The Regatta then took place two years running, but not in 1948, since that was the year the dock gates were removed for repairs. It would appear that the tradition then died until 1971, when Charlestown Estate Ltd reopened the port after the new single gate was fitted, sponsoring the Regatta, which had very little funds, which has continued to date. Village men in reserved occupations, medically unfit or too old for military service, were recruited into the LDV.(Local Defence Volunteers), which was later renamed the Home Guard (better known as Dad's Army). Issued with uniforms, steel helmets, Lee Enfield rifles, Lewis guns and other weapons, they maintained a nightly watch in six day shifts on the battery, sleeping in the upper floor of the old *Content* fish cellar, now *Salamander*.

171

In fact the very first bomb dropped on Cornwall fell on Charlestown, exploding in a field in front of *The Grove* on 5 July 1940, the attention of a German He-111 bomber having been drawn to a squad of soldiers marching up Charlestown Road. The explosion brought down the ceiling of both a classroom and the cloakroom in the village school, but no one was seriously injured. Extracts from the Charlestown Primary School Log Book of the period, give a glimpse of how education has changed in the last 50 years, as well as some of the difficulties of wartime schooling:

'24 May 1939. Empire Day kept up. Children decorated school, lessons given and patriotic songs sung. Nurse Morris visited the school and inspected the children.

'11 Sept 1939. We started a "double-shift", working with the London County Council teachers; this week Charlestown school is working in the morning.'

'11 March 1940. The dentist has paid his annual visit and spent three days here.'

'24 May 1940. Empire Day. At 11 o'clock all the children, including evacuees and infants assembled. Patriotic songs sung and the Union Jack saluted. The children wore red, white and blue rosettes made by them.'

'24 June 1940. Today I admitted 20 children evacuated from East Ham (London), with instructions that they must "merge" with our children.'

'5 July 1940. A bomb from a Nazi plane was dropped in a field nearby. Some slight damage.

'11 Dec 1940. We were in the air-raid shelters from 1.35pm to 2.05pm. Ordinary time table suspended.'[50]

Whilst that period may now seem archaic, a brief look at the old Charlestown School Punishment Book, which ran from 1897 to 1966 reveals how modern attitudes have changed regarding the treatment of children during education:

'22 May 1897. Carrie Chappel had the cane for constantly disobeying & having 13 mistakes in spelling.'

'27 Aug 1901. Punished Carrie Chappel for tearing out leaves of her exercise book after I corrected them.'

'18 Oct 1907. Gave Joseph Wilkinson the cane for answering his teacher back.'

'28 Jan 1914. Gave Reg Walkey, Frank Truscott, Alfred Williams & George Jacobs the stick for playing marbles instead of coming to school when the bell rang.'

'18 July 1933. Morley Taylor, Dennis Williams & Francis Howard, one stroke each for disobedience. Five minutes granted for them to go and see the seaplanes. Instead of coming back, they went out in a boat and were absent 30 minutes.'

'13 Oct 1933. Caned Trevor Best, Gerald West & Willie Oliver for disobedience, also Howard Mills for rushing through the porch, shouting and screaming after being told not to do it.'

'5 Oct 1943. Maureen Pearson, evacuee, one stripe across each hand with a ruler for wilfully scratching her desk.'[51]

The normal outgoing clay and incoming timber and coal trade in the dock was restricted to just two berths for the duration of the war, one unloading berth on the west side and one loading on the east being left empty. The remainder of the dock was taken over by the Admiralty as a fitting out base for minesweepers. Preparation work for this commenced with the entire dock being fenced round with sheets of corrugated iron, part of which was covered over entirely so that the warships would not be visible from the air. Rowse's cooperage buildings and others were requisitioned and filled with naval stores from Plymouth Dockyard and lean-to workshops were erected at dock level and machines installed. The contract for building the new wooden Admiralty Type Motor Minesweepers was given to Frank Curtis of Totnes, who established a building yard in Par Docks. Known as HM. MMS.(Short) and HM. MMS (Long), 119ft and 140ft respectively, the class had been developed to counter the new German magnetic mine, the bare hulls from Par being towed to Charlestown, for outfitting and finishing, the dock holding two at a time.

A Chief Petty Officer ERA. (Engine Room Artificer), and navy engineering lieutenant, would arrive at Charlestown with each basic hull and supervise the installation of the main engine and engine room fittings. At each stage of fitting out more and more navy men arrived, all billeted locally, until each ship was completed, inspected, then taken to sea for trials with a full crew, before being accepted to join the fleet. None of them were named, being identified only by number, a total of 38 sweepers being completed, of which 31 were 'short' class, No's HM. MMS. 26, 28, 74, 75, 139, 140, 149, 150, 167, 168, 169, 170, 204, 205, 224, 225, 226, 227, 228, 268, 269, 270, 271, 282, 285, 286, 292, 294, 295, 296 and 298. The remainder were 'long' class, numbered, HM. MMS. 1032, 1033, 040, 1078, 1079, 1080. Of these only two were lost during the entire war, No. 168 detonating a mine on 25.06.1945 in Genoa Harbour, No. 170 also blown up on 12.10.1944 off Gorgona Island, Italy. The 'short' class were of 165 tons displacement, 119 x 23 x 9.5ft, one shaft diesel engine of 500bhp, 11 knots maximum speed, complement 20 officers and ratings. The 'long' class were of 255 tons displacement, 140 x 26 x 10.5ft, one shaft diesel, 500bhp, 10 knots maximum speed, complement 21 officers and ratings.[52]

Elsewhere in Charlestown, the Indian troops accidently set fire to part of Duporth House whilst having an illegal 'fry up' in a bedroom, and three of their number were killed when a tree was blown down in a gale across an accommodation hut (their headstones are in the old part of Charlestown cemetary). Duporth was taken over by American troops towards D-Day (6 June 1944) and Crinnis Beach was 'attacked' time and time again by waves of Landing Craft and fully armed troops in rehearsals for the forthcoming Normandy landings. On the social side, Charlestown girls were in constant demand to attend dances, parties and socials given by the US service men. Military trucks would call at the village, picking up females of all ages, for dances as far away as Newquay, Perranporth and St. Agnes, where there were were huge military camps, holding thousands of men.

Following the war the clay trade was again slow to pick-up, and Charlestown Estate's income from the port did not revive until the 1950's. The Foundry did well out of the war, having been fitted with a new electrical supply, machines and equipment, and scrapping over 1,000 tons of old and redundant plant, the techniques and tools acquired greatly assisted the company in the years ahead. With delivery times for machinery and castings being quoted elsewhere of 4-5 years, and new machinery for farms and industry unavailable during the war, Charlestown Foundry was fully occupied with orders, the number of full-time employees after the war rising from 30 to 107. A new department was opened to offer major overhauls of the heavy earth moving plant used by the Western Excavating Co, and during 1945-56 the output of the Foundry rose from 251 tons of cast iron to 891 tons and gun-metal castings from 9 tons to 30. The process of drying china clay was also changing from the old slow heat method to high pressure filter presses, and in 1967 the remaining 'lower' china clay dry in Charlestown ceased to be used.[53]

Changes on the dock were also obvious, with the introduction of the Dockers Union agreement and registered dockers, so that Charlestown retained only sufficient men to open and close the dock gates and handle the mooring ropes, the clay work force coming over from Par as required. In the early 1980's English Clays dismissed all its registered dockers at Par & Fowey, taking back only a reduced number of non-union workers. Charlestown Estate employees could now do any job on the dock for themselves, and found they could work 'gate-ho' and load ships with as few as 4-6 men, who might be carpenters, masons, plumbers or labourers as required. 'Gate-ho' was the traditional cry of the Harbour Master, shouted up the dock which creates a natural echo, when a ship wanted to enter or leave. As well as a shout, someone would go round the houses and tap on the windows shouting 'gate-ho', to get the men out if not already at work somewhere. A large bell, hung on an iron gantry at the end of the weighbridge, would be rung by the office Clerk at the appropriate time in the morning for Estate work to start, at noon for the mid-day break and in the afternoon to finish. This bell disappeared around 1946-7, and we would very much like to know where it now is? It was replaced by an electric Klaxton horn which served the same function for a time. Since employment as a dock porter originally required a man to live below the Rashleigh Arms, so that he was close to work, they were always on hand when called out. As time went on, so the work force lived further afield, and time keeping became their own responsibility, the alarm clock taking over from the Charlestown bell.

Charlestown's one and only murder took place in October 1969. Nine year old Debbie Williams, who lived with her mother Margaret, step sister Mandy and step-father Peter Williams, at No. 63 Charlestown Road, one of the old 'Front Row' cottages on the bend in Duporth Road, was reported missing early one evening. A party of villagers volunteered to assist the police in their search of the woods and pond areas, setting out on a cold blustery Saturday night. Just after midnight, Shirley Mathieson found her naked body face down in a ditch on the side of the Tregorrick Road. An immediate murder enquiry was launched, the father, Peter Williams being arrested and charged on the Monday. Williams confessed to a long history of incest with his step-daughter and was sentenced to 17 years in prison, serving somewhat less than the full term.

Management of the Estate continued until Walter Bulteel retired, when a contract to act as estate managing agents was given to Stratton Holborow Ltd, of Truro. Their first appointed agent was a Mr. Wilton, followed by a Mr. Onslow and finally John Newey, who managed the Estate for the directors from 1970 until Charlestown was sold in 1985. During that period there were many problems and changes in the village. By 1971 the old oak gates had to be replaced, a new single steel gate, built by Devoran Engineering, worked by wire cables and an electric winch, being installed. This necessitated a cofferdam across the mouth of the dock entrance, widening of the entrance to take larger vessels and the creation of a concrete 'pit' in the dock floor into which the gate could fit when lowered. The work took some three months, during which time the dock was closed completely, earning no income. Unfortunately, 1971 was a very dry, hot summer, and coupled with the dozens of heavy lorries on the dock side taking away rubble, mud and rock, almost a third of the western wall collapsed into the dock overnight. Removing that material and rebuilding the wall added something like a further £10,000 to the cost of the overall job, the dock remaining closed almost all summer.

Several new companies started in Charlestown around 1970, such as Armech Ltd, Reg March's engineering business, which took over the lower floor of the big building at the entrance to Eleven Doors. Once Skinner's clay crushing mill, upstairs has served as a drill hall, dance hall, dancing school, organ manufacturing works, bicycle works and in many other activities. Reg March also started Charlestown Divers in the old Steamer Store, at the head of Barkhouse Lane, now The Charlestown Gallery (Don Austen). On leaving the Royal Navy in 1971, Richard Larn commenced work on the old Conservative Hall building with Roger Parker, Chairman of Partech Electronics Ltd, fitting it out as an electronic production workshop, later taking over both floors of

Two views of the buildings which now house the Charlestown Shipwreck &
Heritage Centre. Above is shown the old clay stores as they were in 1976,
before it was converted into a two storey building, the upper floor now occupied
by the Bosuns Diner. *The doorway on the left, now leads into the Centre's*
gift-shop.

the building previously occupied by Armech Ltd. Partech Electronics
is now a leading manufacturer of water quality measuring instrumenta-
tion, their equipment installed in sewage and water treatment works in
almost every country in the world. Following on from Partech, Roger
Parker and Richard Larn went on to fit out the Long Store in Duporth
Road as a commercial diving school, opened in 1972 as Prodive Ltd, a
subsidiary of Partech (Electronics) Ltd. With only one other such civil-
ian training establishment in Gt. Britain, and the North Sea oil and gas
industry clamouring for commercial divers, Prodive trained many hundreds of young men for this new industry, setting standards that eventually became enshrined in new HSE legislation regarding diver
training and safety. Recognition of the work done in Charlestown and
at Fort Bovisand, Plymouth, the other diving centre, was rewarded
when both schools were given MSC (Manpower Services Commission)
training recognition, which allowed them to accept trainees on government sponsored commercial diving courses of 12 weeks duration. Many
of the older residents of Charlestown will remember classes of fit, noisy
young men, accommodated in No. 6 Quay Road, between 1972 and
1978, who were fed in the Pier House Hotel; of the early morning physical training sessions on the dock side, diving in the outer basin and
dock in all weathers, often at 3 am, and the long hours they spent

The Charlestown Shipwreck & Heritage Centre as it is today, with the old Scarborough lifeboat, diving observation chamber and armoured diving dress as outside exhibits.

underwater in the huge indoor tank in the Longstore, learning to weld and cut steel. Their final examinations over, they would organise huge end of course parties, frequently lasting all night, in that little cottage overlooking the dock, managed by Keith & Lindsay Righton, managers of the Pier House. The Long Store, once a rigging shop on the lower floor, with block making on top, a china clay store, a cement store, farm store and then a diving school, is now earmarked to be converted into four cottages; a long and interesting history. Prodive Ltd left Charlestown in 1978, moving to larger, more suitable waterfront premises in Falmouth Docks. Other new businesses included J.D.L. Trailers (John Lowe) operating from the old school building, The Cornish Smoked Fish Co, initially the Smoked Mackerel Co (Martin Pumphrey) and the Shipwreck Centre.

The largest development in Charlestown since the building of the Lovering Clay Dries, was the conversion of part of the lower clay dry into a visitors' centre, which today in nationally renowned as the Charlestown Shipwreck & Heritage Centre. After some 30 years Royal Navy, commercial and sport diving activity, the authors had collected a large and varied amount of shipwreck artefacts and relics, which were rapidly turning the old Prodive building into something of a museum. An approach to Charlestown Estate at Easter 1976, to rent a suitable building to open as a shipwreck centre, ended up with an agreement that the authors would supply the contents and the Estate the premises,

177

which they would administer on a day to day basis. On being asked the jackpot question, 'how many visitors do you think such a centre would have in a year?' we guessed at 5,000. After opening for a token three months in 1976 to meet the conditions of a modest tourism grant, the first full season in 1977 showed that 55,000 people had passed through the gate! Building on success, the Centre was doubled in size by the Estate over the winter of 1981, to include an audio-visual theatre, an exhibition area twice its original size, a restaurant and toilets, utilising the old single- storied clay stores attached, which had previously been used as garages. Opened by the Minister for Tourism in spring 1981, the Centre won the award that year for the best tourist development. The Centre is now owned by John & Rita Kneale, with the shipwreck contents owned by the authors, and enjoys an international reputation for the quality and range of its exhibits. The Centre has literally the largest collection of shipwreck artefacts on public display in the United Kingdom, which now includes the John Bevan Historic Diving Collection. Visitors of Charlestown may be surprised to know there are some 23 active commercial businesses trading in the village, with a gross annual turnover of many millions of pounds.

Friendly ghosts of the past haunt every corner of Charlestown. No longer do Dorothy & Hilda Batterscombe run their dancing classes upstairs in what is now Partech (Electronics) office, nor does blind 'Grannie' Lucking clean for Miss Hitchen's at Pond House, having worked there for 23 years for 1s.6d (7.7p) a day without an increase. Poor 'Grannie' contacted measles as a young girl and when her eyes hurt her mother put poultices over them, which literally drew them out of their sockets, blinding her for life. After being burgled, Miss Hitchen's changed night into day, and spent the hours of darkness walking around Charlestown and Porthpean, sleeping all day. No longer are musical concerts held in the upper floor of the Rank Store, and Ben, the son of Joe Wilkinson, the Harbour Master, no longer proudly rides his Harley Davison motor cycle, the first in the area, around Quay Road. Seine nets no longer adorn the outer walls of the quay, nor Looe fishermen sleep overnight on their nets in the *Content* fish cellar, and gone are the days when church concerts, given by the Artillery Volunteer Band and Wesleyan chapel choir were held on the island in the centre of the Higher Pond.

The sound of wheelwrights' tools no longer ring out from the workshop alongside No. 151 Charlestown Road, nor the blacksmiths a few yards higher; postman Pope has long gone from his cottage in Brick Hill; Captain Deacon no longer leaves his old house on the corner at No.103 to take the children for Sunday school in the chapel; his talks so interesting about life at sea, the building was always full. The weighbridge has gone from outside No.107, and the last village policeman, PC Hocking no longer lives there. Another Hocking was the undertaker, who made a mental note of everyone's physical build and, on hear-

Some of the characters of Charlestown, dressed in period costume, engaged as film extras for the making of 'Darwin's Voyage of Discovery' in the port, in the 1970s.

From left to right: 'Hank' Hancock; Dennis Burrows; 'Doug' Side; Gordon Rogers; Donald Littleton; 'Jim' Isbell; 'Dobber' Kellaway; 'Fred' Glover; 'Charlie' Walkey; 'Bill' Charteris; Mark Bawden.

ing of a serious illness would knock up a suitable coffin, then go to the end of the road and wait for the news! – he too has gone. *Angle House*, which once stood just about where the roundabout is at the top of St. Austell by-pass, and where Peter Bishop was born and brought up, has long been pulled down, as have the tennis courts behind Church Lane, and in Skinner's field. Jackie Hosegood no longer lifts 2cwt clay casks by himself to stand them two high, still working with a shovel on the dock at 80 years of age, and we all miss Donald Littleton, the estate foreman and so many of his old staff. Wonderful, lively, irreplacable characters all of them, people that were the heart and soul of this lovely Cornish port. God bless them, may they rest in peace.

By 1984, all imports into Charlestown had ceased, fertiliser being the last incoming cargo. The limitation in length of motor coasters that could enter the dock was now causing a worrying decline in trade for the owners, and it was patently obvious that real money would soon have to be spent on the property generally, especially the housing stock, with many new roofs required. Many properties still had no bathroom, equally as many with flush toilets at the end of the garden, and rents

'Jackie' Hosegood, who died in 1946, aged 91. Grandfather of Arthur Hosegood, 'Jackie', who was illiterate, tattooed all over and always wore two gold ear rings, had been mate of the Dashwood. *He worked as a dock porter at Charlestown after retiring from the sea, always taking a gallon of beer to work each day. Immensely strong, even in later years he could lift and stack 224lb (2cwt) casks of clay on top of each other.*

were still ridiculously low, some in the order of £5 a week. After a lifetime of Estate management, offering low rents, security and, to many, a job for life, there was no reason to suspect that things would ever change. The Crowder family would always be in the background, sleepy little Charlestown, still virtually undiscovered by tourists, would never change. The village was understandably unprepared for what was about to happen.

Chapter 3   Reference sources

No.	Source
1	St. Austell Star, 9.1.1891
2	" " " 16.1.1891
3	" " " 30.1.1891
4	" " " 17.7.1891
5	" " " 25.6.1891
6	" " " 6.9.1891
7	" " " 9.10.1891
8	ibid
9	St. Austell Star, 15.1.1892
10	" " " 22.1.1892
11	" " " 26.2.1892
12	Charlestown Estate Letter Books
13	ibid
14	St. Austell Star, 4.11.1892
15	" " " 15.12.1892
16	" " " 13.1.1893
17	" " " 10.2.1893
18	" " " 7.4.1893
19	Charlestown Estate Letter Books
20	ibid
21	ibid and CCC. CRO. DD.CF.743/1
22	Charlestown Estate Letter Books
23	St. Austell Gazette & Mid Cornwall Advertiser, 25.3.1897
24	" " " " " " 24.6.1897
25	" " " " " " 1.7.1897
26	" " " " " " 29.7.1897
27	ibid
28	Charlestown Estate Letter Books
29	St. Austell Gazette & Mid Cornwall Advertiser, 21.11.1897
30	" " " " " " 28.11.1897
31	Charlestown Estate Letter books
32	ibid
33	120 Years of Engineering at Charlestown, CCC. CRO.
34	ibid
35	Charlestown Estate Letter books
36	Lloyd's War Losses, First World War, p153 & Wooden Ships and Iron Men, Bainbridge. G, 1980 p42

37	Lloyd's War Losses, First World War, p24
38	Lloyd's War Losses, First World War, p201
39	Charlestown Estate Letter Books
40	Transcript of interview with William H. Stark, 1994
41	Charlestown Letter Books
42	St. Austell Star, 30.10.1924 & 6.11.1924
43	" " " 6.11.1924
44	" " " 1.1.1925 p6
45	" " " 11.8.1925 p6
46	" " " 13.11.1924 p7
47	Transcript of interview with Charles Walkie, 1979
48	" " " " Mrs. Facey, 1979
49	120 Years of Engineering at Charlestown, CCC. CRO.
50	Charlestown Primary School Log Book, 1938-1972
51	" " " Punishment Book, 1897-1966
52	Mine Warfare Vessels, Cocker. M.P. 1993, p82-86
53	120 Years of Engineering at Charlestown, CCC. CRO.

CHAPTER 9

The Face of Change. 1985 – 1994

The retirement of Walter Bulteel in 1963, the last of the old fashioned estate managers, brought to an end a long history of squirearchies and tradition. Richard Stratton & Geoffrey Holborow (Stratton & Holborow, Land Agents and Chartered Surveyors) of Truro, were then asked by the directors to carry out a valuation of the property owned by Charlestown Estate Ltd and, well pleased with their work, the Estate invited them to manage their affairs on a part time basis. Initially Mr. Michael Wilton, followed by a Mr. Denzel Onslow, spent one or two days a week in the estate office, the agents then introducing John Newey who, acting on their behalf as sub-Agent, was instrumental in getting the accounts and management of the port on a more business-like footing. His position eventually become that of a full time sub agent, with a contract to manage the entire estate, overseeing the widening of the dock entrance, the installation of the new gate and, in 1976, the conversion of the lower clay dry buildings to a visitors' centre, followed by its expansion in 1981.

By 1984, Petre Crowder, Managing Director of Charlestown Estate Ltd had decided to sell Charlestown, allegedly under pressure from his own two sons and Mrs Ann Smyth-Osbourne's, his sister who was a fellow director in the estate, despite a gross turnover of £529,000. Whilst pure speculation on the part of the authors, the decision was probably based on the certainty that the volume of clay shipped out from Charlestown was already in terminal decline. The new steel dock gate installed in 1971 at great expense was also now three-quarters of the way through its anticipated life span and, if history repeated itself, would soon start to give trouble, eventually requiring replacement sometime in the 1990s. Should the gate collapse or distort due to storm action, so that it could no longer retain the level of water necessary for shipping, then the port would close, and the then average port gross income of £112,752, which yielded a profit of £84,981, would become a loss. In addition there loomed the cost of a new gate, which would certainly exceed £100,000. There was also the problem of an ageing stock of early 19th century housing, which required constant expensive repairs, and whose rental return barely covered the costs. Put into perspective, the majority would probably agree that the directors of Charlestown Estate Ltd were in an unenviable position, and one in which disposal of a mounting liability was the most sensible course of action for them to take.

To this end a private sale document was prepared in 1984, which was

Clay being loaded down chutes from the tramway, mounted on a gantry, running half the length of the dock on the east side. The vessel is the Dutch coaster Twente, *photographed during the late 1950s.*

given a limited distribution to investors who would possibly be interested in the outright purchase of Charlestown; these included the National Trust and English China Clays. Sight of the sale document by a private individual filtered back to the village, causing wide-spread speculation, rumours and a considerable degree of concern amongst the 160 or so tenants, especially since throughout 1984-5 cottages were left empty when occupants moved out. Previously the estate had always maintained a waiting list of those seeking to take on rented property in Charlestown, but now the village took on the air of a ghost town as more and more properties were left empty, the reason for which soon becoming obvious. The potential sale featured on the front page of the Western Morning News on 18 July 1985, when it was suggested that the asking price could be £4 million, a figure on which a spokesman for Stratton & Holborow said he could not comment. The press quickly picked up that the National Trust might be interested, the Trust's regional director in Cornwall, Richard Meyrick, commenting, 'In the event of a sale, the National Trust would consider the case very carefully. Charlestown must be regarded as a very important heritage property.' Stratton & Holborow, who had already opened a branch office in Charlestown, by building an upper storey over part of the old Estate

The interior of an unidentified cooperage, possibly one at Mount Charles, c1930. Charlestown had three cooperages, the largest being that of the Rowse brothers. The dry casks shown being assembled were used solely for china clay.

Office, giving improved accommodation for their increased staff, then sought to secure their position before the village was sold. This led to them obtaining a lease on the entire building, renting back the lower floor to Charlestown Estate Ltd, conducting all the estate business from there.

By late September 1986, a spokesman for the London firm of solicitors, Boodle Hatfield, announced in the press a change of ownership, shareholders and directors. In fact John Tomalin, a London based investor, who specialised in identifying various properties that had 'break-up' potential, had seized on the opportunity offered by Charlestown. Putting together a consortium of ten individuals, which included himself, the Earl of Shaftesbury, who lives at Wimborne, Dorset, and Commander Osborne King, they purchased the property outright under the name of the Charlestown Partnership. Negotiations were completed through Town West Properties, and Charlestown changed hands for an unsubstantiated figure of £2.5 million. At this stage the National Trust's information officer Giles Clotworthy stated publicly that, 'We were given the opportunity of looking at it as a possible acquisition and were then, and still are, concerned about the fate of such a fascinating and historic part of Cornwall's industrial heritage.

However, the main attraction of Charlestown is as a working port. Ownership by the Trust would not help the port to continue to operate. We therefore did not believe the Trust was the right body to take on Charlestown.'

The Crowder's period of ownership can literally be described as a dynasty, which ended more abruptly than Petre Crowder had anticipated. Still living in *Pond House*, his wife was rushed to hospital with a broken hip after falling on the quay, leaving her husband to pack up generations of family history and depart 'by close of business' on the day of sale, or risk the deal falling through, forcing him to make a somewhat hasty and ignominious departure.

The new owners immediately approached Restormel Borough Council's Planning Officer with ideas for widescale development of the village, only to find that things were going to be difficult. In order to achieve a quick profit, a cottage portfolio in two lots was prepared and offered for sale privately, the Charlestown village properties being bought up by the Northumberland & Durham Property Trust Ltd, the Holmbush properties by Laira Properties of Plymouth. The amount raised cleared the investment, so that the remaining property, the port, commercial properties and cottages, including a vast acreage of surrounding green belt farmland, many derelict or empty plots and all the side access roads and lanes in the village represented their profit. Following a further sale of property the following year, they were now taking the long term view. Of the planning applications submitted, only that for Penrice Park was granted, initially for a retail food store, but this land was later purchased by Swan Developments, in order to build the new housing estate opposite Penrice School. They also disposed of the Walled Garden behind the *Beeches*, through Stratton & Holborow, as a building plot, of 0.57 acres, for £58,700, the equivalent of over £100,000 an acre. With interest rates very high and pressure on the directors to return a profit, the partnership instructed Conrad Ritblat, the London auctioneers, to sell the remainder of Charlestown as one lot, including the port, beaches, Rashleigh Arms, Pier House Hotel, all the commercial premises, and some 40 residential properties, according to the sale catalogue of 10 September 1987. However, it should be stressed that Charlestown was just one of some 30-40 similar lots offered for sale at that auction, and was in no way exceptional.

Issued in July, the sale catalogue caught the attention of literally dozens of property developers from all over the country, who saw Charlestown as a wonderful opportunity for asset stripping and potential development. For six weeks prior to the sale, chauffeur driven Rolls Royce, Bentley and BMW cars and even helicopters, disgorged sleek business men who poked into every corner of the village, took hundreds of photographs, patronised the locals and spent most of their time talking to London contacts on their portable telephones, probably trying to raise money. After two centuries of rural obscurity, running

An aerial view of Charlestown taken in 1975. The vessels in dock include the ill-fated Marques, *a sailing brig based here for several years, which sank off the West Indies in 1984 with the loss of 20 lives. There is a wooden fishing boat under construction by John Moore, outside his old Bark House Lane workshop. What is now the car park was still an active coal yard.*

on a shoestring, the village suddenly became the focal point of big business, where everyone seemed to buy for millions, retain the areas they wanted, then sold again for more millions, everyone seemingly making a profit. It is believed that Charlestown Partnership placed a £2.5 million reserve on their sale, which was not reached on the day of auction, since the lot was withdrawn. One of the men at that sale was property developer Stephen Lucas, of Newbury, who approached the auctioneer after the sale closed making an offer of £2.6 million (according to the Cornish Guardian). The offer accepted, Lucas signed an agreement to purchase and wrote out a deposit cheque for £250,000, but when presented to the bank the following day, it bounced, whereupon the matter was placed in the hands of solicitors. It did however serve to buy Stephen Lucas some time, which is probably what he wanted, knowing he did not have the money but was keen not to lose the opportunity. His first move was to ring the Estate Office in Charlestown from his car whilst on the M.1, the day after the sale, to ask exactly where the village was! After a very brief visit to see what he had bought, during which time he hardly got out of his car, he then approached David Bulstrode, the 47-year-old Jersey based millionaire chairman of Marler Estates, which owned three London soccer stadiums, BOM Holdings and Queens Park Rangers. He agreed to put up the purchase money in the name of BOM. Holdings plc (British Oil & Minerals), which must have been a considerable relief to Stephen Lucas, who would otherwise have faced court proceedings. BOM. Holdings was in fact a 'shell' company, whose major asset was an old oil refinery near Southend-on-Sea, on which it was intended to develop a leisure park.

With Queens Park Rangers playing a friendly mid-season match at Truro in January 1988, David Bulstrode, after watching the match and playing a round of golf at Perranporth, took the opportunity to visit Charlestown and was interviewed and photographed by the press standing on the dock gate. Meanwhile, during those four months, asset stripping had already started, with nine vacant properties, including the old Harbour Master's House, being auctioned off by Allsop & Co, at the Mayfair Intercontinental Hotel, London, on 15 December 1987. Those properties alone raised £482,000 and 32 other tenanted properties were sold to Northumberland & Durham Property Trust for an undisclosed sum, probably in the order of £1,200,000. When interviewed by a Western Morning News reporter, Mr Bulstrode commented, 'We intend to retain the leisure aspect of Charlestown and a separate company under my chairmanship, will be formed specifically to look after those interests. Charlestown will become more of a holiday village. That is inevitable. We don't want drastic change but to enliven the village without spoiling its attractiveness – which in itself is a valuable investment and will be protected.' He denied that existing residents in Charlestown would be unable to afford the asking price for the new-look village shops and houses he planned. He did not foresee the

Duporth Manor, Charles Rashleigh's home, being demolished in 1988. Part of the Duporth Holiday Park, the building had fallen into disrepair and had to be taken down. Much of the granite and interior fittings were reused elsewhere.

changes causing any problems in making Charlestown a more attractive place in which to live, work or visit.

Matthew Taylor, the Liberal MP, whose Truro constituency includes Charlestown, sought written confirmation on behalf of residents that the interests of the tenants would be protected. 'Charlestown has an ageing population and many more properties will eventually come onto the market with vacant possession,' he said. 'It seems clear that, with prices being set by London rather than local buyers, many generations rooted in Charlestown will come to an end.' Elsewhere in the country of course, outside of Cornwall, such business dealings are common place. Sentiment plays no part in the buying and selling of people's homes in towns and cities, where community spirit and a sense of belonging were swallowed up long ago in the sprawl of development. In Cornwall, where people frequently live their entire lives within a 10 mile radius of where they were born, taking pride in primarily being Cornish, and then identifying themselves as Charlestown born, such treatment was totally alien.

Overnight, rents, which admittedly were very low, increased considerably and following a second increase, many residents simply left, particularly those with only short-hold leases or no lease at all. Regrettably, the possibility of being unable to continue to afford to live in Charlestown took its toll on at least one resident, Donald Littleton, retired Charlestown Estate foreman and carpenter. Invited to Plymouth to express his views on what was happening in Charlestown in a local television news programme, he was so stressed by the situation that on returning to St. Austell, he stopped to rest on a seat at the top of Charlestown Road, where he died of a heart attack, not being found until some hours later. In fact, many of the fears expressed concerning eviction or of people being priced out of their homes proved to be groundless. Many tenants were given the opportunity to purchase their freehold, becoming property owners for the first time in their lives. If rents now appear high, it must be said that the housing stock of Charlestown is in a better state of repair than it has ever been.

The village was again thrown into confusion in June 1988 when David Bulstrode died of a heart attack, apparently a happy man. Seizing the initiative, Stephen Lucas, of Newbury, Berkshire, and Barry Williamson of Braintree, Essex, borrowed heavily and bought what was left of Charlestown from BOM Holdings. They then created a development plan for Charlestown that was quite unbelievable, involving 1,500 sq.ft of light industrial units, 38,000 sq.ft of retail accommodation, 4,000 sq.ft of offices, 156 new cottages, houses and flats – and a band-stand, the latter being some sort of gesture to the residents, 'who like their brass bands' Lucas was heard to say! Prior to the Lucas/Williamson take over, BOM Holdings had engaged Stratton & Holborow to continue to manage the port for them, but on hearing of the collapse of that company following Mr. Bulstrode's death, when share prices went to the floor, they rightly sought assurances regarding their future position. Receiving no reply, the new owners refusing to put anything in writing or to agree management terms, Stratton & Holborow relinquished the management of the port completely.

Local architect Alan Leather Associates were then engaged to prepare plans for the envisaged development, which were kept secret until unveiled on the day of 'The Party', Tuesday 26 July 1988. In conversation with the authors concerning the Shipwreck Centre earlier in the year, Stephen Lucas had commented, 'I bet this village has never had a real party – I'll tell you what I'm going to do, I will give them a party, one they will never forget.' How right he was – the residents are still talking about it, six years later! Preparation commenced long before the 26th, with gilt edged invitations sent out to over 300 people, which included every resident of the village, the mayor, Restormel Borough Council planning officials, Councillors and others. A huge marquee was hired and erected over the top of a temporary wooden stage floor in the car park, the floor necessary to counter the natural slope and uneveness of the ground beneath. Inside crisp, starched, white tablecloths covered dozens of side tables, loaded down with a magnificent buffet, including lobster, crab, salmon and game. Dozens of boxes of wine of every sort stood ready to be served by uniformed waiters and waitresses, whilst outside a jazz band played, flags fluttered in the breeze, the

The short street in Charlestown known as Eleven Doors *or* China Town, *a Victorian development of farm buildings which saw the front doors of eleven buildings facing onto a small lane. It acquired its nickname from visiting sailors, who sought and presumably found drinking dens and ladies of easy virtue there.*

sun shone, and even the St. John's Ambulance Corps were in attendance in unusual strength – strangely fortuitous in the circumstances, whilst at the entrance security guards denied admission to the press, television, and anyone without a pass.

On every seat in the marquee was a beautifully presented pack of information, 'Charlestown 2000', with loose sheets showing the Lucas/Williamson plan for the village, a superbly arranged, organised, orchestrated attempt to win over the village to support their development plan, which had it been allowed to proceed, would have destroyed the unique nature of Charlestown for ever. On top of each information pack lay a large yellow card bearing the words, 'Yes – I vote for Charlestown', which were intended for a hopefully unanimous show of support when called for. As someone remarked on the day, 'I notice the reverse side doesn't give you a chance to say No!'

The people arrived dressed for a party, the sun continued to shine and it stayed warm and dry. To a packed audience first Stephen Lucas and then Barry Williamson made their presentation, followed by Arthur Hosegood, one of the oldest village residents. The architects were then explaining in detail the development of each individual site, inviting the audience to follow their plan using the individual presentation packs when, without warning, events came to an abrupt and cataclysmic end as the floor groaned, lurched, then collapsed. People were thrown out of their seats, others to the floor, many into the half metre void beneath the floor, women screamed, loudspeakers and the podium fell over, food tables crashed down, glasses broke and panic ensued.

In all fairness the entire presentation was a superb and expensive piece of showmanship, with quality printing, excellent drawings, and very well organised services, on which the owners and architects were to be congratulated. If there is a God in Heaven, the timing was as if He had pointed an exasperated finger down at Charlestown and said, 'Lucas, that's enough,' bringing the whole show to an abrupt end. The staff showed great presence of mind, chairs were whipped outside, the elderly were helped up and sat down with a glass of wine in their hand, the few minor injuries were treated by the ambulance crew, the band played, food was served and the near catastrophe soon forgotten in the heat of the afternoon. In fact the party went on for the rest of the day and well into the evening, until all the food and drink had been consumed, but there never was a 'Charlestown 2000' vote and the little yellow cards never served their intended purpose.

In the meantime, the villagers had rightly formed a Resident's Association under the Chairmanship of Postmaster Geoffrey Beare, whilst various assets within the village continued to be sold off. These included the Rashleigh Arms, Partech Electronics, the Schoolhouse Joinery, the Smoked Mackerel Co, the hairdressers and Post Office etc. which gave the owners some working capital. However, they were already in financial trouble regarding payment of the interest on the money borrowed, let alone repayment of the capital. Restormel Borough Council drastically reduced the sheaf of planning applications submitted, leaving only those which involved the enhancement or refurbishment of existing properties, and the owners announced in the Western Morning News on 3 March 1990, that 'their £12 million scheme for Charlestown had been put on the back-burner'.

During this period the owners were raising various tiers of mortgage on the property, involving a Swiss Bank and the Trustee Savings Bank, who by May 1990 had called in the loan made to Swordhurst Ltd, the company headed by Barry Williamson and Suffolk businessman Peter Clapperton, Stephen Lucas having dropped out of the scene over a year before. The TSB then foreclosed on the property, so that ownership which had been in the hands of its subsidiary Target Holdings Ltd, was passed to Penfelton Ltd, who continued to run the port with Peter Clapperton as manager. The village was now in its fifth ownership in as many years, with uncertainty as to the future of the port itself, since by now there was very little left to sell. Peter Clapperton, acting for Target Holdings, and being paid some £4,000 a month for his services, held

Prior to the 1971 widening of the dock entrance, coasters such as this, the German Magda Wegener, *of Hamburg, would not have been able to enter Charlestown. Even so, there is little room to spare on either side, and when fully loaded, the state of the tide may dictate when a vessel can leave.*

Charlestown together for the next two and a half years, maintaining the flow of shipping – apart from a short period of dispute with a clay company. Peter Clapperton then purchased the port and remaining properties for himself, ownership changing for the sixth time since 1986 into the hands of his new company, Charlestown Heritage & Trading Company Ltd. It was this company that sold the Shipwreck Centre, car park and Ivy House to John & Rita Kneale, owners of the Cliff Head Hotel, and the Pier House Hotel to George & Rodney Morcom, owners of the Rashleigh Arms. Other properties sold included the Wrought Iron workshop, previously a blacksmiths but originally the *Rashleigh* pilchard cellar. Strangely enough, it had been Peter Clapperton who foresaw that Charlestown was ideally suited as a base for sailing ships as far back as March 1990, when he announced he intended to form a new company called Tall Ships Ltd, which would negotiate with sailing ship owners all over the country, to showcase their vessels at Charlestown. When finally the remaining property for sale was reduced to the port and beaches, the clay dry, the old heavy transport yard and a few workshop buildings on the west side of the dock, it was announced that all these, apart from the clay dry, had been purchased by Mr and Mrs Robin Davis, of Square Sail Shipyard Ltd, a Bristol based company with a fleet of square rigged ships. Square Sail took possession of the dock as of 18 October 1993, the seventh and hopefully last owner of the port in seven years, the eighth since it was conceived.

For Charlestown, the sensational attempt of an armed raid on the village Post Office on Saturday 17 April 1993, was indeed big news. The thwarted hold-up was made at 6.45am by Kenneth Hadley, 37, and Tony Cowles, 24, who with another couple, drove overnight from Scunthorpe, all the way to Charlestown to make the raid. Arriving in the village at 5.45am and finding the shop closed, they were forced to drive around for an hour, until it opened. Hadley then pushed an imitation gun into Mrs Gillian Burley's back, while Cowles demanded she open the safe. With immense courage she told them that the keys were upstairs, that it was a bit early and that they should try somewhere else! Mrs Burley advised them that her husband Adrian, along with other male relatives were upstairs, whereupon the two men drove off at speed. A local man, out early to collect his newspaper, noticed the car was not local and suspicious, noted its number. As a result the police stopped and arrested the would-be robbers within 45 minutes. On 1 July 1993, at Truro Crown Court, Judge Graham Neville sentenced both men to five and a half years in prison.

Looking back over these pages, which cover 247 years of history, it can be seen that Charlestown has had its share of troubles and probably always will. Its founder was bankrupted by the port, the Crowders continued their ownership under sufferance, never really making any serious profit after the 1800s simply because the port was never large enough for 20th century shipping. Only during the past eight years have the various owners seen a substantial return on their investment, but only at the expense of their assets. With the port the very heart of Charlestown, the very reason for its inception and for almost 200 years its main employer and source of income, it would appear that whoever its owner there are only a limited number of options as to its future. To continue the existing clay trade for as long as the older, fast disappearing generation of small coasters allow, which is certainly a maximum of ten years, probably less – and then what? Or to make alterations to the basin entrance to allow longer, hence larger coasters to enter, which could prolong the clay trade for many years to come, providing that Charlestown can continue to be competitive. However, the second option, apart from being very expensive, would risk exposing the existing dock gate to heavy weather, with possibly serious damage. The size of the dock and the limitation on any possible expansion, coupled with the fact the gate can only be opened for short periods at each tide, makes Charlestown totally unsuitable as a leisure marina. Square Sail Shipyard's current use of the dock as a base for sailing ships is therefore aesthetically ideal, but whether this generates sufficient income for the company is the owner's business. Had there been sufficient and suitable space close to the sea to create a shipyard, then it is likely that a replica warship of the early 1700s would already be under construc-

The three-masted 450 ton barque Kaskelot, *meaning sperm-whale in Danish, made her first appearance in Charlestown during the summer of 1993, for film-making in connection with* The Three Musketeers, *featuring Charlie Sheen. Here a carriage and four with horsemen arrive alongside at night.*

195

tion in Charlestown by Square Sail's workforce. However, there are now a considerable number of 'tall ships' in this country which, particularly in winter, require a secure sheltered berth with specialised overhaul and maintenance facilities. With a decline in the traditional skills of sailmaking, rigging, splicing, blockmaking, blacksmithing and shipwrights, all of which are now available in Charlestown, the port may yet become a centre for such maritime activity.

For the first time since 1825, the port of Charlestown has a resident owner, instead of an absentee landlord, and without question the port, the very heart of Charlestown, previously cushioned financially by the income of a private estate that no longer exists, has to produce revenue if it is to survive.

Certain privileges within the old estate, understandably taken for granted over 160 years of the Crowder era, may no longer be acceptable to individual freeholders, and some change is inevitable.

As always throughout history, however, it is the people of Charlestown who have made this short account of a Cornish port possible, who continue to fascinate – who give life to the buildings, the work places and the homes. If you close your eyes and reach out, the fingertips of each generation can touch those who have gone before and those who come after – and the story of Charlestown can only continue from here.

A new chapter commences in Charlestown's history. The Kaskelot *enters her home port on 26 March 1994, to join the reproduction* Santa Maria *(ex. Phoenix), part of a fleet of sailing ships owned by Square Sail Shipyard Ltd who now own the port of Charlestown.*

APPENDIX 1

Chronological list of historic events concerning Charlestown.

1747 – Charles Rashleigh born at Menabilly

1764 – Rashleigh became an articled clerk to Francis Polkinghorn

Appointed Steward and Land Agent for Menabilly

Rashleigh's father, Jonathan Rashleigh MP. FRS. FSA. died

1769 – Rashleigh qualified as an Attorney-at-Law in London

Started legal practice at 36 Lincoln's Inn Field, London

Purchased town house in St. Austell (now the *White Hart* Hotel)

1774 – Rashleigh started first St . Austell bank

Rashleigh met Grace Tremayne, of Helligan Manor

1776 – Rashleigh became engaged to Grace Tremayne

Rashleigh married Grace Tremayne

1778 – Rashleigh appointed Under Sheriff of Cornwall (1st term)

1779 – Harriet Rashleigh born at St. Austell (1st daughter)

Rashleigh appointed Deputy Town Clerk for Tregony

Rashleigh purchased land for his Duporth Estate

1781 – Rashleigh's mother Mary died at Menabilly

Rashleigh appointed steward to the Duchy of Cornwall

Martha Rashleigh born at St. Austell (2nd daughter)

Duporth Manor completed, Rashleigh's threw a 'house-warming'

1782 – Rashleigh appointed Under Sheriff of Cornwall (2nd term)

1784 – Rashleigh attends court concerning Manor of Tewington

1786 – Rashleigh acquires lease of Tewington Manor and Porthmear

1789 – Sophia Rashleigh born at Duporth Manor (3rd daughter)

1790 – Work commenced on building outer quay at Porthmear

Joseph Dingle appointed Superintendent of Works at Porthmear

1791 – Rashleigh appointed Under Sheriff of Cornwall (3rd term)

1792 – Work commenced on excavation of inner dock at Charlestown

Cliff battery established for 4×18lb cannon

1793 – Shipwright's yard established, some small vessels launched

1794 – Port leat cut from Luxulyan to Porthmear

1795 – Crinnis Cliff Artillery unit formed

1798 – Local volunteer cavalry and infantry units raised

Rashleigh appointed Recorder to Bodmin & Town Clerk to St.Austell. Purchased the Manor of Tewington from the Duchy

1799 – First dock gates erected

Duporth Cup presented, name of Charles's Town first used

1801 – Rashleigh appointed Steward to the Duchy of Lancaster

1804 – Charlestown's first iron foundry opened

1805 – Balance owing by Joseph Dingle to Rashleigh, now £15,000

1811 – Rashleigh took Joseph Dingle to court, now owed £23,000

1814 – Chancery suit threatened against Rashleigh by nephew William

1818 – Fifty persons left Charlestown to emigrate to America

1820 – Grace Rashleigh died, buried in St. Austell cemetery

Work commenced on the rival port of Pentewan
Joseph Daniel obtained title to Duporth Manor by fraud

1823 – Charles Rashleigh died at Duporth, buried at St. Austell

Charlestown pier suffered severe storm damage

1824 – Second smelting house opened in Charlestown

1825 – Ownership of Charlestown changed hands

First full survey and inventory of Charlestown land

1826 – Pentewan port opened

1833 – Charlestown's 'hot & cold seawater baths' opened

1840 – William Pearse Banks relinquished shipyard to Anthony Luke

1846 – Charlestown Cornish Railway Company agreement

1850 – Wreck of the *John & Henry* schooner in the outer basin

1851 – Rashleigh Arms built on foundations of old clay cellars

St. Paul's Church completed and consecrated

1854 – Wreck of the *Heir of Madron* outside Charlestown Harbour

1857 – Charlestown's Naptha Works offered for sale

1860 – 18 pdr. guns in Battery exchanged for 4×28 pdr's

1861 – Gun Battery became officially No. 4 Battery, Cornwall Artillery Volunteers

1864	–	Proposal to enlarge harbour and bring in a branch rail line
1868	–	14 ton block of granite from Luxulyan shipped in the dock
1869	–	Charlestown Reading Room & Library opened
1871	–	William Luke, shipbuilder and owner, died
		Charlestown had the oldest Methodist alive in the world
1873	–	Dock extended in length
1884	–	28 pdr. cannon in the Battery exchanged for 32 pdrs
1885	–	Foundry changed ownership Henry J. Bulteel appointed estate agent
1887	–	Severe drought caused both leat ponds to dry up.
		Pumps used
1889	–	Wesleyan Methodist Chapel refurbished
1890	–	New dock gates fitted
1891	–	Dock lit by oil lamps, following three drownings
1891	–	The 'Great Blizzard' closed Charlestown Road and dock
		Mount Charles cooper's strike
1892	–	Sale of Charlestown considered to a third party
		Severe gale washed away part of the outer basin wall 68 pdr howitzer gun added to the 32 pdr Battery cannon
1893	–	An estimated 6,000 tons of cliff fell on the eastern beach
1895	–	Charlestown Infants School opened

Vicarage built for St. Paul's church

1897 – Artillery Volunteer's disbanded, Battery closed

1905 – St. Austell Gas Company considered a gasometer at Charlestown

1913 – Duporth Road (Brick Hill) adopted and widened by the Council

1916 – Work force greatly reduced as workers went into the army

1920 – Gas main laid in Charlestown Road, street lighting installed

1924 – Henry Bulteel died, his son Walter appointed estate agent

1924 – Duporth Manor and estate sold at auction

1925 – Charlestown Road surfaced with tarmacadam for first time

1935 – Foundry purchased by English China Clays

1940 – Foundry engaged in war contracts; evacuees in Charlestown

      – Bomb dropped on Charlestown, first in Cornwall

      – Dock taken over for fitting out mine-sweepers

1948 – Dock gates removed for repairs

1961 – Sir John Ellenborough Crowder MP died, buried at Charlestown

1967 – 'Back Row' cottages pulled down, 'Front Row' given bathrooms

1969 – Debbie Williams, of Charlestown, aged nine years, found murdered near Duporth

1971 – New dock gates fitted

1976 – Shipwreck & Visitors Centre opened

1981 – Shipwreck & Heritage Centre enlarged and restaurant built

Lady Florance Gertrude Crowder died, buried at Charlestown

1986 – Charlestown sold to the Charlestown Partnership

1987 – Lower part of Charlestown sold to BOM Holdings plc

1988 – Stephen Lucas & Barry Williamson buy port and buildings

1990 – Target Holdings Ltd assume ownership of port and buildings

1991 – Charlestown Heritage & Trading Ltd purchased port

1993 – Port purchased by Square Sail Shipyard Ltd

APPENDIX 2

1851 Census return of Charlestown residents
in Charlestown Road

It should be noted that until the late 1920's, when the council first gave each property an official number and introduced the first road signs with names, houses in Charlestown were identified only by the occupant, since in such a small compact village everyone knew where everyone else lived. Hence, when the government authority made their 1851 Census return of occupants, the first such record made in the country, they started at Charlestown Mill, calling it No.1, working down hill until they reached No. 151 at the edge of the sea.

This numbering system was applied to all following census returns until, following the Council's intervention, they numbered the properties in reverse, commencing with *Salamander*, at the seaward end of Quay Road as No.1, working up hill.

It is therefore most likely that this 1851 record of property and occupants progressed down hill, along Church Road (Lane) and back, continuing down Charlestown Road, systematically working from side to side as the Census officers passed individual houses. It is unfortunate that only *Charlestown Mill* and the *Rashleigh Arms* are individually identified in the official document.

In the column marked children, 2s = 2 sons; 5d = 5 daughters; the last column 'others' includes relatives, friends etc. who were not paying lodgers, ie. 2gs = 2 grandsons etc.

House No.	Surname	Given Name	Occupation	Wife	Children/Oth	
1	*Charlestown Mill*					
	Gill	Phillip	Miller	Susan	2s. 5d	1
2	Kernick	Samuel	Tin Wks.Man'gr	Ann	1s. 2d	2
3	Curtes	William	Small farmer	Mary		
4	Bolemia	William	Engineer	Ann	2s. 1d	
5	Richards	Richard	Engineer	Mary	1s	
6	Osborne	Sydney	Iron moulder	Caroline	4d	
7	no tenant					
8	Stephens	Luke	Blacksmith	Ann		

204

9	Watts	Isaac	Pattern maker	Biary	1d	
10	Woolwork	Clavery	Not known	Emily		
11	Phillips	John	Miner	Dorothy	2s. 2d	
12	Binone	Richard	Clerk	Mary	1d	
13	Scaul	Edward	Labourer	Ann	2s	
14	Rosevean	–	Out pauper	Elizabeth	4s. 6d	
15	Stephens	–	Iron moulder	Mary	3s. 3d	
16	Hill	Peter	Carpenter	–	2s. 1d	
17	Gates	John	Labourer	–	1s. 2d	
18	Harpers	–	Miners wife	Phillipa	5s. 1d	
19	Tregonning	Joseph	Miner	–	1s. 2d	
20	Hammiss	John	Labourer	–	3s. 3d	
21	Furniger	John	Farmer	–	2s. 2d	
22	Hammiss	George	Blacksmith	–	2s	
23	Richards	James	Cooper	–	4s. 1d	
24	Eddy	Walter	Miner	–	4s. 1d	
25	Friginza	William	Tin miner	–	3s. 2d	
26	Bush	William	Miner & cooper	–	6s. 1d	
27	Williams	Stephen	Miner	–	2d	
28	Jenkins	William	Miner	Mary	3s. 5d	

(lodgers at this address, William Burt & William Rowe)

29	Burn	Richard	Carpenter	–	2s. 3d	
30	Henwood	William	Blacksmith	Jane		
31	Hodge	John	Farmer	–	2s. 2d.	2gs
32	Stanley	Thomas	Tailor	–	1s. 1d	
33	Barrett	William	Labourer	Mary	2s. 2d	
34	Chaganness	Thomas	Labourer	Sarah	2s. 3d	
35	Henrda	John	Labourer	Jane	4s. 2d	
36	Wood	George	Farmer	Elizabeth	3s. 2d	
37	Heal	Charles	Cordwainer	Elizabeth		
38	Lang	John	Iron smith	Catherine	1d	

39	Blewitt	Charles	Iron moulder	Mary	1s. 1d
40	Iewil	James	Blacksmith	Jane	1s. 3d
41	Hore	Philip	Farmer/carrier	Mary	2s. 4d
42	Cornish	–	Mariner's wife	Rachael	1s. 1d
43	Marhive	John	Stone mason	Mary	1s. 1d
44	Melwish	–	Mariner's wife	Eveline	1s
45	Thomas	James	Engineer	Elizabeth	2s. 4d
46	Hase	James	Ropemaker	Elizabeth	1s. 1d
47	Dyess	Nicholas	Labourer	Mary	2d
48	Stephens	John	Roper	Elizabeth	5s. 1d
49	Rowe	John	Cooper	Jane	1s
50	*Rashleigh Arms*				
	Stephens	Thomas	Innkeeper	Mary	2s
	Rodda	Richard	Tea dealer – and servants		
	Harris	–	Barmaid	Susan	
	Bunny	–	House servant	Jane	
	Phillips	–	House Servant	Elizabeth	
	Phillips	–	House servant	Jane	
51	Hodge	John	Carpenter	–	
52	Hammess	William	Carpenter	Jean	
53	Pitwell	William	Cooper	–	2s. 1d
54	Williams	John	Mine agent	Elizabeth	1s. 2d
55	Stephens	James	Cooper	Jane	3d
56	Harris	Thomas	Husbandman	Elizabeth	2d
57	Waine	–	Sailors wife	Elizabeth	1s. 1d
58	Trudgion	–	Sailors wife	Juylina	2s. 2d
59	Broad	–	Sailors wife	Rebene	3s. 1d
60	Inch	Charles	Cooper	Elizabeth	
61	Hammen	–	Independent	Jane	1s
62	Mannen	John	Cooper	Charlotte	
63	Reynolds	James	House proprietor –		

64	Roberts	–	Independent	Mona	2s. 2d
65	Parnell	John	Cooper	Jane	3s
66	Hase	–	Mariners wife	Ann	2d
67	Trudgion	John	Miner	Gertrude	1s
68	Doble	Thomas	Coastguard	–	3s
69	Hoskin	Thomas	Coastguard	Olive	2s. 3d
70	Hodge	James	Labourer	Mary	2s. 1d
71	Roberts	Edward	Carpenter	Mary	1d
72	Trudgion	Samuel	Miner	–	3s
	Harris	Thomas	Moulder	–	(lodger)
73	Hoskins	John	Carpenter	Mary	2s
74	Williams	John	Labourer	Jane	4s. 1d
75	*The Villa*				
	Luke	Anthony	Timber mch't	Anne Marie	3d
	Mitchele	–	House servant	Elizabeth	
76	Broadwish	–	Independent	Betsey	1s
77	Reynolds	–	Mariners wife	Jane	
78	Luke	William	Merchants clerk	Elizabeth	3s.
	Walkey	–	House servant	Mary Ann	
79	Coulpe	Edward	Mariner	–	3s. 4d
80	Hitchins	–	Midwife	Bisula	1s. 2d
81	Banks	Baker	Agent	–	3s. 2d
	Hawkins	–	House servant	Philippa	
82	Holden	Richard	Customs Officer	Emily	
83	Vivian	John	Cordwainer	Mary	
84	Frost	Philip	Blacksmith	Jane	4s
85	Henwood	Thomas	Blacksmith	Mary	1s. 1d
86	Girhard	Michael	–	Elizabeth	1s. 1d
	Pedwell	Edward	Cooper	Sarah	
87	Pedwell	William	Clerk	Eleanor	1s
88	Hutton	–	Labourers wife	Elizabeth	2s
89	Moore	Samuel	Ships carpenter	Jane	1s
90	Houghton	William	Dock Master	–	1s. 1d

91	Houghton	John	Hobbler jumper	Ann	1d
92	Harris	Thomas	Mariner	Mary	1d
93	Wills	William	Labourer	Elizabeth	
	Carpenter	–	Midwife	Elizabeth	(lodger)
	Walkey	Joseph	–	–	(nephew)
	Bennett	–	–	Ellen	(lodger)
94	Clemis	George	Hobbler	Esther	1s
95	Larking	Samuel	Coastguard	Jane	4s. 4d
96	Organ	–	Mariners wife	Mary	1s
	Dutton	William	Mariner	–	(lodger)
97	Dingle	Joseph	Mariner	Mary	1s. 1d
98	Polglap	Thomas	Tailor	Jane	1s. 2d
	Hill	Francis	Tailor	–	(lodger)
99	Rowse	William	Blacksmith	Ursula	
100	Hendra	William	Porter	Catherine	4s. 1d
101	Walkey	John	Shipwright	Catherine	2d
102	Tregonning	Edward	Shoemaker	Harriet	2d
103	Randle	Thomas	Grocer	–	2s. 1d
	Hooper	–	House servant	Ann	
104	Clemas	Richard	Butcher	Jane	2s
	Francies	Joseph	Porter	Mary	3s
105	Newman	William	Lath renderer	Jane	1s
106	Milehill	Joseph	Farmer	Dorothy	1s
107	Organ	William	Cooper	Elizabeth	2s. 1d
108	Roberts	William	Carpenter	Ann	1s. 2d
109	Clemas	William	Carrier	Honor	1d
	Hawke	Peter	Pauper	Susan	
110	Hammion	Philip	–	Elizabeth	2d
	Moore	Mr	Shipwright	Mrs	
111	Williams	Ralph	Mason	–	
	Nicholls	Wallace & Samuel both Masons			(lodgers)
112	Pope	John	Mariner	Jane	1s
	Nicholls	John	Mason	–	(lodger)
113	Harking	John	Carpenter	–	1s
	Roberts	–	House keeper	Jenny	

114	Roach	–	Trinity Pensioner	Elizabeth	1s. 1d
115	Laury	Martin	Miner	Mary	1s
116	Walkey	John	Porter	Grace	2s. 3d
117	Whitten	Henry	Labourer	Elizabeth	2s. 2d
118	Wherry	Nicholas	Sawyer	Jane	1s. 2d
119	Brag	–	–	Martha	2s. 1d
120	Polglap	–	Mariners wife	Elizabeth	1s. 2d
121	Patten	George	Ships carpenter	Martha	
122	Moore	Charles	Ships carpenter	Elizabeth	2s. 2d
123	Walkey	Henry	Labourer	Lorina	4s. 4d
124	Murton	John	Carpenter	Melinda	1s. 2d
125	Dunn	John	Shipwright	Jane	4s. 2d
	Dingle	William	Labourer	–	(lodger)
126	Bale	Roger	Pilot	Jane	
127	Hore	John	Cooper	Mary	
	Nancolis	Robert	Moulder	Elizabeth	1s. 1d
128	Tresselling	William	Baker	Jane	
129	Skews	James	Labourer	Elizabeth	
130	Organ	–	Pauper	Martha	
131	Dowerick	John	Carpenter	Ann	1s. 2d
132	Crowl	William	Labourer	Julia	1s
133	Crowl	John	Labourer	Mary	(mother)
134	Hendra	–	Labourers wife	Rose	1s. 2d
135	Bunt	–	Miners wife	Elizabeth	3s. 2d
136	Jenkin	–	Mariners wife	Mary	
137	Clemes	George	Tailor	Thomadin (?)	
138	Crowl	William	Farmer	Philipa	3s. 2d
	Vian	–	House servant	Martha	
139	Bishop	Henry	Engineer	Grace	1s. 1d
140	Morion	Augustus	Merchant	–	
	Miniass	–	House servant	Jane	

141	Hodge	William	Small farmer	Elizabeth	4s. 2d
142	Cropmass	John	–	Mary	1d
143	Richards	James	Labourer	Elizabeth	6s. 2d
144	Rowse	Edward	Porter	Elizabeth	5s. 2d
145	Eplett	Thomas	Mason	Loveday	1s. 2d
146	Dowerick	William	Blacksmith	Mary	1s. 3d
147	Bennetts	Jacob	Labourer	Elizabeth	3s. 5d
148	Thorn	Samuel	Roper	Jane	
149	Roberts	Charles	Gardener	Susan	3s. 2d
150	Empty				
151	Pearse	John	Sawyer	Martha	1s. 5d

APPENDIX 3

Ships built at Charlestown between 1790 – 1874

A total of six shipbuilders worked in Charlestown, who between them launched 28 vessels, mostly schooners and sloops under 100 tons gross, the largest being the 175 ton *Pride of the Channel*. By comparison with other local shipyards, Charlestown's output was small, but by no means insignificant:

Shipbuilding output of ports in the St. Austell area from 1786–1880.

Mevagissey shipyards launched	– 11,603 tons
Fowey shipyards launched	– 8,443 tons
Polruan and Bodinnick shipyards launched	– 6,128 tons
Charlestown's shipyard launched	– 2,025 tons
Par's shipyard launched	– 1,442 tons
Looe shipyards launched	– 890 tons

Ships' built at Charlestown.

	Ship's name	Type	Builder	Date of Register
No.1	*Speedwell*	Lugger	T. Shepherd	1794
2	name unknown		T. Shepherd	
3	name unknown		T. Shepherd	
4	*Duporth*	Sloop	T. Shepherd	1811

Registered No.10 at Fowey 1811, 58 tons, Charles Rashleigh owned 12/64ths, the Rev. H. Tremayne and John Polkinghorne the remaining 52/64th shares.

5	*Kitty & Clara*	Sloop	William Banks	5.10.1816

Registered No.14 at Fowey in 1816, re-registered Plymouth 1818. 35ft.2ins x 12ft.2ins x 6ft.2ins, 20.5 tons, 1 mast.

6	*Harriot*	Cutter	William Banks	8.7.1818

Registered No.7 at Fowey in 1820. 57ft.1ins x 18ft.10.5ins x 83.4 tons, clinker built. Master J. Pearce, owner Philip Ball, Mevagissey.

7	*Swan*	Schooner	William Banks	1822

8 *Union Packet*   Sloop   William Banks   12.7.1823
Registered No.4 Fowey in 1823, re-registered Fowey 1825. 47ft.
3ins x 16ft.8ins x 8ft. 50 tons gross. Master William banks, owner
William Roach. Vessel went to Minehead in 1827.

9 *Charles Rashleigh*   Schooner   William Banks   1824
Registered No.1 Fowey in 1824, transferred to Truro in 1834.
56ft.5ins x 17ft.11ins x 10ft.1ins, carvel built, 2 masts, single
deck, 73.5 tons. Ownership held between 22 individuals.

10 *Henry*   Schooner   William Banks   2.9.1824
Registered No.20 at Fowey in 1824, registration cancelled in 1846
without reason. 56ft.6ins x 17ft.10ins x 9ft.3ins, 2 masts, single
deck, 74.5 tons.

11 *Gleaner*   Sloop   William Banks   21.3.1827
Registered No.2 at Fowey in 1827, went to Plymouth register in
1843. 43ft.11ins x 15ft.9ins x 7ft.2ins, single mast, single deck,
carvel built, 43 tons. William Banks owned 32/64ths.

12 *Laurel*   Sloop   William Banks   12.9.1832
Registered No.5 at Fowey in 1832, re-registered Fowey in 1839
and again in 1865. 54ft.7ins x 17ft.9ins x 9ft.2ins, single mast,
single deck, carvel built, 70 tons. Ownership shared between 12
individuals.

13 *East Cornwall*   Schooner   William Banks   10.3.1834
Registered No.8 at Fowey in 1834, 66ft.4ins x 19ft.7.5ins x
11ft.7ins, single mast, single deck, 110.3 tons, carried a female
bust figurehead. Ownership shared between 28 individuals.

14 *Busy*   Sloop   William Banks   12.7.1836
Registered No.38 at Fowey in 1836, purchased by John Tredwin
of Padstow in 1847. 42ft x 14ft x 7.8ft, single mast, single deck, 49
tons. Master Coombes, ownership shared between 17 St. Austell
individuals, including A. Luke, of Charlestown.

For reasons unknown, it would appear that apart from one vessel built
in late 1838, by John Knight, a Lostwithiel merchant, all ship construction ceased at Charlestown between 1836 and 1840, possibly due to
the illness of William Pearse Banks, who handed over the lease of the
shipyard to Anthony Luke in 1841.

15 *Uzella*   Schooner   John Knight   24.1.1839

16 *Engineer*   Sloop   Anthony Luke   6.9.1841
Registered No.8 at Fowey 1841, re-registered Fowey 1844.
49ft.7ins x 16ft.4ins x 8ft, carvel built, single mast, single deck,
44 tons. Master Coombes, later Charles Hodge. Anthony Luke

retained over half shares in this vessel. Wrecked at Bedruthan Steps, North Cornwall, 4.3.1897.

17 *Merchant*   Brigantine   Anthony Luke   27.1.1844
Registered No.1 at Fowey 1844, re-registered Fowey 1856, ownership transferred to Newhaven in 1869. 80ft.2ins x 20ft.9ins x 14ft.2ins, two masts, single deck. Master A. Luke.

18 *Pentewan*   Sloop   Anthony Luke   25.8.1844
Registered No.10 at Fowey, 49ft.8ins x 17ft.5ins x 6ft, single mast, single deck, carvel built, 34 tons. Master Roger Hodge, later Thomas Hodge. Owned between 14 St. Austell traders.

19 *Pet*   Schooner   Anthony Luke   26.10.1848
Registered No.12 at Fowey 1848, transferred to Folkstone 1868. 62ft.4ins x 17ft.2ins x 10ft.10ins, two masts, single deck, carvel built, 83 tons. Female bust figurehead. Anthony Luke owned over half her shares.

20 *Jessie*   Schooner   Anthony Luke   9.5.1855
Registered No.5 at Fowey 1855. 70ft.3ins x 17ft.9ins x 8ft.7ins, two masts, one deck, carvel built, 66.59 tons. Female bust figurehead. Master John Luke, who bought Anthony Luke's shares in the vessel. Wrecked at the entrance to Looe Harbour, Cornwall, 14 May 1855.

21 *William & Anthony* Brig   Anthony Luke   23.10.1862
Registered No.14 at Fowey 1862, re-registered Fowey 1869, went to Faversham 1872. 97ft x 24ft x 13ft, two masts, one deck, carvel built, 200.64 tons. Male bust figurehead. Anthony Luke died leaving this vessel incomplete, which was finished off by his friend John Stephens. Totally owned by William Luke.

22 *Maria Louisa*   Schooner   William Luke   16.8.1866
Registered No.12 at Fowey in 1866, re-registered Fowey 1869. 86ft.3ins x 20ft x 11ft, two masts, one deck, carvel built, 108.84 tons. Female bust figurehead. Rebuilt in 1869, tonnage reduced. Owned totally by William Luke. Wrecked in the Azores, 01.12.1889.

23 *Mary Lizzie*   Schooner   William Luke   22.8.1868
Registered No.4 at Fowey 1868, then from 1870 at St. John's, Newfoundland. 102ft x 21ft x 12ft 2ins, two masts, one deck, carvel built. Female bust figurehead. William Luke owned 56/64th shares. Vessel sold to a London ship owner June 1872.

24 *Teazer*   Dandy   William Luke   26.10.1868
Registered No.6 at Fowey 1868, transferred to Hull 1872. 75ft.8ins x 18ft.3ins x 9ft.5ins, two masts, one deck, carvel built, 65.27 tons. Owned entirely by William Luke.

25 *Little Fred*   Smack   William Luke   5.3.1870
Registered No.2 at Fowey, 1870. 60ft.3ins x 18ft.4ins x 8ft.3ins, one mast, one deck, carvel built, 42.66 tons. Left Pentewan for Cork on 6.8.1896, never heard of again.

26 *Challenge*   Schooner   William Luke   20.10.1870
Registered No.6 at Fowey 1870. 80ft x 20ft x 9ft.8ins, two masts, one deck, carvel built, 78.81 tons. Female bust figurehead. William Luke owned the entire vessel. Left Oporto for Fowey 27.10.1901, never heard of again.

27 *Pride of the Channel* Brigantine   W. Luke/J.Stephens 12.5.1873
Registered No.8 at Fowey 1873. 109ft.7ins x 24ft.5ins x 12ft.10ins, two masts, but converted to three masts from 23.7.1885, one deck, carvel built, 175.52 tons. Female bust figurehead. William Luke died during the vessels construction, which was completed by John Stephens. Owned by Elizabeth Luke and later John Stephens. Lost off the Paulliac coast, France, 3.3.1897.

28 *Flying Spray*   Schooner   John Stephens   4.5.1874
Registered No.12 at Fowey 1874. Lost off Tangier 11.1875. This was the last vessel built at Charlestown, launched down a slipway on the western beach (see text for details of launch).

APPENDIX 4

List of mines and shafts, in alphabetical order.

A great many of these mines and individual shafts were local to Charlestown, others were further afield, but all are listed in the *Black Tin Books*, of the Charlestown Smelting Company, as having sent ore to the village for refining, assay and coining, where blowing house and smelting services were offered for almost 100 years.

Account House	Care Marsh	Great Hewas
Annie's	Cavear Moor	Great Polgooth
Barker's	Charlestown United	Gripes
Barrat's	Come-by-Luck	Hallavick Moor
Bartliver Moor	Conse Moor	Hancocks
Beacon	Crinnis	Handfire
Beam	Cuddra Consolidated	Happy Union
Bell Moor	Dingle's	Higher Molinnes Moor
Best to Agree	Drakewall's	Job's
Bob Engine Shaft	East Beam	Kirron
Boscarne	East Poole	Little Good Luck
Bowling Green	East Poole	Lobb's
Brown Willie	Gardiner's	Middlemoor's
Burthy Row Moor	Gover	Milinnes
Came by Chance	Gowan's East	New Adventure
Carclaze	Hancock's	New Criggan
Nina Moor	Rosevean	Wheal Eliza
Northey's	Smythe's	Wheal Friendship
North Towan	Strawberry	Wheal Frederick
Old Buckler's	Temple	Wheal Polmear
Pendalow	Three Men's Venture	Wheal Prosper
Pentruff	Tickell's	Wheal Rose

Perry's

Phoenix

Pit Moor

Poor Man's Endeavour

Porkellis Moor

Remery's

Restugga Moor

Tremayne's

Viaduct Stream

Walker's

West Polmear

Wet & Weary

Wheal Anna

Wheal Arthur

Wheal Sovereign

Wheal Treasure

Wheal Virgin

GENERAL INDEX

218